GREAT RECIPES FOR GREAT WEEKENDS

FOOD&WINE®
MAGAZINE

GREAT RECIPES FOR GREAT WEEKENDS

Written and edited by
MARDEE HAIDIN REGAN

Photography by
MICHAEL GEIGER

Design by
CARBONE SMOLAN ASSOCIATES

MAGAZINE
American Express Publishing Corporation, NY

Great Recipes for Great Weekends

Editorial Director: Susan Crandell
Writer/Editor: Mardee Haidin Regan
Art Director: Leslie Smolan
Designer: Allison Muench
Photographer: Michael Geiger
Food Stylists: Helga Weinrib, Anne
Disrude (page 69 and cover)
Rick Ellis (pages 75, 128 and 143), John
Robert Massie (page 43)
Assistant Editor: Jessica King
Editorial Assistant: S. Kirk Walsh

Publisher: Claire Gruppo
Associate Publisher:
Victoria Smith Walsh

The text of this book was set in Trump
by TypoGraphic Innovations, Inc., New
York, N.Y. The four color separations
were done by International Colour,
Rochester, N.Y. The book was printed and
bound in Italy by A.M.E Publishing Ltd.

Published by American Express Publishing Corporation, 1120 Avenue of the
Americas, New York, New York 10036

Library of Congress Cataloging-in-
Publication Data
Regan, Mardee Haidin.
Great recipes for great weekends.
Includes index.
1. Cookery. 2. Menus. I. Geiger,
Michael.
II. Smolan, Leslie. III. Title.
TX714.R44 1989   641.5   89-6912
ISBN 0-916103-10-2

CONTENTS

MAKING WEEKENDS GREAT

What is it about weekends that makes so many people act totally different from the way they do during the other five days of the week? What turns the wiliest deal-maker into someone who looks like a hobo and is content to spend whole days polishing the wood on a boat? What transforms a gentle man into a basketball fanatic who can out-dunk people a head and a half taller than he? What makes the most impatient people you know able to sit in traffic for hours in 90-degree weather then arrive at their weekend retreat with a smile? There must be something to it. The only logical answer is: It's the weekend.

Ah, the weekend—that brief span that begins most Fridays around six and lasts almost until Monday morning. The weekend—that indescribably delicious time that's ours to savor; the time when we can indulge the Walter Mitty side of ourselves, sleep as late as we wish and cook and eat what we want.

There's a difference between weekend and weekday cooking, too. Monday to Friday, most of us are merely producing meals; weekday cooking often is slapdash, catch-as-catch-can sort of fare. But on weekends, we all have the chance to relax, to cook and entertain for the pure enjoyment and satisfaction of doing so.

Great Recipes for Great Weekends is meant to give weekend cooks both a gleam of inspiration and a helping hand. It offers abundant ideas, many menus and a wide variety of well-constructed, tasty recipes. These dishes and menus are ideal for entertaining friends, family or just yourself. Some suggest preparing foods that will make getting through the week easier—and extending some of that special weekend feeling into the workweek. We have created and photographed menus for 26 special occasions—more than two dozen memorable meals, each one conveying a particular spirit. All could happily be applied to other seasons and other events. Not every reader will be interested in celebrating Bastille Day nor will everyone be poverty-stricken at tax time, but we do think most readers will call on the menus

that motivate these offbeat celebrations. Not everybody will be hosting a small wedding this June (but our dinner could fete a new Phi Beta Kappa or anyone else who deserves a party of some sort), nor will most people be inviting the boss for dinner this spring. But think about it. Chances are you will be entertaining someone you care about, and our Dinner to Impress the Boss might be just perfect.

Throughout the book, we've given suggestions for meals that don't require a lot of forethought or trouble. These can be as handy on a Wednesday as on a Saturday or Sunday, and if you follow the guidelines set forth in A Procrastinator's Dinner, your life can be simplified—on weekdays and weekends.

—Mardee Haidin Regan

SPRING

■ ■ ■

A
FORMAL DINNER
WITH MUSIC

Experienced hosts and hostesses seem to have every tenet of entertaining down pat. They are utterly unflappable, adept at everything. Talented cooks, they can also arrange flowers (which they probably grew themselves), set a beautiful table, keep the conversation lively, eat without gaining weight, read all of the latest books, run in the marathon and give to the needy. They even know precisely what music will make the meal just right. ~ If you aspire to those abilities, then let us help as much as we can. Next time you plan a spiffy dinner party, prepare this relatively easy menu, which looks more elaborate than it really is. And if you're concerned about playing the proper music, we have prevailed upon conductor Sir Colin Davis and violinist Sanford Allen to give us their suggestions for an evening of Mozart selections chosen specifically to suit this meal. We think you'll find their choices particularly helpful. Turn to the music menu on page 15.

■ ■ ■

Chocolate Pâté
with
Pistachio Sauce

Lemon-Frosted
Grapes

10

BUCKWHEAT BLINI
WITH SMOKED SALMON
AND TWO CAVIARS

Serve the blini in a napkin-covered basket surrounded by the accompaniments so that guests can help themselves. Each guest fills a blini, folds it over, then dips it in the melted butter and eats it. This is most definitely finger food, so be sure to provide large napkins.

1 PACKAGE (¼ OUNCE) ACTIVE DRY YEAST
1 TEASPOON SUGAR
2½ CUPS LUKEWARM BUTTERMILK
  (105° TO 110°)
1 CUP SIFTED BUCKWHEAT FLOUR
1 TEASPOON BAKING SODA
¼ POUND (1 STICK) PLUS 2 TABLESPOONS
  UNSALTED BUTTER, MELTED AND
  COOLED
4 EGGS, SEPARATED
1 CUP SOUR CREAM
1½ CUPS SIFTED ALL-PURPOSE FLOUR
1 TEASPOON SALT
½ CUP MILK
ABOUT ½ CUP VEGETABLE OIL, FOR THE
  SKILLET

ACCOMPANIMENTS:
½ POUND (2 STICKS) UNSALTED BUTTER,
  CLARIFIED
1 CUP SOUR CREAM
¾ CUP MINCED SHALLOTS
½ POUND THINLY SLICED SMOKED SALMON
4 OUNCES RED CAVIAR
4 OUNCES BLACK CAVIAR
4 LEMONS, CUT INTO THIN WEDGES

1~ Stir the yeast and sugar into ½ cup of the buttermilk and let stand until the yeast begins to bubble, about 5 minutes.

2~ In a large bowl, combine the buckwheat flour and the baking soda with the remaining 2 cups buttermilk. Add the yeast liquid, stirring well to break up any lumps. Cover the bowl with a kitchen towel and let stand in a warm, draft-free place until the mixture doubles in volume, about 2 hours.

3~ In a medium bowl, combine 6 tablespoons of the melted butter with the egg yolks and sour cream. Stir in the all-purpose flour and salt; mix well to break up any lumps. Gradually fold into the buckwheat mixture. Stir in the milk. Cover the bowl and let stand in a warm, draft-free place for 2 hours. *(The recipe may be prepared to this point up to 1 day ahead. Cover and refrigerate. To continue, let return to room temperature; stir in ¼ to ½ cup water, if the batter has thickened, to return it to its original consistency.)*

4~ Beat the egg whites until stiff but not dry. Fold gently into the batter. Loosely cover the bowl with plastic wrap and let stand in a warm draft-free place for 30 minutes.

5~ Preheat the oven to 250°. Lightly brush one or two heavy skillets or griddles, preferably non-stick, with some of the vegetable oil. Warm over high heat until barely smoking, 1 to 2 minutes.

6~ For each pancake, ladle 2 to 3 tablespoons of batter onto the skillets, allowing plenty of room in between, to form pancakes about 3 inches in diameter. Cook over moderately high heat until bubbles break on the surface and the top is almost dry, 2 to 3 minutes. Turn and cook until golden brown on the bottom, 1 to 2 minutes. Lightly brush each blini with a little of the remaining 4 tablespoons melted butter. Stack on a plate and keep warm in the oven. Brush the skillet with more vegetable oil and repeat with the remaining batter.

7~ The blini should be served as soon as possible after they are cooked. Place the clarified butter in a small chafing dish or butter warmer and arrange the remaining accompaniments in serving bowls.

SERVES 8
RECIPE BY W. PETER PRESTCOTT

POTATO CASES WITH SHIITAKE AND MOREL FILLING

For this recipe, the potatoes are cut into rectangular boxes and then oven-roasted. Just before serving, you spoon in the rich mushroom filling.

8 BAKING POTATOES (10 OUNCES EACH), ABOUT 5 INCHES BY 2 INCHES
½ OUNCE DRIED MORELS
2 TABLESPOONS UNSALTED BUTTER, MELTED AND CLARIFIED
3 TABLESPOONS EXTRA-VIRGIN OLIVE OIL
3 GARLIC CLOVES, SLICED
¾ POUND FRESH SHIITAKE MUSHROOMS— STEMMED, CAPS CUT CROSSWISE INTO SLICES AND THEN HALVED
¼ CUP DRY WHITE WINE
¼ CUP CHICKEN STOCK OR CANNED BROTH
⅓ CUP HEAVY CREAM
1 TEASPOON FRESH LEMON JUICE
½ TEASPOON SALT
⅛ TEASPOON FRESHLY GROUND PEPPER
1 TABLESPOON MINCED FRESH PARSLEY

1~ With a paring knife, trim the potatoes to make straight-sided rectangular boxes (3 by 1½ by 1½ inches). Holding the paring knife vertically, cut completely around the inside of the potato box, leaving a shell ⅛ to ¼ inch thick. Insert the paring knife horizontally ⅛ to ¼ inch from the bottom of the box. Work the knife back and forth in a swiveling motion to loosen the inside piece. If necessary, insert the paring knife in several different spots. Keep the potato cases submerged in cool water while you prepare the filling.

2~ Preheat the oven to 450°.

3~ Soak the morels in 2 cups of hot water until softened, about 10 minutes. Remove the morels, squeezing gently. Strain the soaking liquid through a double layer of dampened cheesecloth into a small saucepan. Rinse the morels and trim. Chop coarsely and add to the saucepan. Boil gently until the liquid is completely absorbed, about 20 minutes. Set aside.

4~ Meanwhile, pat the potato cases dry and brush completely with the butter. Place on a baking sheet and bake for 20 minutes, or until golden brown, turning the cases on a different side every 5 minutes.

5~ In a large heavy skillet, heat the oil. Add the garlic and cook over moderately high heat until light golden, about 1 minute. Add the morels and the shiitake. Cook, stirring frequently, until the shiitake are softened, about 2 minutes.

6~ Add the wine and stock and cook over moderately high heat until the liquid is slightly reduced, about 1 minute. Stir in the cream and boil until thickened, about 2 minutes. Add the lemon juice, salt and pepper. Keep warm.

7~ To serve, season the potato cases lightly with salt. Stir the parsley into the filling. (If the filling is too thick, stir in 1 to 2 tablespoons additional cream, stock or water.) Place 2 potato cases on each serving plate. Spoon filling into each potato and serve.

MAKES 8 FIRST-COURSE OR 4 SIDE-DISH SERVINGS
RECIPE BY ANNE DISRUDE

Tarragon Veal Chops

Turnips Anna

12

Thick, juicy veal chops make a beautiful presentation in this meal. You might want them to hold "center stage" and pass the side dishes separately.

4 VEAL CHOPS, CUT 1 INCH THICK
(ABOUT 2½ POUNDS), AT ROOM
TEMPERATURE
½ TEASPOON SALT
¼ TEASPOON FRESHLY GROUND PEPPER
4 TEASPOONS CRUMBLED DRIED TARRAGON
2½ TABLESPOONS UNSALTED BUTTER
½ CUP DRY RED WINE (PREFERABLY THE
WINE OF DINNER)

1~ Season the veal chops with the salt and pepper. Press 1 teaspoon of the tarragon onto both sides of each chop.
2~ In a large heavy skillet, melt the butter over moderate heat. When it foams, add the chops. Sauté the chops, turning several times, until browned on the outside, tender and slightly pink near the bone, 8 to 10 minutes. Remove to warmed dinner plates.
3~ Pour the wine into the skillet and cook, stirring and scraping up any browned bits from the bottom of the pan, until the liquid is reduced to about ¼ cup, 3 to 4 minutes.
4~ Spoon the sauce over the chops and serve at once.

SERVES 4
RECIPE BY SHIRLEY SARVIS

This is Pommes Anna's almost identical twin —made with turnips instead of potatoes.

5 TABLESPOONS UNSALTED BUTTER,
MELTED
¼ CUP BACON DRIPPINGS (FROM ABOUT
6 STRIPS OF COOKED BACON)
6 TABLESPOONS ALL-PURPOSE FLOUR
6 TABLESPOONS FRESHLY GRATED
PARMESAN CHEESE
¾ TEASPOON SALT
½ TEASPOON GROUND GINGER
¼ TEASPOON DRY MUSTARD
¼ TEASPOON FRESHLY GROUND PEPPER
¼ TEASPOON FINELY CRUMBLED THYME
¼ TEASPOON FINELY CRUMBLED ROSEMARY
PINCH OF FRESHLY GRATED NUTMEG
1½ POUNDS MEDIUM TURNIPS, PEELED
AND SLICED PAPER THIN

1~ Preheat the oven to 450°. Brush the bottom and sides of a 9-inch glass pie plate generously with some of the melted butter; set aside.
2~ In a small bowl, combine the bacon drippings and the rest of the melted butter. In another bowl, combine the flour, Parmesan cheese, salt, ginger, mustard, pepper, thyme, rosemary and nutmeg; spoon about ¼ cup of this mixture onto a small plate.
3~ Pick out the prettiest and most uniform turnip slices. Dip one into the bacon fat and butter, then press one side into the seasoned flour on the plate. Lay the slice, floured-side up, in the center of the pie plate. Repeat dipping and placing the most uniform slices, overlapping them slightly and working out from the center in concentric rings, to cover the bottom and sides of the pie plate.
4~ Continue layering the remaining turnip slices, in slightly overlapping concentric rings, brushing each layer with the bacon fat and butter and scattering a little of the seasoned flour evenly on top, until all of the turnips have been used.
5~ Brush bacon fat and butter on the shiny side of a 9-inch square of aluminum foil and place, buttered-side down, on top of the turnips. Place a heavy 8- or 9-inch skillet on top and press firmly; fill the skillet with pie weights or dried beans.
6~ Bake in the middle of the oven for 30 to 35 minutes, until the bottom and sides are richly browned. (Set a pan on the rack below to catch any juices.)
7~ Remove from the oven, lift off the skillet and peel off the foil. With a thin spatula, carefully loosen the turnip cake around the edges. Let cool for 5 minutes, then invert onto a heated serving plate. Cut into wedges and serve at once.

SERVES 6 TO 8
RECIPE BY JEAN ANDERSON

ROASTED GARLIC

Roasted garlic marries beautifully with the veal and turnips in this dinner. Feel free to double or triple the recipe as desired.

2 LARGE HEADS OF GARLIC
1 TABLESPOON OLIVE OIL
SALT AND FRESHLY GROUND PEPPER

1~ Preheat the oven to 350°.
2~ Peel off the outer layer of skin on the heads of garlic to expose the cloves, but do not peel the cloves. Rub the whole heads with the oil and place in a small baking pan. Add enough water to reach halfway up the heads.
3~ Bake the garlic until very tender but not brown, 1½ to 2 hours. Remove from the pan and let cool.
4~ Peel the cloves and season with salt and pepper to taste. *(The garlic can be cooked 1 day ahead. Once cool, cover and store at room temperature. Reheat the cloves in olive oil on top of the stove before serving.)*

SERVES 4
RECIPE BY MOLLY O'NEILL

GREEN GULCH LETTUCES WITH GOAT CHEESE

You'll need a break after that generous main course—this salad is just the ticket.

1 BUNCH OF WATERCRESS
1 SMALL HEAD OF RED LEAF LETTUCE
1 SMALL HEAD OF BOSTON OR BUTTER LETTUCE
1 SMALL HEAD OF ROMAINE LETTUCE
¾ CUP PECAN HALVES (ABOUT 3 OUNCES)
3 LARGE NAVEL ORANGES
1 TABLESPOON BALSAMIC VINEGAR
½ CUP LIGHT OLIVE OIL
1 TEASPOON MINCED SHALLOT
SALT AND FRESHLY GROUND PEPPER
5 OUNCES OF SONOMA GOAT CHEESE OR OTHER MILD GOAT CHEESE

1~ Preheat the oven to 350°.
2~ Trim, rinse and dry the watercress, red leaf, Boston and romaine lettuces. Tear into bite-size pieces.
3~ Arrange the pecans on a baking sheet and bake until they begin to brown, 5 to 8 minutes.
4~ Remove the orange zest from one of the oranges and chop enough to measure ½ teaspoon. Peel the remaining oranges over a bowl to catch the juices. Remove the outer membranes from the orange sections and cut the individual segments apart. Reserve 3 tablespoons of the juice.
5~ In a small bowl, whisk together the vinegar, oil, shallot, salt and pepper and the reserved orange juice and orange zest.
6~ In a large bowl, toss together the greens, orange segments, pecans and vinaigrette. Arrange the salad on serving plates and crumble some of the goat cheese over the top of each serving.

SERVES 6
RECIPE BY ANNIE SOMERVILLE
GREENS, SAN FRANCISCO

13

LEMON-FROSTED GRAPES

14

Make these sparkling clusters and you'll be serving the prettiest grapes in town.

3 TABLESPOONS SUGAR
1½ TEASPOONS GRATED LEMON ZEST
1 EGG WHITE
½ POUND SEEDLESS GREEN GRAPES,
    DIVIDED INTO SMALL BUNCHES

1~ In a small bowl, combine the sugar and lemon zest. Put the egg white in another small bowl and beat until frothy.
2~ Hold each bunch of grapes by the stem and dip the grapes into the egg white, allowing any excess to drip off. Then dip the grapes into the lemon-sugar, making sure they are completely covered. (Use a fork to dip any stray single grapes.)
3~ Arrange the grapes on a baking sheet lined with waxed paper and freeze until hard, about 30 minutes. Cover with plastic wrap and store in the freezer for up to 1 week.

SERVES 4
RECIPE BY MARCIA KIESEL

CHOCOLATE PÂTÉ WITH PISTACHIO SAUCE

It seems only proper that an intense meal herald an intense dessert. Here's a knockout.

15 OUNCES BITTERSWEET CHOCOLATE,
    SUCH AS TOBLER EXTRA BITTERSWEET,
    BROKEN INTO PIECES
1 CUP HEAVY CREAM
4 TABLESPOONS UNSALTED BUTTER, CUT
    INTO TABLESPOONS
4 EGG YOLKS
1 CUP CONFECTIONERS' SUGAR, SIFTED
½ CUP MYERS DARK RUM
PISTACHIO SAUCE (AT RIGHT)
SPRIGS OF FRESH MINT AND CHOPPED
    TOASTED PEELED PISTACHIOS, FOR
    GARNISH

1~ In a double boiler or in a medium bowl set over simmering water, combine the chocolate, cream and butter. Cook over low heat, stirring occasionally, until the chocolate is melted and the mixture is smooth, about 10 minutes. Remove from the heat.
2~ One at a time, whisk the egg yolks into the chocolate until well blended. Gradually whisk in the confectioners' sugar and then the rum.
3~ Line the bottom and sides of a 4-cup loaf pan with a sheet of plastic wrap. Pour the hot chocolate mixture into the pan. Let cool to room temperature, then cover and refrigerate overnight.

4~ Invert the pâté onto a platter to unmold and peel away the plastic wrap. Refrigerate until ready to serve. Cut with a cold knife or a wire cheese cutter into ½-inch slices. Serve each slice with a couple of tablespoons of Pistachio Sauce and garnish with mint sprigs and chopped pistachios.

SERVES 8 TO 12
RECIPE BY JIMMY SCHMIDT
THE RATTLESNAKE CLUB, DENVER

PISTACHIO SAUCE

You can serve this rich sauce under or over nearly any special dessert.

¾ CUP PISTACHIO NUTS (ABOUT 4 OUNCES)
1¾ CUPS HALF-AND-HALF, SCALDED
5 EGG YOLKS, AT ROOM TEMPERATURE
¼ CUP SUGAR
¼ TEASPOON VANILLA EXTRACT
PINCH OF SALT
2 TABLESPOONS PISTACHIO LIQUEUR OR
   FRANGELICO (HAZELNUT LIQUEUR)

1~ Place the pistachios in a small heatproof bowl and cover them with boiling water. Drain the nuts and slip off their skins. Place the peeled pistachios in a medium skillet and cook over moderately high heat, tossing, until lightly toasted, 2 to 3 minutes.

2~ In a blender or food processor, combine the toasted pistachios and 1 cup of the half-and-half. Blend until the nuts are coarsely chopped. Add the remaining ¾ cup half-and-half and process for 30 seconds. Let cool completely.

3~ Strain the half-and-half through a fine mesh sieve into a heavy-bottomed saucepan, pressing on the nuts to extract as much liquid as possible; discard the nuts. Bring the pistachio-flavored half-and-half to a boil.

4~ In a medium heatproof bowl, combine the egg yolks, sugar, vanilla and salt. Whisk briefly to blend. Gradually whisk in the hot half-and-half. Return the mixture to the saucepan and cook over moderate heat, stirring constantly, until the custard thickens enough to coat the back of a spoon lightly, 2 to 3 minutes; do not let boil. Remove the sauce from the heat and whisk until it is slightly cooled, about 2 minutes.

5~ Strain the sauce into a medium bowl. Stir in the pistachio liqueur. Let the sauce cool to room temperature, then cover and refrigerate until cold. *(The sauce can be prepared a day ahead.)*

MAKES ABOUT 2 CUPS
RECIPE BY JIMMY SCHMIDT
THE RATTLESNAKE CLUB, DENVER

15

A Mozart Menu
for Music
Throughout the Meal

WITH THE HORS D'OEUVRE:
Sonata for Two Pianos in D Major, K.448

WITH THE FIRST COURSE:
selections from Don Giovanni, especially to include the sextet from Act II

WITH THE ENTRÉE:
String Quartet in B-flat Major ("The Hunt Quartet"), K.458

WITH THE SALAD:
"Posthorn" Serenade, K. 320

WITH THE DESSERT:
the overture and selections from The Magic Flute

WITH THE COGNAC:
Divertimento in E-flat for Violin, Viola and Cello, K. 563

—selected especially for this meal by Sir Colin Davis and Sanford Allen

■ ■ ■

A
PULITZER
BREAKFAST

16   To many of us, from Monday through Friday, breakfast is a time, not a meal, and might not involve food at all. But on Saturdays and Sundays, breakfasts have a deliciously different protocol. There's time to sip some juice, munch on a muffin or piece of coffee cake, drink copious amounts of coffee or tea and read those multi-sectioned weekend newspapers. Big newspapers are synonymous with weekends, and that's why this breakfast is named in honor of journalist Joseph Pulitzer. ～ Our menu works just fine for virtually any at-home breakfast, but everyone will find it especially endearing on the weekend because of the freedom it accords guests and hosts alike. Guests are free to rise when they want to and do as they please. Breakfast and fresh reading materials are furnished. You, as host, commit only to getting up before anyone else does, to set out the essentials, brew coffee into a thermal carafe and unpack the coffee cake and muffins, which you so wisely prepared ahead of time. Then you can sneak back to bed, knowing you have provided your guests with sustenance (juice, fresh-baked breadstuffs and coffee) and entertainment (newspapers, newspapers, newspapers). This Pulitzer is definitely a prize.

■ ■ ■

Sour Cream
Coffee Cake with
Bee-Sting Glaze

Assorted Muffins

Three-Berry
Preserves

Breakfast Tatin

BLUEBERRY MUFFINS WITH STREUSEL TOPPING

18

When breakfast is over, don't forget that broken-up, leftover muffins make an excellent base for a late-night scoop of vanilla ice cream. If you use frozen berries here, leave them frozen or only partially thawed—otherwise they'll make the muffins too soggy.

¾ CUP SUGAR

2 TEASPOONS GRATED LEMON ZEST

2¼ CUPS ALL-PURPOSE FLOUR

7 TABLESPOONS PLUS 1 TEASPOON
  UNSALTED BUTTER

1 TABLESPOON BAKING POWDER

1 EGG

½ CUP MILK

2 CUPS BLUEBERRIES, FRESH OR FROZEN

1~ Preheat the oven to 400°. Generously butter twelve 2½-inch muffin cups.

2~ In a small bowl, combine ¼ cup of the sugar and 1 teaspoon of the lemon zest; crush them together until the sugar absorbs some of the lemon flavor, about 1 minute. Add ¼ cup of the flour and 2 tablespoons of the butter. Cut the butter into the mixture until it forms coarse crumbs. Set this streusel topping aside.

3~ In a large bowl, combine the remaining ½ cup sugar and 1 teaspoon lemon zest, crushing them together until the sugar absorbs the lemon flavor, about 1 minute. Add the remaining 2 cups flour and the baking powder and toss to blend well.

4~ In a small saucepan, melt the remaining 5 tablespoons plus 1 teaspoon butter; let cool slightly.

5~ In a medium bowl, whisk together the egg, milk and melted butter. Pour the liquid over the flour mixture and fold lightly, 3 or 4 times with a rubber spatula, to partially combine. Sprinkle the blueberries over the batter and distribute evenly, using as few strokes as possible (the mixture should not be perfectly smooth and will be quite dry).

6~ Quickly divide the batter among the prepared muffin cups. Sprinkle about 1 tablespoon of the streusel topping over each.

7~ Bake in the middle of the oven until the tops of the muffins are golden and spring back when lightly pressed, about 25 minutes for fresh berries, 35 for frozen.

8~ Let the muffins cool in the pan for 2 minutes. Using a blunt knife, ease the muffins onto a wire rack and let cool for 15 to 20 minutes.

MAKES 12 MUFFINS
RECIPE BY DIANA STURGIS

RASPBERRY MUFFINS

Raspberry lovers won't find it easy to set aside a small amount for the next day's breakfast, but, if the truth be told, these muffins are well worth it.

1¾ CUPS ALL-PURPOSE FLOUR
¾ CUP YELLOW CORNMEAL
⅔ CUP SUGAR
1 TABLESPOON BAKING POWDER
2 EGGS
½ CUP MILK
5 TABLESPOONS UNSALTED BUTTER,
  MELTED
1 to 1¼ CUPS SMALL RASPBERRIES

1~ Preheat the oven to 400°. Generously butter twelve 2½-inch muffin cups.
2~ In a bowl, mix together the flour, cornmeal, sugar and baking powder.
3~ In a medium bowl, whisk together the eggs, milk and melted butter. Pour over the dry ingredients and fold lightly with a spatula until just blended; there may be some dry streaks in the batter.
4~ Spoon half of the batter into the prepared muffin cups. With a dampened finger, make a slight depression in each one. Place 5 or 6 raspberries in each depression, away from the cup sides. Spoon the remaining batter on top, dividing it evenly among the 12 cups. Do not spread the batter; it will even out as it bakes.
5~ Bake the muffins until golden and well risen, about 20 minutes. Remove from the pan while still hot and serve warm or at room temperature.

MAKES 12 MUFFINS
RECIPE BY DIANA STURGIS

APPLE, CINNAMON AND RAISIN MUFFINS

Seek out good, tart apples for these muffins; the payoff in flavor is worth an extra minute or two of searching at the greengrocer.

2 CUPS ALL-PURPOSE FLOUR
⅔ CUP PACKED DARK BROWN SUGAR
1 TABLESPOON BAKING POWDER
½ TEASPOON FRESHLY GRATED NUTMEG
1 EGG
⅓ CUP SAFFLOWER OIL
⅔ CUP UNSWEETENED APPLE JUICE
1 TART COOKING APPLE, SUCH AS GRANNY
  SMITH OR GREENING, UNPEELED AND
  FINELY DICED (1 CUP)
1 TEASPOON GROUND CINNAMON
½ CUP RAISINS
½ CUP CHOPPED NUTS, SUCH AS PECANS
  OR WALNUTS

1~ Preheat the oven to 400°. Generously butter twelve 2½-inch muffin cups.
2~ In a large bowl, sift together the flour, brown sugar, baking powder and nutmeg.
3~ In a medium bowl, combine the egg, oil and apple juice. Whisk until blended.
4~ In another medium bowl, toss together the apple and cinnamon until evenly coated. Stir in the raisins and nuts.
5~ Pour the egg mixture over the sifted dry ingredients and fold lightly, 3 or 4 times with a rubber spatula, to partially combine. Add the apple mixture and distribute evenly, using as few strokes as possible (the batter should not be perfectly smooth).
6~ Quickly divide the batter among the prepared muffin cups. Bake in the middle of the oven until the tops of the muffins are golden and spring back when lightly pressed, 23 to 25 minutes.
7~ Let the muffins cool in the pan for about 2 minutes. Using a blunt knife, ease the muffins onto a wire rack and let cool for 15 to 20 minutes.

MAKES 12 MUFFINS
RECIPE BY DIANA STURGIS

19

DATE-BRAN MUFFINS

Lest we forget, muffins are around-the-clock foods—a good replacement for after-school cookies and an excellent midnight snack.

1 EGG
¼ CUP SAFFLOWER OIL
1⅓ CUPS MILK
1⅓ CUPS HIGH-FIBER BRAN CEREAL
1 CUP CHOPPED PITTED DATES
⅓ CUP CURRANTS
1½ CUPS ALL-PURPOSE FLOUR
1 TABLESPOON BAKING POWDER
⅓ CUP SUGAR

1~ In a medium bowl, lightly whisk the egg, safflower oil and milk. Stir in the bran cereal and set aside to soften, about 20 minutes.
2~ Meanwhile, preheat the oven to 400°. Generously grease twelve 2½-inch muffin cups.
3~ In a small bowl, combine the dates and currants. In a medium bowl, toss together the flour, baking powder and sugar. Pour the bran mixture over the flour and fold lightly, 3 or 4 times, to partially combine. Sprinkle the date/currant mixture over the batter and mix, using as few strokes as possible (the batter should not be perfectly smooth).
4~ Quickly divide the batter among the prepared muffin cups. Bake in the middle of the oven until the muffins are lightly browned and the tops spring back, about 20 minutes.
5~ Let the muffins rest in the pan for about 2 minutes. Ease the muffins onto a wire rack and let cool for 15 to 20 minutes.

MAKES 12 MUFFINS
RECIPE BY DIANA STURGIS

THREE-BERRY PRESERVES

Offering homemade preserves to friends and family is a pleasing gesture—especially when it's this fresh-berry concoction.

1½ CUPS RASPBERRIES OR LOGANBERRIES
     (ABOUT ½ PINT)
1½ CUPS STRAWBERRIES (ABOUT ½ PINT),
     HALVED OR QUARTERED IF LARGE
1½ CUPS GOOSEBERRIES (ABOUT ½ PINT),
     ENDS TRIMMED WITH SCISSORS
½ CUP SUGAR

1~ In a medium nonreactive saucepan, combine the raspberries, strawberries, gooseberries and sugar. Bring to a boil over moderate heat, stirring to dissolve the sugar. Cook for 20 minutes, stirring occasionally.
2~ Press the cooked berries through a sieve to remove the seeds. Measure the berry mixture. If you have more than 1½ cups, return to the saucepan and boil until reduced to 1½ cups.
3~ Pour the preserves into a heatproof glass jar and cover. The preserves will keep in the refrigerator for up to 3 weeks.

MAKES ABOUT 1½ CUPS
RECIPE BY DIANA STURGIS

SOUR CREAM COFFEE CAKE WITH BEE-STING GLAZE

Your taste buds will be stung by the good flavors and textures you'll find in this old-fashioned German coffee cake recipe.

2 ENVELOPES (¼ OUNCE EACH) ACTIVE DRY
     YEAST
¼ CUP LUKEWARM WATER (105° TO 115°)
½ POUND (2 STICKS) PLUS 4 TABLESPOONS
     UNSALTED BUTTER, SOFTENED
¾ CUP GRANULATED SUGAR
2 WHOLE EGGS
2 EGG YOLKS
½ TEASPOON SALT
1 TEASPOON VANILLA EXTRACT
½ CUP WARM MILK
½ CUP SOUR CREAM
4 TO 5 CUPS ALL-PURPOSE FLOUR
⅔ CUP PACKED LIGHT BROWN SUGAR
¼ CUP PLUS 2 TABLESPOONS HEAVY CREAM
¼ CUP PLUS 2 TABLESPOONS HONEY
¼ TEASPOON FRESH LEMON JUICE
1⅓ CUPS SLICED BLANCHED ALMONDS
     OR 1⅓ CUPS ALMONDS WITH THEIR
     SKINS, COARSELY CHOPPED

1~ In a small cup, sprinkle the yeast over the lukewarm water; set aside.
2~ In a large bowl, cream together 1½ sticks of the butter and the granulated sugar until light and fluffy. Beat in the whole eggs, 1 at a time, mixing well after each addition. Add the egg yolks, salt, vanilla, milk, sour cream and dissolved yeast. Beat until smooth, about 2 minutes.

BREAKFAST TATIN

3~ Using a wooden spoon, gradually stir in 4 cups of the flour until a very soft dough forms. (The dough will not be firm enough to pull away from the sides of the bowl.) Continue to stir, adding additional flour, if necessary, until the dough is smooth and elastic, 8 to 10 minutes. Place the dough in an oiled bowl, turn to coat and cover with a damp towel. Set aside in a warm place to rise until doubled, about 45 minutes, or cover and refrigerate overnight.

4~ Melt 2 tablespoons of the butter. Punch down the dough and divide it in half. Place each piece of dough in a buttered 9-inch square pan. Brush the top of each cake with 1 tablespoon of the melted butter. Cover and set aside in a warm place to rise until doubled, 40 to 50 minutes.

5~ Preheat the oven to 375°.

6~ In a small heavy saucepan, stir together the brown sugar, cream, honey and the remaining 6 tablespoons butter. Bring to a boil for 30 seconds. Remove from the heat and stir in the lemon juice and almonds. Let cool slightly, 8 to 10 minutes. Drizzle the topping evenly over both cakes.

7~ Bake for 30 to 35 minutes, or until the cakes are golden brown. Let cool in the pans on a rack. If desired, wrap one cake in plastic wrap and freeze for up to 2 weeks.

MAKES TWO 9-INCH SQUARE CAKES, ABOUT 16 SERVINGS
RECIPE BY RICHARD SAX

The *tarte Tatin* is a classic French tart in which the ingredients are layered and cooked under a top crust of pastry. A tatin is inverted for serving, not unlike the ubiquitous all-American upside-down cake. Don't try to prepare this tart ahead of time—wait until you're up and functioning.

1¾ CUPS ALL-PURPOSE FLOUR
2½ TEASPOONS BAKING POWDER
¼ TEASPOON SALT
½ CUP PLUS 1 TABLESPOON SUGAR
10 TABLESPOONS COLD UNSALTED BUTTER, CUT INTO SMALL PIECES
6 TO 8 COOKING APPLES, SUCH AS GOLDEN DELICIOUS—PEELED, CORED AND QUARTERED
1 CUP MILK
WHIPPED CREAM (OPTIONAL)

1~ In a food processor, blend the flour, baking powder, salt and 1 tablespoon of the sugar. Add 6 tablespoons of the butter and process just until crumbly. Remove to a bowl, cover and refrigerate until ready to bake the tart.

2~ Place the remaining ½ cup sugar and 4 tablespoons butter in a 9- to 10-inch heavy ovenproof skillet, preferably cast iron, and melt over moderate heat. Remove from the heat. Arrange the apple quarters in overlapping concentric circles, rounded-side down. (The apples will shrink as they cook, so don't worry that they seem crowded in the pan when you start.)

3~ Cook over moderately high heat, rotating the pan occasionally for even browning, until the apples are soft and well browned on the bottom and the liquid that remains is thick and syrupy, about 30 minutes. *(The recipe can be made several hours ahead to this point. Set aside at room temperature until ready to bake.)*

4~ Preheat the oven to 450°.

5~ Add the milk to the biscuit mixture and blend just to incorporate. Distribute the biscuit mixture evenly over the top of the apples. Bake in the middle of the oven for about 15 minutes, or until browned on top.

6~ Let the tatin rest for 5 minutes, and then invert onto a large round serving plate. (If the apple pieces don't come out evenly or some cling to the pan, just stick them back on where they belong.)

7~ Cut into wedges and serve with whipped cream if desired.

SERVES 6 TO 8
RECIPE BY ANNE DISRUDE

■ ■ ■

A
TAX-TIME
DINNER

Celebrate tax time? What's to celebrate, you may well ask. April 15 may not be a festive occasion in and of itself, but there's no reason why the weekend after need be lonely, dull or morose. Why not telephone some equally "strapped" friends and invite them over for an evening of reduced-circumstances revelry? It just happens that every ingredient in this meal is inexpensive, so whether you actually need to watch your pennies or not, this menu makes for a tasty casual dinner and an amusing evening with friends. ∼ You can capitalize on the poverty theme of this meal and have fun with it, or you can ignore it altogether. Bring out your finest china, crystal and linens, or opt for paper plates, jam-jar glasses and well-worn but clean dish towels as napkins. Either way, everyone at your table is sure to enjoy the main-course offerings – barbecued ribs, potato salad, applesauce and corn bread. Later on, a plate of Depression Cookies and a pot of chicory-laced coffee will add a fitting end to an entertaining evening.

■ ■ ■

23

*Spareribs with
Molasses-Mustard
Glaze*

Rosy Applesauce

Corn Bread

*Tangy Potato
Salad*

24

A
TAX-TIME
DINNER

Serves 4

DOMESTIC BEER, JUG WINE
AND TAP WATER
Spicy Pumpkin Seeds

*Pan-Fried Parsley Cakes with
Tomato-Anchovy Sauce*

Spareribs with Molasses-Mustard Glaze
Rosy Applesauce
Tangy Potato Salad
Corn Bread

CHICORY COFFEE
Depression Cookies

SPICY PUMPKIN SEEDS

These seeds are deliciously addictive. Make a double or triple batch to have on hand for nibbling.

1 GARLIC CLOVE, MINCED
1 TABLESPOON OLIVE OIL
2 TEASPOONS GROUND CUMIN
1 TEASPOON SWEET PAPRIKA
½ TEASPOON CAYENNE PEPPER
½ CUP SHELLED PUMPKIN SEEDS (PEPITAS)*
1 TEASPOON COARSE (KOSHER) SALT
*AVAILABLE IN LATIN AMERICAN GROCER-
   IES AND HEALTH FOOD STORES

1~ Preheat the oven to 400°.
2~ In a small skillet, cook the garlic in the oil over low heat for about 5 minutes without browning. Strain the oil through a fine sieve and discard the garlic. Return the garlic-flavored oil to the skillet and add the cumin, paprika and cayenne. Cook over low heat, stirring occasionally, until fragrant, about 1 minute.
3~ Place the pumpkin seeds on a baking sheet. Scrape the spice mixture over the seeds, sprinkle with the salt and toss to coat evenly. Spread the seeds in a single layer. Bake in the oven for about 5 minutes, or until they turn light brown. The seeds will pop and dance while cooking.

MAKES ABOUT ½ CUP
RECIPE BY MARCIA KIESEL

PAN-FRIED PARSLEY CAKES WITH TOMATO-ANCHOVY SAUCE

Parsley may be the most underestimated ingredient on earth. Though it appears as a garnish here, it's also the main ingredient.

4 CUPS PARSLEY, LARGE STEMS REMOVED,
   PLUS 1 TABLESPOON CHOPPED PARSLEY
4 TABLESPOONS UNSALTED BUTTER
1 SMALL ONION, MINCED
½ CUP HEAVY CREAM
¾ TEASPOON SALT
¾ TEASPOON FRESHLY GROUND PEPPER
1⅓ CUPS FINE BREAD CRUMBS
⅓ CUP GRATED SWISS CHEESE
½ CUP ALL-PURPOSE FLOUR
1 EGG, LIGHTLY BEATEN
¼ CUP OLIVE OIL
1 TEASPOON ANCHOVY PASTE
1 TEASPOON MINCED GARLIC
2 TEASPOONS CHOPPED CAPERS
½ CUP CHOPPED CANNED ITALIAN PEELED
   TOMATOES
2 TEASPOONS FRESH LEMON JUICE
¼ CUP DRY WHITE WINE
SPRIGS OF PARSLEY, FOR GARNISH

1~ In a medium saucepan, bring 6 cups of water to a boil. Add the 4 cups of parsley and blanch until wilted, about 3 minutes; drain and coarsely chop.
2~ In a medium skillet, melt 2 tablespoons of the butter over moderate heat. Add the onion and reduce the heat to low. Cook until softened but not browned, about 5 minutes. Add the blanched parsley and the heavy cream. Cover and simmer over low heat until most of the cream is absorbed, about 10 minutes.

3~ Place the parsley mixture in a medium bowl. Stir in ½ teaspoon of the salt, ½ teaspoon of the pepper, ⅓ cup of the bread crumbs and the Swiss cheese. Cover and refrigerate until chilled, about 45 minutes.

4~ When the parsley mixture is cold, press it into 8 round cakes, 2 inches in diameter. Dredge the parsley cakes in the flour, dip in the egg and then dredge in the remaining 1 cup bread crumbs.

5~ In a medium saucepan, heat 2 tablespoons of the olive oil over low heat. Add the anchovy paste and garlic and cook until aromatic, about 1 minute. Add the capers, tomatoes, lemon juice and wine. Simmer over moderate heat, stirring occasionally, until the flavors are combined, about 4 minutes. Remove from the heat and stir in the remaining 2 tablespoons butter. Season with the remaining ¼ teaspoon each salt and pepper. Add the 1 tablespoon chopped parsley; keep warm.

6~ In a large skillet, heat the remaining 2 tablespoons olive oil over moderately high heat. Add the parsley cakes and cook until the first side is well browned, about 2 minutes. Turn and cook until browned on the second side, about 2 minutes longer. Drain the cakes on paper towels. Reheat the sauce over low heat and divide among 4 warm plates. Place 2 parsley cakes on each and garnish with parsley sprigs.

SERVES 4
RECIPE BY MARCIA KIESEL

SPARERIBS WITH MOLASSES-MUSTARD GLAZE

There's something about spareribs that just automatically makes you feel better—maybe because it's perfectly proper to use your fingers to eat them. Tax time or not, these are a treat.

2 RACKS (ABOUT 6 POUNDS) BABY PORK
    SPARERIBS, TRIMMED OF EXCESS FAT
    AND CRACKED
1 TEASPOON SALT
1¼ TEASPOONS FRESHLY GROUND PEPPER
¾ CUP MOLASSES-MUSTARD GLAZE
    (AT RIGHT)

1~ Preheat the oven to 350°. Season the ribs on both sides with the salt and pepper and lay them meaty-side down on a large roasting pan or jelly-roll pan. Bake on the middle rack of the oven for 1 hour, turning once after 30 minutes. Drain off any excess fat.

2~ Increase the oven temperature to 400°. Generously brush the meaty side of the ribs with the Molasses-Mustard Glaze and bake for 5 minutes; repeat 2 more times, letting the ribs bake for 10 minutes after their third coating.

3~ Remove the ribs from the oven. When cool enough to handle, cut the ribs apart with a thin, sharp knife. Serve warm. *(The ribs can be made ahead and reheated loosely covered with foil.)*

SERVES 4
RECIPE BY MICHAEL MCLAUGHLIN

MOLASSES-MUSTARD GLAZE

The glaze can be stored, covered, in the refrigerator for several weeks, although the flavors will diminish.

½ CUP DIJON-STYLE MUSTARD
⅓ CUP CIDER VINEGAR
⅓ CUP PACKED DARK BROWN SUGAR
½ CUP UNSULPHURED MOLASSES
1 TEASPOON HOT PEPPER SAUCE,
    OR TO TASTE
1 TEASPOON DRIED THYME
1 TABLESPOON POWDERED MUSTARD
½ TEASPOON SALT

1~ In a small nonreactive saucepan, whisk all of the ingredients together until thoroughly mixed. Bring to a boil over moderate heat. Reduce the heat and simmer, uncovered, for 5 minutes.

2~ Remove the glaze from the heat, transfer immediately to a bowl and let cool to room temperature before using.

MAKES ABOUT 1½ CUPS
RECIPE BY MICHAEL MCLAUGHLIN

Housekeeping Hints You Probably Didn't Know

Age-honored wisdom from Buckeye Cookery *and Practical Housekeeping, Buckeye Publishing Co., Minneapolis, 1880.*

NUTMEGS—Always grate nutmegs at the blossom end first.

TO PRESERVE MILK—A spoonful of grated horse-radish will keep a pan of milk sweet for days.

CORN STARCH is a good substitute for eggs in cookies and doughnuts. One table-spoon of the starch is equal to one egg.

SILVER POLISH—To one quart rain-water add two ounces ammonia and three ounces of precipitated chalk. Put into a bottle, keep well corked and shake before using.

TO FRESHEN WALNUTS—When walnuts have been kept until the meat is too much dried to be good, let them stand in milk and water eight hours, and dry them, and they will be as fresh as when new.

WASHING DISHES—Care must be taken not to put tumblers which have had milk in them into hot water, as it drives the milk into the glass, whence it can never be removed. They should be first rinsed well in tepid water.

ROSY APPLESAUCE

When cooked with the peel, then strained, applesauce can range from a blushing golden shade to sparkling burgundy, depending on which variety of apples you choose. It even seems to taste better when the color is pronounced.

2 POUNDS APPLES (CHOOSE CORTLAND FOR
  CANDY-PINK SAUCE OR EMPIRE FOR A
  DEEP ROSE COLOR), CORED AND CUT
  INTO CHUNKS, BUT NOT PEELED
2 TEASPOONS TO 2 TABLESPOONS SUGAR,
  TO TASTE
⅛ TEASPOON GROUND CORIANDER OR
  PINCH OF CINNAMON (OPTIONAL)

1~ In a heavy medium saucepan, combine the apples with ¼ cup of water. Cover and cook gently over moderately low heat, stirring occasionally, until the apples are very soft. (Cooking time will vary from 15 to 30 minutes, depending on the variety of apples used.)
2~ Let the apples cool, uncovered, for about 15 minutes.
3~ Press the apples through a food mill into a bowl. For a coarse sauce, use the wide disk, being careful not to push through the skins. For a smoother, all-purpose texture, a medium disk will do.
4~ Stir in the sugar gradually, adjusting to taste; stir in the coriander. If you prefer a stiffer texture, return the sauce to the pan and cook over moderate heat for a few minutes, stirring constantly, to evaporate some of the liquid.

SERVES 4
RECIPE BY ELIZABETH SCHNEIDER

TANGY POTATO SALAD

There is a rule that, even though unwritten, is a culinary absolute: You must serve potato salad with spareribs. You must. This tart potato salad is simple as can be, but if you want to, dress it up by adding celery, hard-cooked eggs, scallions or whatever else comes to mind.

2 POUNDS BOILING POTATOES (5 TO 6
  MEDIUM)
⅓ CUP MAYONNAISE
⅓ CUP SOUR CREAM
2 TABLESPOONS HOT DIJON-STYLE MUSTARD
3 TABLESPOONS GRATED ONION
1 TEASPOON POWDERED MUSTARD
½ TEASPOON SALT
½ TEASPOON FRESHLY GROUND PEPPER
1 SMALL BUNCH OF PARSLEY, CHOPPED, FOR
  GARNISH

1~ Place the potatoes in a medium saucepan and add cold water to cover. Bring to a boil over high heat. Reduce the heat to moderately low and simmer for 20 to 30 minutes, or until the potatoes are fork-tender.
2~ Meanwhile, in a large serving bowl, blend together the mayonnaise, sour cream, Dijon mustard, onion, powdered mustard, salt and pepper.

3~ When the potatoes are cooked, drain them and set under cold running water to cool. Peel the potatoes and cut into ¼-inch slices. As they are cut, place the slices in the bowl and coat with some of the dressing. Taste and correct the seasonings, if necessary.

4~ Sprinkle on the parsley and serve the potato salad warm or at room temperature.

SERVES 6
RECIPE BY FOOD & WINE

CORN BREAD

Fingers of corn bread are a tasty addition to any meal—especially if they are served warm and slathered with whipped honey butter.

1½ CUPS YELLOW CORNMEAL
½ CUP ALL-PURPOSE FLOUR
1 TABLESPOON BAKING POWDER
1 TEASPOON SALT
3 EGGS
1¼ CUPS MILK
1 TABLESPOON SUGAR
4 TABLESPOONS UNSALTED BUTTER,
    MELTED

1~ Preheat the oven to 400°. Lightly butter a 13-by-9-inch baking dish.

2~ In a large bowl, sift together the cornmeal, flour, baking powder and salt. In another bowl, beat the eggs with the milk and sugar. Add the egg mixture to the dry ingredients and mix thoroughly. Stir in the melted butter and pour the batter evenly into the prepared pan.

3~ Bake the corn bread for 12 to 15 minutes, or until a toothpick inserted in the center comes out clean. Serve warm or at room temperature.

SERVES 4 TO 6
RECIPE BY FOOD & WINE

DEPRESSION COOKIES

Don't let the name fool you. Neither you nor the United States need be depressed to serve these cookies—they work just as well when you're happy and the Dow Jones is on the rise.

½ POUND (2 STICKS) UNSALTED BUTTER,
    SOFTENED
1 CUP SUGAR
1 EGG
¼ CUP DARK UNSULPHURED MOLASSES
2 CUPS SIFTED ALL-PURPOSE FLOUR
2 TEASPOONS BAKING SODA
2 TEASPOONS GROUND CLOVES
1 TEASPOON GROUND GINGER

1~ Preheat the oven to 300°. Grease 2 or more baking sheets.

2~ In a medium mixer bowl, beat the butter with the sugar until light and creamy, about 5 minutes. Add the egg and the molasses and beat until well blended.

3~ In a small bowl, combine the flour, baking soda, cloves and ginger. Gradually add the dry ingredients to the butter and beat until well blended. Cover and refrigerate for 20 minutes.

4~ Remove the dough from the refrigerator. Drop rounded teaspoons of the dough onto the prepared baking sheets, leaving 2 inches in between. Bake for 15 to 18 minutes, until the cookies are a deep golden brown. Let cool for 1 minute, then transfer to a rack to cool completely. *(These cookies will keep for up to one week at room temperature in a tightly covered tin.)*

MAKES 6 DOZEN
RECIPE BY KEN HAEDRICH

■ ■ ■

A PROCRASTINATOR'S DINNER

2 8

Here's a menu that will appeal to the wily side of all true procrastinators. If you can get organized to do a little bit of preparation every couple of months, the payoff is wanton procrastination after that. The trick is this: Buy, pound flat and freeze a large number of boneless chicken breasts. By doing so, you will be prepared to make Spontaneous Chicken at a moment's notice. ∼ You can serve this entrée with confidence as a planned dinner for guests, an impromptu meal with the neighbors or a Saturday night family supper. If you want to dress it up, you can: Stir in some braised wild mushrooms, douse it with brandy or crumble some crisped pancetta on top. Or maybe what makes Spontaneous Chicken so right is its adaptability. You might choose to serve the chicken on a bed of rich egg noodles, next to a mound of sautéed Vidalia onions or over Mighty Quick Biscuits (page 51). The remainder of our menu relies on pantry staples and a few fresh ingredients from the greengrocer (no need to brave the supermarket). The result? An incredibly easy three-course meal for six.

Green Bean and Tomato Salad

Spontaneous Chicken with Mustard Sauce

Sage and Walnut Corn Cakes

■ ■ ■

30

A PROCRASTINATOR'S DINNER

Serves 6

SAUVIGNON BLANC
Sage and Walnut Corn Cakes
Green Bean and Tomato Salad
Spontaneous Chicken
with Mustard Sauce

Pineapple Brûlé

SAGE AND WALNUT CORN CAKES

Don't think this recipe makes more than you and your guests can eat. You'll all gobble these corn cakes right up.

1 CUP MILK
1 EGG
5 TABLESPOONS EXTRA-VIRGIN OLIVE OIL
1 CUP ALL-PURPOSE FLOUR
1 CUP FINELY GROUND CORNMEAL
2½ TEASPOONS BAKING POWDER
1½ TABLESPOONS SUGAR
1 TEASPOON SALT
20 FRESH SAGE LEAVES
⅔ CUP CHOPPED WALNUTS

1~ In a bowl, combine the milk, egg and 3 table-spoons of the oil; beat well.

2~ In a medium bowl, whisk together the flour, cornmeal, baking powder, sugar and salt. Make a well in the center; stir in the milk mixture.

3~ Heat a griddle, preferably cast iron, over moderate heat. Add 1 tablespoon of the oil and swirl to coat. When the oil shimmers, scatter 10 of the sage leaves over the griddle and sprinkle on ⅓ cup of the walnuts. Pour half the batter onto the griddle to just cover the nuts and sage leaves. (The batter should be no more than ½ inch thick.)

4~ Cook until bubbles appear on the surface, 5 to 7 minutes; the top should be barely wet. Slide the cake onto a plate and carefully invert onto the griddle. Cook the second side for about 4 minutes, until browned. Transfer to a rack and repeat with the remaining oil, sage, walnuts and batter. Serve warm.

MAKES TWO 10-INCH CAKES
RECIPE BY ANNE DISRUDE

GREEN BEAN AND TOMATO SALAD

You can procrastinate all you want before making this dish, as long as you take five seconds to pour the vinegar over the shallots a few hours in advance. Halve the recipe unless leftovers make tomorrow sound easier.

2 LARGE SHALLOTS, THINLY SLICED
¼ CUP RED WINE VINEGAR
1 TABLESPOON DIJON-STYLE MUSTARD
¼ TEASPOON SALT
1 TEASPOON FRESHLY GROUND PEPPER
½ CUP EXTRA-VIRGIN OLIVE OIL
1½ POUNDS THIN GREEN BEANS, TRIMMED
½ CUP FINELY SHREDDED FRESH BASIL
3 PINTS RED AND YELLOW CHERRY OR PEAR
   TOMATOES, HALVED LENGTHWISE

1~ In a medium bowl, cover the shallots with the vinegar and let macerate for 2 to 3 hours, or overnight. Whisk in the mustard, salt and pepper. Gradually whisk in the olive oil.

2~ In a large pot of boiling salted water, cook the green beans until tender but still firm to the bite, 1½ to 2 minutes after the water returns to a boil. Drain, rinse under cold running water and drain well. *(The recipe can be prepared to this point up to 2 days ahead. Cover and refrigerate the dressing and beans separately.)*

3~ Stir the basil into the dressing. In a bowl, toss the beans with half of the dressing. Arrange them on one side of a large platter. Toss the tomatoes with the remaining dressing and mound them next to the beans.

SERVES 12
RECIPE BY BOB CHAMBERS

SPONTANEOUS CHICKEN WITH MUSTARD SAUCE

On one of those rare enterprising days, the habitual procrastinator can prepare to indulge his or her inclination to delay. The chicken for this dish is frozen for at least an hour—or for up to two months—before cooking.

CHICKEN:
6 BONELESS CHICKEN BREAST HALVES
6 TABLESPOONS UNSALTED BUTTER
1½ TABLESPOONS VEGETABLE OIL

MUSTARD SAUCE:
2 BUNCHES OF SCALLIONS (WHITE PART
    AND ABOUT 2 INCHES OF THE GREEN),
    THINLY SLICED (ABOUT 1½ CUPS)
1½ CUPS HEAVY CREAM
¾ CUP DRY WHITE WINE
1 TABLESPOON MUSTARD SEEDS
1½ TABLESPOONS STRONG DIJON-STYLE
    MUSTARD
SALT AND FRESHLY GROUND PEPPER
1 LEMON, THINLY SLICED, FOR GARNISH

1~ *Prepare the Chicken:* Trim off and discard any excess fat from each chicken breast.
2~ Place each chicken breast half between two sheets of waxed paper and pound until flattened to about ¼ inch. Peel off the paper and place the cutlet on a baking sheet or any flat surface. Place in the freezer for 1 hour. *(Wrapped tightly in foil and stacked in the freezer, these pounded cutlets can be frozen for up to 2 months. It's worthwhile doing a large batch, so that the makings for a meal are always close at hand.)*

3~ *Cook the Chicken:* In a large skillet set over moderate heat, melt the butter with the oil until foamy. Working in batches as necessary, sauté the cutlets for 1 minute on each side. Remove from the skillet and set aside.
4~ *Make the Mustard Sauce and complete the dish:* Add the scallion to the skillet and sauté over moderate heat, stirring, for 2 minutes, until soft. Add the cream, wine and mustard seeds and cook, stirring frequently, for 5 minutes.
5~ Stir in the mustard; season with salt and pepper to taste. Working in batches, return three of the chicken cutlets to the skillet and turn to coat them with the sauce. Reduce the heat to low and simmer gently for 2 to 3 minutes, or until the chicken is just cooked through. Cook the remaining chicken in the same manner.
6~ Serve with some of the sauce spooned over the top of each cutlet. Tuck the lemon slices between the cutlets.

SERVES 6
RECIPE BY W. PETER PRESTCOTT

PINEAPPLE BRÛLÉ

Fresh pineapple is a treat all by itself. Quickly jazzed up with some rum, sugar and butter, it's a sight and sensation to behold.

4 TABLESPOONS UNSALTED BUTTER
1¼ CUPS LOOSELY PACKED DARK BROWN
    SUGAR
½ CUP DARK RUM
½ TEASPOON LEMON JUICE
¼ TEASPOON ALMOND EXTRACT
2 RIPE PINEAPPLES, QUARTERED LENGTH-
    WISE, WITH LEAFY TOPS ATTACHED

1~ In a small saucepan, melt the butter over low heat. Add 1 cup of the brown sugar, the rum, lemon juice and almond extract. Cook, stirring frequently, for 10 minutes; set aside.
2~ Using a sharp knife, cut the flesh of the pineapple away from the skin, leaving a ½-inch shell. Cut away and discard the core. Cut the pineapple into wedges about 1 inch thick. Return the wedges to the shell and push every other wedge from the center toward the opposite side of the shell to create a pattern.
3~ Preheat the broiler. Wrap the leafy tops in foil to prevent them from burning. Place as many pineapple quarters as will fit in a large, shallow baking or roasting pan. Spoon about 2 tablespoons of the rum sauce over each quarter and sprinkle each serving with some of the remaining ¼ cup brown sugar.
4~ Broil 6 inches from the heat for 4 to 5 minutes, or until the sugar begins to bubble. Broil the remaining batches in the same manner. Remove the foil and serve hot.

SERVES 8
RECIPE BY W. PETER PRESTCOTT

POTLUCK SUPPER

If you're in the mood to entertain a large number of people in a casual way, there's nothing quite as free and easy as a potluck supper. The constraints are few: A potluck meal can be served indoors or out, in the afternoon or evening, at any time of year. ~ By definition, a potluck doesn't promise the moon and stars–just whatever you feel like cooking at the time. And as long as you offer at least a few foods that have universal appeal, no one will go hungry. The entrées here (glazed country ham, chile-roasted turkey, ten-chile chili) and the accompaniments (stuffed eggs, baked beans, potato salad, pasta salad, coleslaw, biscuits) offer something to please every appetite. And when dessert time rolls around, your guests will want to sample both kinds of pie, plus the ice cream and the rice pudding. ~ Potluck suppers are easy because you select do-ahead recipes, saving on last-minute angst. Remember to triple and quadruple recipes that have relatively small yields to avoid running out. Your potluck supper should be as generous in quantity as it is in spirit.

■ ■ ■

*Glazed
Country Ham*

Pasta Salad

Ten-Chile Chili

Calico Corn Salad

*Spiced Baked
Beans*

Chile-Roasted

GLAZED COUNTRY HAM

34

POTLUCK SUPPER

Serves 40

BEER, WINE, LEMONADE, LIMEADE
AND ICED TEA

Glazed Country Ham

Chile-Roasted Turkey

Ten-Chile Chili

Disheveled Eggs

Calico Corn Salad

Spiced Baked Beans

Green Potato Salad

Caraway Coleslaw

Pasta Salad

Buttermilk Biscuits

*Deep-Dish All-American Cinnamon
Apple Pie*

Strawberry-Rhubarb Pie

Vanilla Lover's Vanilla Ice Cream

Rice Pudding with Orange and Bay

Blueberry-Bay Compote

Nothing could be finer than a platter stacked with thin slices of a well-cured country ham from Carolina—or Virginia.

1 COUNTRY-STYLE CURED HAM, AT LEAST
  14 POUNDS
1 QUART FRESH UNPASTEURIZED CIDER OR
  UNSWEETENED APPLE JUICE
30 WHOLE CLOVES
3 BAY LEAVES
1 CUP BOURBON
1 CUP BITTER-ORANGE MARMALADE
¼ CUP DIJON-STYLE MUSTARD

1~ Wash the ham under tepid running water, using a brush to scrub away any surface mold or dust. Place the ham in a large pot and cover with cold water. Set aside in a cool place (do not refrigerate); let soak, changing the water at least twice, for about 48 hours.

2~ Remove the ham and discard the soaking water. Place the ham in a large stockpot. Add the cider, 12 of the cloves, the bay leaves and 4 cups of water. Set the pot over moderate heat and bring the water to a boil. Cover, reduce the heat to moderately low and simmer until the shank bone is loose enough to move in its socket, 3 to 4 hours, or about 15 minutes per pound. Remove the ham from the cooking liquid, drain and let cool for about 10 minutes, until it can be handled.

3~ Using a large sharp knife, remove the skin and enough fat from the ham so that only a ½-inch coating remains. Score the ham fat with criss-cross lines to form a diamond pattern.

4~ Preheat the oven to 400°.

5~ In a small nonreactive saucepan, combine the bourbon, marmalade and mustard. Cook over moderate heat, stirring occasionally, until just boiling, about 5 minutes. Set the glaze aside.

6~ Garnish the ham with the remaining 18 cloves, inserting one in each corner of the diamonds. Using a small brush, coat the ham evenly with the glaze. Place the ham in a large roasting pan. Bake on the lowest shelf of the oven until nicely browned, 20 to 30 minutes.

7~ Remove the ham from the oven and let stand for at least 30 minutes before carving. To carve, make a deep vertical cut at the shank end about 4 inches from the end of the bone. Thinly slice the ham on the diagonal toward the shank end. Serve warm, at room temperature or chilled.

SERVES 25 TO 30
RECIPE BY NANCY HARMON JENKINS

CHILE-ROASTED TURKEY

The method for cutting up this turkey is easier done than said, and the effort is worthwhile since by doing so you'll save hours of cooking time.

6 ANCHO CHILES (ABOUT 3 OUNCES)
1 CUP BOILING WATER
3 GARLIC CLOVES, SMASHED
1 MEDIUM ONION, QUARTERED
1 TABLESPOON FRESH LIME JUICE
1 TABLESPOON CORN OIL
½ TEASPOON SALT
12-POUND TURKEY, PREFERABLY FRESH

1~ Preheat the oven to 350°. Arrange the ancho chiles on a baking sheet and heat in the oven until softened, about 2 minutes. Cut open the chiles and discard the stems, seeds and ribs. Rinse the chiles and place in a small bowl; cover with the boiling water and let soak for 30 minutes.

2~ In a food processor, combine the chiles with ¼ cup of their soaking liquid, the garlic, onion, lime juice, corn oil and salt. Puree until smooth, about 2 minutes, scraping down the sides of the bowl once or twice. *(The chile puree can be made up to 3 days ahead and refrigerated in a covered container.)*

3~ Cut up the turkey: Pull the turkey leg away from the body and, with a sharp knife, cut through the hip joint to remove the thigh and drumstick in one piece. Repeat with the other leg. Starting at the neck, cut the meat from one half of the breast, cutting and scraping against the bone and keeping the blade of the knife as close to the rib cage as possible. Cut through the wing joint and remove the wing and boneless breast half in one piece. Repeat with the other side. There will be 4 large pieces of turkey. Discard the neck, giblets and carcass or reserve them for stock.

4~ Score the turkey skin at 1-inch intervals. Rub the chile puree all over the pieces of turkey. Let marinate at room temperature for 1 hour, or in a large plastic bag in the refrigerator for up to 24 hours. Let return to room temperature before cooking.

5~ Preheat the oven to 450°. Arrange the turkey pieces, skin-side up, in a single layer in a large shallow baking pan and place in the middle of the oven. Reduce the oven temperature to 325° and bake for 1½ hours, or until the thickest part of the thigh registers 170° on an instant-reading thermometer and the juices run clear.

6~ Remove the turkey from the oven and let cool for at least 15 minutes. Separate the wings from the breast and carve each breast into thin slices. Cut the remaining meat off the thigh and leg bones. *(The turkey is, of course, best when freshly cooked, but it can be made up to 2 days ahead, wrapped well and refrigerated. Let return to room temperature before serving.)*

SERVES 16
RECIPE BY DIANA STURGIS

DISHEVELED EGGS

Stuffed eggs often look too perfect, as if an artist made them rather than an ordinary cook. These eggs aren't fancy, but they are deliciously disheveled.

1½ TEASPOONS CARAWAY SEED
12 EGGS
¼ POUND BACON (ABOUT 6 SLICES)
6 TABLESPOONS MAYONNAISE
2 TABLESPOONS PREPARED MUSTARD
¼ TEASPOON SALT
¼ TEASPOON FRESHLY GROUND PEPPER

1~ Place the caraway seed in a small saucepan. Add 1 cup of water and bring to a boil over high heat. Reduce the heat slightly and boil until the liquid is nearly evaporated; set aside to cool.

2~ Place the eggs in a large heavy saucepan and add water to cover by 1 inch. Bring to a boil over moderate heat. Reduce the heat and simmer for 10 minutes. Rinse the eggs under cold running water until cool enough to handle; remove the shells.

3~ Meanwhile, cut the bacon into ¼-inch squares, and fry them in a large skillet over moderate heat until crisp and brown. Drain on paper towels.

4~ Slice the eggs in half lengthwise and remove the yolks. Mash the yolks in a medium bowl. Add the caraway seed and liquid, the bacon, mayonnaise, mustard, salt and pepper; blend well. Fill the egg white halves with the yolk mixture. Refrigerate until chilled.

MAKES 2 DOZEN
RECIPE BY W. PETER PRESTCOTT

35

TEN-CHILE CHILI

This chili will knock your socks off—not because it's wildly hot and spicy, but because of the mix of complex flavors it contains.

⅓ CUP CUMIN SEED

2 TABLESPOONS CORIANDER SEED

2 ANCHO CHILES

2 MULATO CHILES

4 PASILLA CHILES

6 POUNDS TRIMMED BEEF CHUCK,
    CUT INTO 1½-BY-¼-INCH STRIPS

½ POUND THICKLY SLICED LEAN BACON,
    CUT CROSSWISE INTO THIN JULIENNE

¾ POUND HAM, FINELY DICED

1½ TABLESPOONS CORN OIL

3 POUNDS LARGE YELLOW SPANISH ONIONS,
    FINELY DICED

¾ CUP DICED CELERY

1 CUP GROUND ANCHO CHILE POWDER*

½ TEASPOON CAYENNE PEPPER

5 BAY LEAVES

1 PEQUIN CHILE (OPTIONAL)

3 JALAPEÑO PEPPERS, SEEDED AND MINCED

3 SERRANO PEPPERS, SEEDED AND MINCED

½ CAN (3½ OUNCES) CHIPOTLE CHILES IN
    ADOBO SAUCE,* COARSELY CHOPPED

1 SMOKED HAM HOCK

2 CANS (35 OUNCES EACH) ITALIAN PEELED
    TOMATOES, DRAINED

½ CUP GOLDEN TEQUILA

2 CUPS BEEF STOCK OR CANNED BROTH

½ TEASPOON ROSEMARY

1 TEASPOON CRUMBLED SAGE LEAVES

1 TEASPOON OREGANO

POBLANO AND ANAHEIM CHILE JULIENNE

*AVAILABLE AT LATIN AMERICAN MARKETS

1~ Preheat the oven to 500°.

2~ In a medium skillet, toast the cumin and coriander seed over moderate heat until fragrant, 1 to 2 minutes. Immediately remove from the heat. Grind to a powder in a spice grinder or food processor.

3~ Place the ancho, mulato and pasilla chiles on a baking sheet and toast them in the oven until fragrant and puffed up, about 2 minutes. Remove the stems and seeds and grind the chiles in a spice grinder or food processor until powdered.

4~ In a stockpot or large stovetop casserole, combine the beef, bacon, ham and corn oil. Cook over moderate heat until the fat is rendered and the bacon is golden, about 20 minutes.

5~ Add the onions and cook, stirring occasionally, until the onions are golden brown, about 20 minutes.

6~ Add the celery, ground chiles and ancho chile powder. Cook, stirring frequently, until the celery is softened and the chile powder is fragrant, about 10 minutes.

7~ Stir in the cayenne, bay leaves, pequin chile, jalapeño and serrano peppers, chipotle chiles, ham hock, tomatoes, tequila, stock, rosemary, sage and oregano. Simmer, uncovered, over low heat, stirring occasionally, for 4 hours.

8~ Serve the chili, garnished with poblano and Anaheim chile julienne.

SERVES 12 TO 18
RECIPE BY BRENDAN WALSH

CALICO CORN SALAD

Though this recipe is best when sweet corn is in season, it still satisfies a craving for corn when only frozen is available. If you use fresh corn, reserve the husks and mound the salad in them to serve.

1 CUP MEDIUM CRACKED WHEAT (BULGUR)

2 CUPS BOILING WATER

⅔ CUP OLIVE OIL

2½ TO 3 CUPS CORN KERNELS

1 CUP MINCED SCALLIONS

1 CUP MINCED FRESH PARSLEY

1 CUP MINCED MINT LEAVES

1 TABLESPOON FINELY MINCED LEMON ZEST

1 CUP FINELY CHOPPED RED BELL PEPPER

⅓ CUP FRESH LEMON JUICE

1½ TO 2 TEASPOONS SALT

FRESHLY GROUND PEPPER

1~ Place the cracked wheat in a bowl with the boiling water and let rest for 1 hour. Drain in a fine sieve, rinse under cold water and, with the back of a large spoon, press out all excess moisture; transfer to a large bowl and set aside.

2~ In a medium skillet, heat 3 tablespoons of the oil over moderately high heat. Add the corn and sauté for 2 minutes, stirring frequently. Remove from the heat and let cool to room temperature.

3~ Add the corn, scallions, parsley, mint, lemon zest and bell pepper to the cracked wheat and gently combine. Mix in the remaining oil. Add the lemon juice, salt and pepper to taste; mix again. Chill, covered, for several hours or overnight.

SERVES 8
RECIPE BY FOOD & WINE

SPICED BAKED BEANS

This is a cross between old-fashioned Boston baked beans and a bean dish from the Piedmont region of Italy. Since these beans improve with age, you can safely make them a couple of days in advance and reheat in a slow oven before serving.

2 CUPS (1 POUND) NAVY, PEA OR SMALL
    WHITE BEANS, SOAKED AND DRAINED
2 CUPS CHICKEN OR BEEF STOCK
1 MEDIUM ONION, FINELY CHOPPED
    (ABOUT 1 CUP)
4 SMALL GARLIC CLOVES, MINCED
8 SLICES BACON, PREFERABLY NITRITE-FREE,
    CHOPPED
1 TEASPOON SALT
½ TEASPOON GROUND CUMIN
¼ TEASPOON GROUND MACE
¼ TEASPOON GROUND CLOVES
½ TEASPOON FRESHLY GROUND PEPPER
¼ CUP BLACKSTRAP MOLASSES

1~ Preheat the oven to 300°.
2~ In a 3- to 5-quart ovenproof casserole, combine all of the ingredients and stir until mixed. Add 4 cups of water and bring to a simmer on top of the stove. Cover and bake for 6 hours.
3~ Increase the oven temperature to 350°. Uncover the casserole and continue baking until the beans have absorbed all of the liquid and formed a slight crust on top, 45 minutes to 1 hour.

SERVES 8
RECIPE BY MICHÈLE URVATER

GREEN POTATO SALAD

Guests will give their "green light" of approval for this basic, homey potato salad.

⅓ CUP OLIVE OIL
2 TABLESPOONS RED WINE VINEGAR
1 TEASPOON DIJON-STYLE MUSTARD
1 TEASPOON CARAWAY SEEDS
½ TEASPOON SALT
½ TEASPOON FRESHLY GROUND PEPPER
2 POUNDS SMALL RED POTATOES
¼ CUP MINCED FRESH PARSLEY
1 MEDIUM GREEN BELL PEPPER, CUT INTO
    ⅛-INCH DICE
4 MEDIUM SCALLIONS, THINLY SLICED
½ POUND BACON (ABOUT 12 SLICES),
    COOKED UNTIL CRISP, AND DRAINED

1~ In a small bowl, whisk together the oil, vinegar, mustard, caraway seeds, salt and pepper. Set the dressing aside.
2~ Place the potatoes in a medium saucepan of cold water. Bring to a boil and cook over moderate heat until tender but slightly resistant in the center when pierced with a knife, about 20 minutes. Do not overcook. Drain and transfer to a bowl; cover with foil or a towel to keep warm.
3~ Peel the potatoes and cut into ¼-inch slices. Place the slices in a shallow dish. Sprinkle on the parsley, bell pepper and scallions.
4~ Whisk the dressing to blend and pour over the vegetables while the potatoes are still warm; toss gently. Crumble the bacon over the salad. Serve immediately or set aside at room temperature for up to 6 hours.

SERVES 6
RECIPE BY DIANA STURGIS

CARAWAY COLESLAW

37

Even the fussiest eater won't turn away from this popular rendition of a long-playing American favorite.

2½ POUNDS CABBAGE, CORED AND FINELY
    SHREDDED
1 MEDIUM CARROT, GRATED
1 TABLESPOON PLUS 1 TEASPOON CARAWAY
    SEEDS
½ CUP PLAIN YOGURT
½ CUP MAYONNAISE, PREFERABLY
    HOMEMADE
½ TEASPOON FRESHLY GROUND PEPPER
¾ TEASPOON SALT

1~ In a large bowl, combine the cabbage, carrot and caraway seeds. Stir in the yogurt, mayonnaise, pepper and salt, tossing until throughly combined.
2~ Serve at once or refrigerate, covered, overnight. Stir again before serving.

SERVES 8 TO 10
RECIPE BY FOOD & WINE

PASTA SALAD

38

You can select just about any shape of pasta for this recipe, but be sure to cook it only until it's al dente.

1 POUND SHAPED PASTA, SUCH AS PENNE
½ CUP MAYONNAISE
½ CUP SOUR CREAM
3 TABLESPOONS DIJON-STYLE MUSTARD
1 TABLESPOON WHITE WINE VINEGAR
DASH OF WORCESTERSHIRE SAUCE
DASH OF TABASCO SAUCE
2 TABLESPOONS POWDERED MUSTARD
2 TABLESPOONS CELERY SEED
1 TABLESPOON SUGAR
SALT AND FRESHLY GROUND PEPPER
⅔ CUP DICED YELLOW BELL PEPPER
⅔ CUP SLICED SCALLIONS (THE WHITE AND
    ABOUT 2 INCHES OF THE GREEN)
1 LARGE CELERY RIB, DICED
2 HARD-COOKED EGGS, CHOPPED

1~ Cook the penne according to package directions. Drain well.
2~ Meanwhile, in a large bowl, combine the mayonnaise, sour cream, mustard, vinegar, Worcestershire, Tabasco, powdered mustard, celery seed and sugar. Season with salt and pepper to taste.
3~ While still warm, add the penne to the dressing and toss well. Add the bell pepper, scallions, celery and hard-cooked eggs and toss again.
4~ Cover and chill before serving.

SERVES 6
RECIPE BY FOOD & WINE

BUTTERMILK BISCUITS

In the South, ham is traditionally served with fresh home-baked biscuits. First you split them in half, then you slather them with butter or mustard and top it off with thin-sliced ham.

1¾ CUPS ALL-PURPOSE FLOUR
2 TEASPOONS BAKING POWDER
½ TEASPOON BAKING SODA
½ TEASPOON SALT
¼ CUP SHORTENING
⅔ CUP BUTTERMILK

1~ Preheat the oven to 450°. Lightly grease a baking sheet.
2~ In a medium bowl, combine the flour, baking powder, baking soda and salt. Toss to blend well.
3~ Add the shortening and rub it into the flour with your fingertips until well combined. Pour in the buttermilk and stir the mixture until it forms a dough.
4~ On a lightly floured surface, roll out the dough ½ inch thick. Using a 2½-inch round cutter, cut out 8 biscuits. Roll out the scraps and cut out 2 more. Arrange the biscuits on the prepared baking sheet and bake for 12 minutes, or until golden on top and dry on the sides. Serve warm.

MAKES 10 BISCUITS
RECIPE BY DIANA STURGIS

DEEP-DISH ALL-AMERICAN CINNAMON APPLE PIE

Trust us—this may be the all-time ultimate apple pie.

PÂTE BRISÉE PIE SHELL (AT RIGHT),
    TRIMMED TO A 16-INCH CIRCLE AND
    FITTED INTO A 9-BY-2-INCH QUICHE OR
    SPRINGFORM PAN WITH A REMOVABLE
    BASE AND BAKED AS DIRECTED
⅓ CUP MELTED, SIEVED APRICOT PRESERVES
6 LARGE GREENING OR GRANNY SMITH
    APPLES (2½ TO 3 POUNDS)—PEELED,
    QUARTERED, CORED AND SLICED ¼ INCH
    THICK
¼ CUP PACKED LIGHT BROWN SUGAR
¼ CUP GRANULATED SUGAR
1½ TEASPOONS GROUND CINNAMON
¼ TEASPOON NUTMEG,
    PREFERABLY FRESHLY GRATED
¼ TEASPOON SALT
2 TABLESPOONS UNSALTED BUTTER
1 TABLESPOON PLUS 1 TEASPOON
    CORNSTARCH

1~ Brush the baked pie shell with 2 tablespoons of the apricot preserves.
2~ In a large bowl, combine the apples, brown sugar, granulated sugar, cinnamon, nutmeg and salt; toss to mix. Let stand for 30 to 60 minutes, until the apples exude about ½ cup of liquid. Drain the liquid into a small heavy saucepan. Add the butter and boil over moderately high heat until the liquid is reduced to ⅓ cup, 3 to 5 minutes.
3~ Preheat the oven to 425°.

PÂTE BRISÉE PIE SHELL

4~ Toss the drained apples with the cornstarch. Place half of the apples in the crust and drizzle with half of the reduced syrup. Arrange the remaining apples in overlapping concentric circles on top and drizzle with the remaining syrup (the apples will be heaped above the crust but will sink down during baking).

5~ Cut a round of foil to fit over the apples and crimp in 3 or 4 places to create a dome. Cover the top of the pie with the foil and bake for 1 to 1¼ hours, or until the juices are thick and bubble up the sides of the dish. The pie is done when the apples are tender when pierced with a skewer.

6~ Remove the foil and bake for 5 minutes, or until the top of the apples are golden brown. Remove from the oven.

7~ Warm the remaining apricot preserves and brush over the top of the hot pie. Serve warm or at room temperature.

SERVES 6 TO 8
RECIPE BY ROSE LEVY BERANBAUM

Here is an excellent pie pastry recipe, one that should be included in your collection of most dependable basics. Use it for almost any open-crust pie.

1⅓ CUPS ALL-PURPOSE FLOUR
¼ POUND (1 STICK) COLD UNSALTED
    BUTTER, CUT INTO SMALL PIECES
½ TEASPOON SALT
3 TO 5 TABLESPOONS ICE WATER

1~ In a food processor, process the flour, butter and salt, turning the machine quickly on and off, until the mixture resembles small peas, about 8 seconds. Sprinkle 3 tablespoons of ice water over the surface of the mixture and process for 3 seconds. Toss lightly with a fork to mix in any dry particles of flour. If the dough does not hold together when pinched, sprinkle with 1 to 2 more tablespoons of ice water and process for 3 short bursts. (Do not overmix; the dough should not form a ball.)

2~ Turn the dough out onto a lightly floured work surface and knead lightly, just until it holds together. Form into a ball. Wrap loosely in plastic wrap and flatten into a 6-inch disk. Refrigerate for at least 45 minutes. (The dough can be made up to a day ahead. Let stand at room temperature for 10 to 15 minutes until malleable before rolling out.)

3~ On a lightly floured surface, roll out the dough into a large round, ⅛ to ¼ inch thick. Cut out a 13-inch circle. Dust the circle lightly with flour and fold in quarters. Place it in a 9½- or 10-inch tart pan about 1 inch high, with a removable bottom. Open up the pastry and fit into the pan, folding down the excess to reinforce the sides. Press the pastry against the fluted sides of pan; trim off any excess dough. Cover with plastic wrap and refrigerate for at least 1 hour. To maintain the best shape, freeze for at least 15 minutes.

4~ Preheat the oven to 425°. Line the pastry with foil and fill with pie weights or dried beans, making sure they are pushed up well against the sides.

5~ Bake for 20 to 25 minutes, until the pastry is almost dry. Remove the foil and weights, prick the bottom and sides all over with a fork and continue baking for 5 to 8 minutes, or until the crust is golden brown. For extra crispness, turn off the oven, leave the door slightly ajar and let the pastry sit in the hot oven for 15 minutes.

MAKES A SINGLE 9½- TO 10-INCH CRUST
RECIPE BY ROSE LEVY BERANBAUM

40

Celebrating
with a Crowd

*A traditional potluck dinner allows unex-
pected guests to join in and partake of what's
available at a given meal. Our party is a bit
more than that: a planned event for a gang of
friends and family, with foods chosen for
their wide appeal. If you are daunted by the
prospect of so much cooking, organize a covered dish dinner: each guest (or family group)
brings a dish of food large enough to serve
everyone. Besides the dishes in our potluck
menu, these other recipes would make good
offerings for a covered dish dinner (increase
the recipes as necessary):*

STRAWBERRY-RHUBARB
PIE

Rhubarb—either you love it or you hate it.
Teamed with strawberries, as it is here, surely
it will please the majority of your family and
friends.

1 POUND FRESH RHUBARB, CUT INTO
    ½-INCH PIECES (4 CUPS), OR 4 CUPS
    INDIVIDUALLY QUICK-FROZEN RHUBARB
    WITH NO SUGAR ADDED, THAWED, WITH
    ITS LIQUID RESERVED (SEE *NOTE*)
¾ CUP SUGAR
PINCH OF SALT
1 TABLESPOON PLUS 1 TEASPOON
    CORNSTARCH
PÂTE BRISÉE PIE SHELL (PAGE 39)
⅓ CUP PLUS 2 TABLESPOONS RED
    CURRANT JELLY, MELTED
1 PINT STRAWBERRIES, SLICED

1~ In a heavy medium saucepan, combine the
fresh rhubarb, sugar and salt; toss to mix. Let
stand at room temperature for at least 15 minutes, or until the rhubarb exudes some juice.

2~ In a small bowl, combine the cornstarch with
¼ cup of cold water; stir until smooth. In a
medium nonreactive saucepan, combine the
dissolved cornstarch with the fresh rhubarb
and its juices. Bring to a boil over moderately
high heat, stirring constantly. Reduce the heat
to moderately low, cover and simmer, stirring
occasionally, until the rhubarb is tender and
the liquid thickened, about 10 minutes.
Remove from the heat and let cool without
stirring.

3~ Paint the baked pie shell with 2 tablespoons of
the melted jelly. Pour the rhubarb filling into
the pie shell. Arrange the strawberry slices on
top in concentric circles, saving the smaller
slices for the center rings. Brush with the
remaining currant jelly to glaze the top. Serve
at room temperature or slightly chilled.
*Note: If using frozen rhubarb, skip Step 1.
Increase the cornstarch to 2 tablespoons and
do not dissolve it in water. In Step 2, in the
saucepan, combine the thawed rhubarb and its
liquid with the sugar, salt and cornstarch.
Bring to a boil, stirring constantly. Reduce the
heat and simmer uncovered, stirring occasionally, until tender, 7 to 10 minutes.*

SERVES 6 TO 8
RECIPE BY ROSE LEVY BERANBAUM

VANILLA LOVER'S VANILLA ICE CREAM

People who think vanilla ice cream is plain tend to skimp on the flavoring itself and overcompensate with too much sugar, cream and eggs. No wonder they don't love vanilla ice cream. This is for people who do.

2 CUPS HEAVY CREAM
1 CUP MILK
½ CUP SUGAR
PINCH OF SALT
3 EGG YOLKS
1 TABLESPOON PLUS 1 TEASPOON VANILLA
   EXTRACT

1~ In a heavy medium saucepan, combine the cream, milk, sugar and salt. Cook over moderate heat, stirring frequently with a wooden spoon, until the sugar dissolves and the mixture is hot, 6 to 8 minutes.
2~ In a large bowl, beat the egg yolks lightly. Gradually whisk in the hot cream in a thin stream. Return the mixture to the saucepan and cook over moderately low heat, stirring constantly, until the custard thickens enough to lightly coat the back of a spoon, 5 to 7 minutes. (Do not let the temperature exceed 180°.)
3~ Strain the custard into a metal bowl. Set the bowl in a basin of ice and water and let stand, stirring occasionally, until cooled to room temperature. Stir in the vanilla. Cover and refrigerate for at least 4 hours, or until very cold.
4~ Pour the custard into an ice cream maker and freeze according to the manufacturer's instructions.

MAKES ABOUT 1 QUART
RECIPE BY LESLIE NEWMAN

RICE PUDDING WITH ORANGE AND BAY

Basmati rice adds a delicious, nutty flavor to this uncommonly light pudding. Serve the pudding plain or with the Blueberry-Bay Compote.

1 CUP BASMATI RICE
4 BAY LEAVES
PINCH OF SALT
3 CUPS MILK
¾ CUP SUGAR
1 TEASPOON GRATED ORANGE ZEST
1 TEASPOON VANILLA EXTRACT
⅓ CUP HEAVY CREAM
2 TABLESPOONS CONFECTIONERS' SUGAR

1~ In a large saucepan, combine the rice with 2½ cups of water. Add the bay leaves and salt and bring to a boil over high heat. Reduce the heat to low, cover and cook, without removing the lid, for 20 minutes. Remove from the heat and keep covered for 10 minutes longer.
2~ Stir the milk and sugar into the rice and simmer over low heat, stirring occasionally, until the mixture is thick and creamy and the rice is very soft, about 45 minutes. Spoon the pudding into a bowl and stir in the orange zest and vanilla. Keep the bay leaves in the pudding and cool to room temperature, stirring occasionally. Place plastic wrap directly over the surface of the pudding and refrigerate overnight.
3~ Place the cream and confectioners' sugar in a chilled bowl and beat until stiff peaks form. Remove the bay leaves from the pudding and fold in the whipped cream. Serve slightly chilled.

SERVES 6
RECIPE BY MARCIA KIESEL

BLUEBERRY-BAY COMPOTE

Serve this compote with ice cream, pound cake or the rice pudding recipe that precedes.

2 CUPS FRESH ORANGE JUICE
½ CUP SUGAR
2 BAY LEAVES, BROKEN IN HALF
1 PINT FRESH BLUEBERRIES

1~ In a medium nonreactive saucepan, combine the orange juice, sugar and bay leaves. Bring to a boil over high heat and cook until reduced to about ⅔ cup, about 15 minutes.
2~ Remove and discard the bay leaves. Stir in the blueberries and remove from the heat. Serve warm or cold.

MAKES ABOUT 3 CUPS
RECIPE BY MARCIA KIESEL

41

■ ■ ■

A
DINNER TO
IMPRESS THE BOSS

Inviting the boss to dinner is a ritual that has deep roots in American business, roots that have threatened to strangle many an ambitious employee. The menu we suggest should get you off the hook. ∼ Designing the meal, from the menu through the music, is easier if you already know that the boss is allergic to shellfish, hates broccoli or gets headaches from red wine. If you don't have such information, your goal should be to serve a tasty, tasteful meal that's not too anything–not too trendy, not too alcoholic, not too exotic or spicy or expensive or in any way extreme. The good news is: That's not at all difficult. ∼ This spring menu has it all: The asparagus is a seasonal treat; the fish is healthful yet stylish and the butter is gorgeous; the potatoes on rosemary branches and the peas and mushrooms in croustades are common ingredients served in uncommonly attractive ways. The green salad with Stilton sets up the palate for a simple but special fresh fruit dessert and some friendly after-dinner conversation. You definitely deserve a raise.

■ ■ ■

*Tiny Potatoes
Roasted
on Rosemary
Branches*

*Grilled Tilefish
with Nasturtium
Butter*

*Peas and
Mushrooms in
Croustades
with Chervil*

2

4 4

A DINNER TO IMPRESS THE BOSS

Serves 4

California Fumé Blanc or
a not-very-oaky Chardonnay
Skillet Asparagus

Grilled Tilefish with Nasturtium Butter

*Peas and Mushrooms in Croustades
with Chervil*

*Tiny Potatoes Roasted on Rosemary
Branches*

Green Salad with Stilton Cheese

COFFEE
*Warm Blackberries with
Cold Almond Cream*

SKILLET ASPARAGUS

You don't need any special equipment to make this first-course dish. Skittish cooks can feel sure of a success with this easy preparation. You can cut the recipe by half if you're serving all of the other dishes in this menu.

2 POUNDS ASPARAGUS
2 TABLESPOONS UNSALTED BUTTER
SALT
LEMON WEDGES, FOR GARNISH

1~ Wash the asparagus but do not dry; trim the ends. With a swivel-bladed vegetable peeler, peel the thick bottom ends of the spears.
2~ In a large skillet, melt the butter over moderately high heat. Add the asparagus spears with just the water that clings to them. Sprinkle with salt to taste and cover tightly. Reduce the heat to moderate and cook, shaking the pan occasionally, for about 4 minutes. The cooking time will vary depending on how crisp you like your asparagus and how thick the spears are, so if you are in doubt, take a peek after a couple of minutes and pierce one with the point of a knife. Serve garnished with a wedge of lemon.

SERVES 6
RECIPE BY LEE BAILEY

GRILLED TILEFISH WITH NASTURTIUM BUTTER

Tilefish meat is lean, moist and firm textured, not unlike white sea bass, which can be substituted. To adjust the recipe to serve four rather than six, just buy four fish fillets and leave everything else as is.

6 TILEFISH FILLETS (ABOUT 2 POUNDS),
    EACH CUT ¾ INCH THICK
2 TABLESPOONS HUNGARIAN OR OTHER
    SWEET IMPORTED PAPRIKA
2 TEASPOONS DRY MUSTARD
¼ TEASPOON FRESHLY GROUND PEPPER
2 TABLESPOONS EXTRA-VIRGIN OLIVE OIL
2 GARLIC CLOVES, MINCED
1 TABLESPOON VEGETABLE OIL
NASTURTIUM BUTTER (AT RIGHT)

1~ Place the fish fillets in a glass or ceramic dish. In a small bowl, combine the paprika, mustard and pepper and sprinkle over both sides of the fillets.
2~ In another small bowl, combine the olive oil and garlic and brush over the fish. Cover and let stand at room temperature for 1 hour.
3~ Light a charcoal grill or preheat the broiler. Brush the grill rack or broiler pan lightly with the vegetable oil and cook the fish fillets directly on the grill or broiling pan, about 4 inches from the heat, turning once, until the fish is opaque throughout and flakes easily with a fork, 3 to 5 minutes on each side. Serve with the Nasturtium Butter.

SERVES 6
RECIPE BY PHILLIP STEPHEN SCHULZ

NASTURTIUM BUTTER

Though you may substitute shredded watercress leaves for the nasturtium, if you do you'll lose the beautiful colors. When nasturtiums are abundant, you might want to double or triple this recipe, shape it into a log and freeze it for future use.

5 TABLESPOONS UNSALTED BUTTER,
  SOFTENED
1 SHALLOT, MINCED
⅛ TEASPOON HOT PEPPER SAUCE
½ CUP NASTURTIUM LEAVES AND
  BLOSSOMS OR WATERCRESS, SHREDDED
¼ TEASPOON SALT

1~ In a bowl, cream the butter until light. Stir in the shallot, hot pepper sauce, nasturtium leaves and blossoms and salt.
2~ If desired, shape into a log. Cover and refrigerate for up to 4 days. Let stand at room temperature for at least 30 minutes before serving.

MAKES ABOUT ½ CUP
RECIPE BY PHILLIP STEPHEN SCHULZ

PEAS AND MUSHROOMS IN CROUSTADES WITH CHERVIL

These vegetable-filled croustades have a lovely chervil flavor. Who wouldn't be impressed by this deliciously simple mixture presented in its own bread bowl.

5 TABLESPOONS UNSALTED BUTTER
8 THIN SLICES OF FIRM-TEXTURED WHITE
  BREAD, CRUSTS REMOVED
¼ POUND FRESH WHITE MUSHROOMS, CUT
  INTO DICE
3 TABLESPOONS MINCED FRESH CHERVIL
½ POUND FRESH OR FROZEN SHELLED
  YOUNG PEAS
¾ CUP HEAVY CREAM
¼ CUP CRÈME FRAÎCHE OR SOUR CREAM
1 TEASPOON FRESH LEMON JUICE
¼ TEASPOON SALT
¼ TEASPOON FRESHLY GROUND PEPPER

1~ Preheat the oven to 400°.
2~ Melt 4 tablespoons of the butter. Brush over both sides of the bread slices. Gently press the bread into eight 2½-inch muffin cups. Bake until golden brown and crisp, about 20 minutes. Carefully lift the croustades from the cups and set aside. *(The croustades can be made up to 5 hours ahead. Store at room temperature in an airtight tin.)*
3~ In a medium saucepan, melt the remaining 1 tablespoon butter over high heat. Add the mushrooms and sauté, without stirring, until brown, about 2 minutes. Reduce the heat to moderate and cook until tender, about 1 minute longer. Remove the mushrooms to a small bowl and toss with 1 tablespoon of the chervil. Set aside for at least 10 minutes or up to 1 hour.
4~ In a medium saucepan with a steamer basket, steam the peas until almost tender, 4 to 8 minutes depending on their size. Remove the basket and discard the cooking water. Return the peas to the saucepan. Add the heavy cream and boil over high heat, stirring, until the cream is thick and reduced by half, about 3 minutes. Add the mushrooms and crème fraîche and stir to combine.
5~ Remove from the heat, season with the lemon juice, salt, pepper and the remaining 2 tablespoons chervil. Divide the warm mixture evenly among the croustades and serve at once.

SERVES 4
RECIPE BY MARCIA KIESEL

45

TINY POTATOES ROASTED ON ROSEMARY BRANCHES

46

What a charming idea! The tiniest new potatoes often are called "creamers." Keep an eye out for them—especially if you live where potatoes are grown.

1½ POUNDS TINY NEW POTATOES, SCRUBBED
4 LONG BRANCHES OF ROSEMARY, 6 TO 8 INCHES EACH
1 TABLESPOON OLIVE OIL
⅛ TEASPOON SALT
¼ TEASPOON FRESHLY GROUND PEPPER

1~ Preheat the oven to 400°.
2~ In a medium pot of boiling water, cook the potatoes over high heat until partially cooked, about 5 minutes. Drain and cool slightly.
3~ Remove most of the leaves from the center of the rosemary branches, leaving a cluster of leaves at either end. Starting at the thicker end, skewer the potatoes onto the branches. Place the potatoes on a baking sheet and drizzle with the olive oil; roll the branches to distribute the oil evenly. Season with the salt and pepper and bake until the potatoes are golden brown and crisp, about 25 minutes.

SERVES 4
RECIPE BY MARCIA KIESEL

GREEN SALAD WITH STILTON CHEESE

To adjust this recipe to serve four, use a small head of radicchio and just two endives.

1 BUNCH OF MÂCHE (LAMB'S LETTUCE), TORN INTO BITE-SIZE PIECES
1 HEAD OF RADICCHIO, TORN INTO PIECES
3 BELGIAN ENDIVES, SLICED ½ INCH THICK
1½ TABLESPOONS WHITE WINE VINEGAR
1½ TEASPOONS DIJON-STYLE MUSTARD
3 TABLESPOONS EXTRA-VIRGIN OLIVE OIL
1½ TABLESPOONS SAFFLOWER OIL
¼ TEASPOON SALT
FRESHLY GROUND PEPPER
WEDGE OF STILTON CHEESE

1~ In a large bowl, combine all the greens.
2~ In a small bowl, whisk together the vinegar, mustard, olive oil, safflower oil and salt. Pour onto the greens and toss to coat well. Season with pepper to taste. Pass Stilton cheese on the side.

SERVES 6
RECIPE BY LEE BAILEY

WARM BLACKBERRIES WITH COLD ALMOND CREAM

Warming these fresh summer berries brings out their full flavor.

1 CUP HEAVY CREAM
⅓ CUP PLUS 2 TABLESPOONS SUGAR
¼ TEASPOON ALMOND EXTRACT
3 TABLESPOONS RED CURRANT JELLY
1 TABLESPOON FRESH LEMON JUICE
3 CUPS BLACKBERRIES

1~ Preheat the oven to 250°.
2~ In a large bowl, beat the cream until it thickens. Sprinkle in 2 tablespoons of the sugar and the almond extract and continue beating until stiff. Cover and refrigerate the almond cream for up to 3 hours.
3~ In a large nonreactive ovenproof skillet, combine the remaining ⅓ cup sugar, the currant jelly and the lemon juice. Cook over moderately high heat, stirring constantly, until the sugar and jelly dissolve, about 2 minutes. Add the berries and toss with a rubber spatula to coat with the glaze.
4~ Set the skillet in the oven and bake until the berries are warmed through but still retain their shape, about 5 minutes.
5~ Serve the berries in bowls, with a large dollop of the chilled almond cream.

SERVES 4 TO 6
RECIPE BY MARY MARSHALL HYNSON

SUMMER

■ ■ ■

A SMALL
SUMMER WEDDING

Summer evenings have an intimate quality. The harsh light and heat of day are gone, replaced by a subtler radiance, cooler temperatures and often a gentle breeze. Picture a billowing white tent, add to that image some sparkling fireflies, a chirping cricket or two and the mellow notes of a string trio. Stir in the scent of all sorts of white flowers and the light of dozens of white candles. Add a bride and groom, and what you have is a flawless setting for a memorable summer wedding. ~ Whether this dinner is your gift to the lucky couple or their gift to their guests, it's a stylish way to honor the wedding tradition. With the exception of the biscuits, every aspect of this meal can be wholly or partly prepared ahead of time, then finished and served by hired staff or friendly volunteers. And though this dinner seems formal and sophisticated, it's really just three courses, all based on fresh, straightforward ingredients. There's drama to every dish: The soup is rich and appealing; the scallop pies in crêpe bonnets are charming to behold, and the wedding cake (frosted simply and decorated with flowers) leads into the requisite Champagne toasts for happiness, good health and long life.

■ ■ ■

*Scallop Pies
in Crêpe Bonnets*

Roast Asparagus

*Jicama, Mango
and Papaya Salad*

CORN AND SHRIMP CHOWDER WITH TOMATOES AND HERBS

A SMALL SUMMER WEDDING

Serves 16

CHAMPAGNE THROUGHOUT

Corn and Shrimp Chowder with Tomatoes and Herbs

Mighty Quick Biscuits

Roast Asparagus

Scallop Pies in Crêpe Bonnets

Jicama, Mango and Papaya Salad

Lemon Celebration Cake

This handy recipe (which can be doubled or halved at will) is one you'll use during sweet corn season every year. Its rich texture results from pureeing some of the solids, not from the addition of cream or thickeners.

11 EARS OF CORN
2 TEASPOONS VEGETABLE OIL
12 OUNCES THICKLY SLICED BACON, CUT CROSSWISE INTO ½-INCH STRIPS
3 LARGE ONIONS, COARSELY CHOPPED
5 SLENDER CARROTS, SLICED ON THE DIAGONAL ¼ INCH THICK
3 CELERY RIBS, SLICED ON THE DIAGONAL ¼ INCH THICK
1 POUND NEW OR SMALL BOILING POTATOES, PEELED AND CUT ½ INCH THICK
3¾ CUPS CHICKEN STOCK OR 2½ CANS (13 TO 14 OUNCES EACH) CANNED BROTH
3 SPRIGS OF FRESH THYME OR ½ TEASPOON DRIED
3 CUPS MILK
1¼ POUNDS MEDIUM SHRIMP, PEELED AND DEVEINED
½ TEASPOON SALT
¼ TEASPOON FRESHLY GROUND PEPPER
3 DASHES OF HOT PEPPER SAUCE
3 LARGE RIPE TOMATOES—PEELED, SEEDED AND CUT INTO ½-INCH DICE
3 TABLESPOONS FRESH CHIVES, CUT INTO ½-INCH LENGTHS

1~ Using a sharp knife, slice the corn kernels off the cobs. Scrape the cobs with the dull side of the knife to release any milky corn juice (you should have 7 cups of corn and juice). Cut 4 of the scraped corn cobs in half and set aside.

2~ In a large heavy saucepan, heat the oil over moderate heat. Add the bacon and sauté until lightly golden but not yet crisp, 10 to 15 minutes. Drain on paper towels and pour off all but 2 tablespoons of fat from the pan.

3~ Add the onions, carrots and celery to the pan and sauté until softened, about 5 minutes. Add the potatoes, chicken stock, thyme and reserved corn cobs. Reduce the heat to low, cover and simmer, skimming occasionally, until the potatoes are tender but still hold their shape, about 15 minutes. Discard the cobs.

4~ Uncover the soup and stir in the corn kernels and juices. Simmer until the corn is just tender, about 3 minutes. Using a slotted spoon, transfer about 3½ cups of the solids to a blender or food processor and puree coarsely. Return the puree to the soup, add the milk and simmer over low heat until warm, about 5 minutes. *(The chowder can be made to this point up to 2 days ahead. Store the soup and cooked bacon separately in the refrigerator; return the soup to a simmer before proceeding.)*

5~ Stir the reserved bacon into the chowder and add the shrimp. Cover and simmer over low heat until the shrimp are opaque throughout, about 3 minutes. Season with the salt, pepper and hot pepper sauce. Stir in the tomatoes and half of the chives. Cook over low heat until the tomatoes are warm, about 1 minute. (If the soup is too thick, add a little milk or water.)

6~ Ladle the chowder into shallow soup plates and garnish with the remaining chives.

SERVES 16
RECIPE BY RICHARD SAX

MIGHTY QUICK BISCUITS

These biscuits are quick to make because the dough is dropped on a baking sheet, not rolled and cut out. You can put together several batches in a flash.

2 CUPS ALL-PURPOSE FLOUR
1 TABLESPOON BAKING POWDER
1 TEASPOON SALT
¼ CUP MAYONNAISE
1 CUP MILK

1~ Preheat the oven to 450°.
2~ In a medium bowl, sift the flour, baking powder and salt. Stir in the mayonnaise and milk until just blended.
3~ Drop the mixture by tablespoonfuls onto a large, ungreased baking sheet, spacing them about 1 inch apart.
4~ Bake for 10 minutes, or until the biscuits are golden.

MAKES TWENTY 1½-INCH BISCUITS
RECIPE BY JO NORTHRUP

ROAST ASPARAGUS

Roasting fresh asparagus spears enriches their flavor in a whole new way and maintains a pleasingly firm texture. This cooking technique was suggested by Johanne Kileen and George Germon, chef/owners of Al Forno in Providence, Rhode Island. It's an excellent way to prepare whatever quantity of asparagus you need.

1 POUND FRESH ASPARAGUS,
    TRIMMED AND PEELED HALFWAY UP
    FROM THE BOTTOM
1 TABLESPOON EXTRA-VIRGIN OLIVE OIL
1 LEMON, CUT INTO WEDGES
FRESHLY GROUND BLACK PEPPER

1~ Preheat the oven to 500°.
2~ Place the asparagus in a single layer on a baking sheet or shallow pan. Drizzle with the olive oil.
3~ Roast the asparagus in the middle of the oven, turning the spears occasionally for even cooking and to avoid browning, for 8 to 10 minutes, depending on the thickness of the stalks.
4~ Serve hot with lemon wedges and pass a pepper mill at the table.

SERVES 3 TO 4
RECIPE BY RICHARD SAX

51

Some Premium Champagnes

Champagne is the name given sparkling wines that are made by the méthode champenoise *and produced within the delimited area of the Champagne region of France. Some of the most highly esteemed bottlings include the following:*

Billecart-Salmon Blanc de Blancs
Bollinger R.D. or Vieilles Vignes
Charbaut Certificate
Krug Clos du Mesnil
Moët & Chandon Dom Pérignon
Mumm René Lalou
Perrier-Jouët Belle Époque
Louis Roederer Cristal or Cristal Rosé
Pol Roger Blanc de Chardonnay or
    Sir Winston Churchill
Dom Ruinart Blanc de Blancs
Taittinger Comtes de Champagne
Veuve Clicquot La Grande Dame
    or Brut Rosé

SCALLOP PIES
IN CRÊPE BONNETS

These little pot pies are ideal as a first course or brunch dish. To prepare them as an entrée for 16, quadruple the recipe and use 8-ounce ramekins.

CRÊPE BONNETS:
1 EGG
6 TABLESPOONS MILK
3 TABLESPOONS CORNSTARCH
1½ TEASPOONS VEGETABLE OIL
½ TEASPOON BAKING POWDER
PINCH OF SALT
6 LONG SCALLION GREENS

SCALLOP FILLING:
1½ POUNDS BAY SCALLOPS, TRIMMED
3 TABLESPOONS ALL-PURPOSE FLOUR
5 TABLESPOONS UNSALTED BUTTER
1½ TABLESPOONS VEGETABLE OIL
⅓ CUP DRY WHITE WINE
1 SMALL ONION, MINCED
2 LARGE GARLIC CLOVES, MINCED
1 LARGE TOMATO—PEELED, SEEDED AND
    CHOPPED
5 SCALLIONS, CHOPPED
⅛ TEASPOON DRIED THYME
½ TEASPOON GRATED LEMON ZEST
½ TEASPOON SALT
¼ TEASPOON FRESHLY GROUND PEPPER

1~ *Make the Crêpes:* In a blender, combine the egg, milk, cornstarch, oil, baking powder and salt. Blend until smooth.

2~ Lightly oil a 6-inch crêpe pan or nonstick skillet (use a 7-inch pan if this is to be an entrée) and heat over moderately high heat. Pour about 2 tablespoons of the crêpe batter into the center of the pan and swirl to coat the bottom evenly. Cook until the underside is lightly browned and the edges are dry, about 20 seconds. Turn and cook the other side for 5 seconds. Transfer to a paper towel and repeat with the remaining batter, stacking the crêpes between paper towels.

3~ Using a sharp knife, slit the scallion greens lengthwise, leaving 1 inch attached at the top. In a small saucepan, blanch the greens in boiling water until just wilted, 5 to 10 seconds. Drain and pat dry.

4~ *Make the Filling:* Rinse the scallops under cold water. Drain and pat dry with paper towels. Sprinkle with the flour.

5~ In a large nonreactive skillet, melt 3 tablespoons of the butter in the oil over moderately high heat. Add half of the scallops and sauté, tossing, until lightly browned, 1 to 1½ minutes. Using a slotted spoon, transfer to a bowl and repeat with the remaining scallops.

6~ Increase the heat to high and stir in the wine. Add the onion and cook until softened slightly, about 1 minute. Stir in the garlic and cook for 2 minutes longer. Add the tomato, chopped scallions, thyme and any accumulated scallop juices. Cook over moderate heat until the sauce thickens, about 5 minutes. Add the scallops, lemon zest and salt and pepper.

7~ Preheat the oven to 350°.

8~ Divide the scallop mixture among six 4-ounce ramekins. Place a crêpe over the top of each ramekin and tie around the edges with a butterflied scallion green. Trim the crêpes neatly with scissors, if necessary.

9~ Melt the remaining 2 tablespoons butter. Set the ramekins on a baking sheet and brush the tops with the melted butter. Bake in the preheated oven for 15 to 20 minutes, or until piping hot.

SERVES 6
RECIPE BY PHILLIP STEPHEN SCHULZ

Jicama, Mango and Papaya Salad

Clive du Val III serves this sweet-tart salad at his snazzy Latin restaurant, Tila's, in Houston, Texas, and at its sister establishment in Washington, D.C. For a fragrant variation on the lime-sesame dressing, he sometimes replaces the sesame seeds with the pulp of two passion fruits. Triple the recipe if you are preparing the menu for A Small Summer Wedding.

3 TABLESPOONS HULLED SESAME SEEDS

2½ TABLESPOONS FRESH LIME JUICE

2½ TABLESPOONS FRESH ORANGE JUICE

1 TABLESPOON HONEY

½ TEASPOON SALT

1 LARGE SHALLOT, MINCED

⅛ TEASPOON CAYENNE PEPPER

⅔ CUP LIGHT OLIVE OIL

1 SMALL HEAD OF ROMAINE LETTUCE, TORN
    INTO STRIPS

1 SMALL HEAD OF BIBB LETTUCE,
    TORN INTO STRIPS

1 MEDIUM JICAMA, PEELED AND CUT INTO
    3-INCH JULIENNE

1 LARGE OR 2 SMALL PAPAYAS—PEELED,
    HALVED, SEEDED AND CUT INTO LONG,
    THIN SLICES

2 SMALL MANGOES, PEELED AND CUT INTO
    LONG, THIN SLICES

1~ In a small nonstick skillet, toast the sesame seeds over low heat, stirring, until golden, 6 to 8 minutes. Let cool.

2~ In a small jar, combine the lime juice, orange juice, honey, salt, shallot and cayenne; cover and shake to mix. Add the oil and the sesame seeds and shake until thoroughly blended.

3~ In a large bowl, toss the romaine and Bibb lettuce with half the dressing. Arrange the salad on 6 plates and divide the jicama, papaya and mango over the greens. Spoon the remaining dressing evenly over the salads and serve.

SERVES 6
RECIPE BY ELIZABETH SCHNEIDER

53

A Calendar of Anniversary Gifts

Tradition dictates the proper gift for each of the first 15 anniversaries and then special ones after that. This list might help you next time you're searching for just the right gift.

1ST	paper	14TH	ivory
2ND	cotton	15TH	crystal
3RD	leather	20TH	china
4TH	linen	25TH	silver
5TH	wood	30TH	pearls
6TH	iron	35TH	jade
7TH	wool	40TH	rubies
8TH	bronze	45TH	sapphires
9TH	willow	50TH	gold
10TH	tin	55TH	emeralds
11TH	steel	60TH	diamonds
12TH	silk	75TH	more diamonds
13TH	lace		

LEMON CELEBRATION CAKE

Be sure you have seven large, unblemished lemons on hand before you start the recipe for this versatile cake. Depending on how you choose to decorate it, this cake could be served at any type of celebration—baby shower, birthday or retirement.

GÉNOISE:
1¾ CUPS SIFTED ALL-PURPOSE FLOUR
8 WHOLE EGGS, AT ROOM TEMPERATURE
1¼ CUPS SUGAR
1 TEASPOON GRATED LEMON ZEST
½ CUP CLARIFIED BUTTER, TEPID

BOURBON SYRUP:
1 CUP SUGAR
¼ CUP FRESH LEMON JUICE
1 TEASPOON CHOPPED LEMON ZEST
¼ CUP BOURBON

LEMON CURD:
1 TEASPOON MINCED LEMON ZEST
7 TABLESPOONS FRESH LEMON JUICE
1 CUP SUGAR
1 WHOLE EGG
3 EGG YOLKS
4 TABLESPOONS UNSALTED BUTTER, CUT
    INTO 6 PIECES

MERINGUE BUTTERCREAM:
4 EGG WHITES, AT ROOM TEMPERATURE
¼ TEASPOON CREAM OF TARTAR
1 CUP SUGAR
1 TEASPOON LEMON EXTRACT
¾ POUND (3 STICKS) UNSALTED BUTTER,
    AT ROOM TEMPERATURE

CANDIED LEMON PEEL (OPTIONAL):
ZEST OF 2 LARGE UNBLEMISHED LEMONS,
    CUT INTO JULIENNE
¼ CUP SUGAR

1~ *Make the Génoise:* Preheat the oven to 350°. Lightly butter a 10-inch springform pan. Cover the bottom with a round of parchment or waxed paper. Lightly butter the paper. Dust the entire pan with flour; tap out any excess.

2~ Sift the flour two more times onto a sheet of waxed paper; set aside.

3~ In a double boiler, combine the eggs, sugar and lemon zest. Cook over barely simmering water, whisking occasionally, until the mixture is smooth and syrupy, deep yellow in color and feels warm to the touch, 5 to 8 minutes. Remove from the heat.

4~ Pour the mixture into a large mixing bowl and beat at high speed until the mixture is pale yellow, tripled in volume and holds a ribbon for a full 10 seconds after the beaters are lifted. (This will take 10 to 15 minutes with a stand mixer or 15 to 20 minutes with a hand beater.)

5~ Sprinkle on half of the flour and lightly fold in. Pour the tepid butter on top and fold in quickly.

Sprinkle on the remaining flour and fold in quickly and delicately so as not to deflate the batter. Pour into the prepared pan and tap the pan on a hard surface to settle the batter.

6~ Bake in the middle of the oven for 40 to 45 minutes, until the cake is golden brown on top and a cake tester inserted in the center comes out clean.

7~ Transfer to a wire rack for 5 minutes. Remove the sides of the pan; invert the cake and remove the bottom. Peel off the parchment. Invert the cake and let cool, right-side up, for 2 to 3 hours. *(If making ahead, wrap airtight and store in a cool, dry place for up to 3 days, or freeze.)*

8~ *Make the Bourbon Syrup:* In a small nonreactive saucepan, combine the sugar, lemon juice and lemon zest with ¼ cup water. Bring to a boil over moderate heat, stirring to dissolve the sugar. Boil for 1 minute. Remove from the heat and strain out the zest.

9~ Let the syrup cool for 10 minutes. Stir in the bourbon. *(If making ahead, pour into a jar, cover and set aside.)*

10~ *Make the Lemon Curd:* In a small nonreactive saucepan, combine the lemon zest, lemon juice and sugar. Let stand for about 10 minutes, until the sugar partially dissolves.

11~ Beat in the whole egg and egg yolks. Stir in the butter. Cook over low heat, stirring occasionally, until the mixture is warm, about 10 minutes. Continue cooking, stirring constantly and scraping the bottom of the pan, until the curd reaches 180° on a candy thermometer or is thick enough to coat the back of a spoon, about 10 minutes. Do not allow the mixture to boil.

12~ Strain the curd into a bowl. Place a sheet of waxed paper directly on the surface and let cool to room temperature. The curd will thicken as it cools. *(The curd can be made ahead of time. Refrigerate, covered, and let return to room temperature before using.)*

13~ *Make the Meringue Buttercream:* In a large mixer bowl, beat the egg whites with the cream of tartar until soft peaks form.

14~ In a small heavy saucepan, combine the sugar with ¼ cup water. Warm over low heat, stirring to dissolve the sugar. Bring to a boil over high heat and boil, without stirring, until the temperature reaches the soft-ball stage, 240° on a candy thermometer, about 15 minutes. Immediately remove from the heat.

15~ With the mixer running at moderately high speed, pour a thin stream of the hot syrup into the egg whites. Add the lemon extract. Beat until the buttercream is glossy and cool, 8 to 10 minutes.

16~ Beat in the butter, 2 tablespoons at a time, until smooth and creamy. *(The buttercream can be made up to 6 hours ahead of time. Cover and hold at cool room temperature.)*

17~ *Make the Candied Lemon Peel:* In a small saucepan of boiling water, cook the zest julienne until softened, about 15 minutes. Drain.

18~ Meanwhile, in a small heavy saucepan, combine the sugar with 1 cup water. Cook over low heat, stirring to dissolve the sugar. Increase the heat to moderate and bring to a boil. Add the drained zest and boil until the liquid reduces to a syrupy glaze, about 10 minutes. Remove from the heat.

19~ Using tongs or a slotted spoon, transfer the julienne to waxed paper and spread out to dry. *(The zest can be candied ahead of time. Wrap loosely in foil until ready to use.)*

20~ *Assemble the cake:* Using a serrated knife, slice the thin brown crust, or sugar bloom, off the top of the génoise.

21~ Split the cake layer horizontally in half to make 2 thin layers.

22~ Brush one side of each layer with the Bourbon Syrup. Transfer the bottom layer, syrup-side up, to a large cake platter.

23~ Evenly spread the Lemon Curd over the bottom layer, leaving a ⅜-inch border around the edges. Place the second layer on top, syrup-side up.

24~ Spread 1 cup of the Meringue Buttercream evenly over the sides of the cake. Spread 1 cup of buttercream over the top. Pipe the remaining buttercream over the cake to decorate it appropriately for the celebration. Decorate with the Candied Lemon Peel, if desired.

SERVES 18
RECIPE BY DIANA STURGIS

55

The Recipe Within the Recipe

The Lemon Celebration Cake (at left) has a thick blanket of lemon curd as a filling between two of its layers of génoise. But whether you make this big cake or not, there's no reason for you to miss out on the lemon curd. This tart but sweet custardy mixture is famed throughout the British Isles as a flavorful spread for bread, toast, cakes or cookies and a filling for tartlets or full-size tarts.

To make just the curd and not the cake, follow the directions in Steps 10 through 12 to produce about one cup (you might want to double or triple the recipe). The ingredients are simply stirred together on stovetop—an easy combination of lemon juice and zest, eggs, sugar and butter. Spoon the curd into a jar and seal airtight. You can keep it on hand in the refrigerator for up to three weeks or so. If orange curd or lime curd appeals to you, just substitute the juice and grated zest of these other fruits for the lemon.

■ ■ ■

A
GARDEN PARTY
TEA

It's summer, the garden is in full bloom, and almost everything is right with the world. Your only quandary is this: You owe several people invitations, and it seems like the ideal time to throw a party, but you've already attended a multitude of every conceivable type – picnics, barbecues, cookouts, clambakes, even croquet contests. ∿ Consider instead a calm and civilized garden party tea. Etiquette does not limit the size of the guest list for a proper tea (indeed, Queen Elizabeth II's are magnificent affairs), so feel free to invite as few or as many guests as you desire. And making your party an outdoor tea offers several distinct advantages: You can show off your horticultural successes to a number of people (who need not know each other beforehand); you can limit the menu to tea sandwiches and a host of desserts (all of which can be made ahead of time), and you get to buy and wear a new hat. ∿ Best of all, your guests will be fed, partied and gone by the time the sun sets, leaving you the better part of the evening to speculate as to why crustless sandwiches are one of the best foods on earth.

Poppy Seed
Tante Cake

Lemon Yogurt
Cake

Cranberry Tea
Bread

Brown Butter
Cardamom
Shortbread Cookies

■ ■ ■

58

A GARDEN PARTY TEA

Serves 16 to 20

SELECTION OF TEAS
SPICED CITRUS TEA

Smoked Salmon and Dill Tea Sandwiches

Cucumber and Tomato Tea Sandwiches

*Roquefort, Walnut
and Cognac Tea Sandwiches*

*Goat Cheese
and Fresh Herb Tea Sandwiches*

radishes and whipped sweet butter

Cream Cheese and Cherry Tea Biscuits

*Brown Butter Cardamom
Shortbread Cookies*

Lemon Yogurt Cake

Cranberry Tea Bread

Poppy Seed Tante Cake

SPICED CITRUS TEA

This fragrant infusion is refreshing either hot or chilled.

1 LEMON
1 ORANGE
1 GRAPEFRUIT
1 CINNAMON STICK
4 CLOVES
¼ TEASPOON FENNEL SEED
2 HEAPING TABLESPOONS NILGIRI, DARJEELING OR ASSAM TEA (OR A COMBINATION)

1~ With a swivel-bladed vegetable peeler, cut 3 strips of the colored zest about 3 inches long and ½ inch wide from the lemon, orange and grapefruit.

2~ Bring 6 cups of water to a boil in a medium nonreactive saucepan. Add the cinnamon, cloves, fennel seed and the 9 strips of citrus zest. Remove from the heat, cover the pan and let steep for about 30 minutes.

3~ A few minutes before serving the tea, return the spice brew to a boil, remove from the heat and add the tea leaves. Steep the leaves for 3 to 5 minutes, depending on how strong and tannic you like your tea.

4~ Meanwhile, bring 2 cups of water to a boil. Rinse out a teapot with the boiling water, strain the prepared tea into the teapot and serve hot.

SERVES 8
RECIPE BY JULIE SAHNI

SMOKED SALMON AND DILL TEA SANDWICHES

While this spread makes an excellent sandwich, it can also be piped into cucumber cups, cherry tomatoes, hard-cooked egg halves or small pastry puffs—perfect teatime dainties.

¼ POUND (1 STICK) UNSALTED BUTTER, SOFTENED
3 OUNCES CREAM CHEESE, SOFTENED
¼ CUP SOUR CREAM
5 OUNCES SMOKED SALMON, CHOPPED
3 TABLESPOONS MINCED FRESH DILL
2 TEASPOONS FRESH LEMON JUICE
⅛ TEASPOON FRESHLY GROUND WHITE PEPPER
1 LOAF THIN-SLICED BREAD, CRUSTS REMOVED AND BREAD CUT INTO SHAPES IF DESIRED

1~ In a medium bowl, combine the butter, cream cheese and sour cream; blend thoroughly. Stir in the smoked salmon, dill, lemon juice and white pepper.

2~ Use immediately or cover and refrigerate. Let the spread soften for about 30 minutes before spreading on the bread and assembling the sandwiches.

MAKES ABOUT 1½ CUPS OF FILLING
RECIPE BY DIANA STURGIS

CUCUMBER AND TOMATO TEA SANDWICHES

These tiny mouthfuls are a classic teatime savory. For best results use very thinly sliced fresh bread, flavorful red vine-ripened tomatoes and bright green fresh coriander leaves with no signs of wilting.

10 TABLESPOONS UNSALTED BUTTER, AT
    ROOM TEMPERATURE
1 TEASPOON PREPARED ENGLISH MUSTARD
½ TEASPOON FRESHLY GROUND PEPPER
½ TEASPOON SALT
¾ TEASPOON FRESH LEMON JUICE
3 TABLESPOONS MINCED FRESH CORIANDER
¼ CUP ALFALFA OR RADISH SPROUTS
    (OPTIONAL)
1 LARGE RIPE TOMATO (ABOUT ½ POUND)
1 CUCUMBER, PREFERABLY SEEDLESS
8 VERY THIN SLICES OF WHITE BREAD (SEE
    NOTE)
8 VERY THIN SLICES OF WHOLE WHEAT
    BREAD (OR SUBSTITUTE WHITE BREAD)

1~ In a small bowl, combine the butter, mustard, pepper, salt, lemon juice and coriander. Blend well. Stir in the sprouts.
2~ Thinly slice the tomato and drain on paper towels. Peel the cucumber; cut ½ inch off the ends and discard. Cut the cucumber crosswise into 3-inch sections. Thinly slice each piece lengthwise.

3~ Spread the flavored butter on one side of each bread slice. Arrange the tomato slices in a single layer on 4 slices and the cucumber in a single layer on 4 slices. (There may be extra tomato and cucumber slices.) Cover the sandwiches with the remaining 8 buttered slices of bread and press gently together.
4~ Using a sharp knife (preferably serrated), trim the sides to remove the crusts and reveal the filling. Quarter each sandwich diagonally to make 4 little triangles. Serve immediately or stack the sandwiches carefully, wrap in plastic wrap to prevent drying out, and store in the refrigerator for up to 2 hours. Remove from the refrigerator at least 15 minutes before serving.
Note: If you cannot find thinly sliced bread, flatten slices with a rolling pin.

MAKES 32 TEA SANDWICHES
RECIPE BY JULIE SAHNI

ROQUEFORT, WALNUT AND COGNAC TEA SANDWICHES

59

This rich sandwich filling is equally tasty when piped or spread on sliced ripe pears.

¼ POUND (1 STICK) UNSALTED BUTTER,
    SOFTENED
4 OUNCES ROQUEFORT CHEESE, SOFTENED
3 OUNCES CREAM CHEESE, SOFTENED
⅓ CUP FINELY CHOPPED WALNUTS
2 TABLESPOONS COGNAC OR BRANDY
1 LOAF THIN-SLICED BREAD, CRUSTS
    REMOVED AND BREAD CUT INTO SHAPES
    IF DESIRED

1~ In a medium bowl, combine the butter, Roquefort and cream cheese; blend thoroughly. Stir in the walnuts and Cognac.
2~ Use immediately or cover and refrigerate. Let the spread soften for about 30 minutes before spreading on the bread and assembling the sandwiches.

MAKES ABOUT 1½ CUPS OF FILLING
RECIPE BY DIANA STURGIS

GOAT CHEESE AND FRESH HERB TEA SANDWICHES

While this filling is tempting on its own, it's fabulous layered with a slice of ham. For 30 tea sandwiches, you'll need about a quarter pound of ham, thinly sliced; lightly spread the top slice of bread with softened butter so that the ham will adhere.

¼ POUND (1 STICK) UNSALTED BUTTER, SOFTENED
5 OUNCES GOAT CHEESE, SUCH AS BUCHERON, SOFTENED
¼ CUP MINCED PARSLEY
1 TABLESPOON MINCED FRESH TARRAGON OR 1 TEASPOON DRIED
SOFTENED UNSALTED BUTTER, FOR SPREADING
1 LOAF THIN-SLICED BREAD, CRUSTS REMOVED AND BREAD CUT INTO SHAPES IF DESIRED

1~ In a medium bowl, combine the butter and goat cheese; blend thoroughly. Stir in the parsley and tarragon.
2~ Use immediately or cover and refrigerate. Let the spread soften for about 30 minutes before spreading on the bread and assembling the sandwiches.

MAKES ABOUT 1½ CUPS OF FILLING
RECIPE BY DIANA STURGIS

CREAM CHEESE AND CHERRY TEA BISCUITS

When you add cream cheese to biscuit dough and then a dollop of cherry preserves, you end up with these tasty one-bite teatime treats.

1 CUP ALL-PURPOSE FLOUR
2 TEASPOONS BAKING POWDER
½ TEASPOON SALT
¼ POUND (1 STICK) UNSALTED BUTTER, AT ROOM TEMPERATURE
1 SMALL PACKAGE (3 OUNCES) CREAM CHEESE, AT ROOM TEMPERATURE
ABOUT 2 TABLESPOONS CHERRY PRESERVES

1~ Preheat the oven to 400°. Lightly flour a baking sheet.
2~ In a small bowl, sift together the flour, baking powder and salt.
3~ In a medium bowl, blend the butter with the cream cheese until well combined. Stir in the flour mixture until well blended.
4~ On a heavily floured surface, roll out the dough into a ½-inch-thick circle. With a floured 1¼-inch round cutter, cut out as many biscuits as possible. The dough will be very soft and will stick to the cutter. Using your finger or the handle of a table knife, push the biscuits out of the cutter onto the prepared baking sheet. Form a small indentation in the center of each biscuit. Spoon ¼ teaspoon of the preserves into each indentation.
5~ Bake in the middle of the oven for 10 to 12 minutes, or until the biscuits are pale gold.

MAKES ABOUT 2 DOZEN
RECIPE BY JO NORTHRUP

BROWN BUTTER CARDAMOM SHORTBREAD COOKIES

These buttery cookies with a hint of cardamom are not as heavy as traditional shortbread.

½ POUND (2 STICKS) UNSALTED BUTTER
3 CUPS ALL-PURPOSE FLOUR
6 CARDAMOM PODS, PEELED, SEEDS CRUSHED INTO A FINE POWDER
½ CUP SUPERFINE SUGAR
½ TEASPOON SALT
¼ CUP MILK
1 TEASPOON VANILLA EXTRACT

1~ Preheat the oven to 325°.
2~ In a small saucepan, simmer the butter over moderately low heat until the moisture from the fat evaporates and the milk solids brown and settle at the bottom of the pan, 25 to 30 minutes. Strain the clear clarified butter into a shallow bowl or lipped plate and chill until firm; discard the browned solids at the bottom of the pan.
3~ In a large bowl, stir together the flour, cardamom, sugar and salt. Cut the clarified butter into small dice and add to the flour mixture. Rub with your fingertips until the mixture forms a coarse meal. Sprinkle on the milk and vanilla while tossing to blend. Gather the dough into a ball.

LEMON YOGURT CAKE

4~On a lightly floured surface, roll out the dough about ⅛ inch thick. Using a 2-inch round cookie cutter, cut into rounds. Gather up the scraps of dough and reroll to make more cookies. Repeat until all of the dough is used.

5~Arrange the cookies on ungreased baking sheets. Bake for 35 to 40 minutes, or until very lightly browned on the edges. Let cool. Store in an airtight container.

MAKES ABOUT 3½ DOZEN COOKIES
RECIPE BY JULIE SAHNI

Lemony and moist, this cake is a dessert worth waiting for. It is wonderful on its own, but if you want to splurge, serve it with fresh berries and cream on the side.

½ POUND (2 STICKS) UNSALTED BUTTER, SOFTENED
1½ CUPS SUGAR
4 EGGS
1 TABLESPOON GRATED LEMON ZEST
1 TEASPOON VANILLA EXTRACT
2½ CUPS ALL-PURPOSE FLOUR
1 TEASPOON BAKING POWDER
1 TEASPOON BAKING SODA
½ TEASPOON SALT
1 CUP PLAIN YOGURT
¾ CUP GROUND BLANCHED ALMONDS
½ CUP FRESH LEMON JUICE

1~Preheat the oven to 350°. Butter and flour a 10-inch tube pan.

2~In a large mixer bowl, beat the butter until light and fluffy. Slowly beat in 1 cup of the sugar. Add the eggs, 1 at a time, beating thoroughly after each addition. Beat in the lemon zest and vanilla.

3~Sift together the flour, baking powder, baking soda and salt into a medium bowl. Fold one-third of the dry ingredients into the butter mixture and then fold in one-third of the yogurt. Repeat 2 more times with the remaining flour and yogurt. Fold in the ground almonds. Spoon the batter into the prepared tube pan.

4~Bake for 1 hour, or until a toothpick inserted in the center comes out clean. Set the pan on a rack to cool.

5~Meanwhile, in a small nonreactive saucepan, heat the remaining ½ cup sugar with the lemon juice over moderate heat, stirring occasionally, until the sugar dissolves, about 5 minutes.

6~Slowly pour the hot lemon syrup evenly over the cake. Let the cake cool completely in the pan before unmolding.

SERVES 8
RECIPE BY PHILLIP STEPHEN SCHULZ

61

CRANBERRY TEA BREAD

62

How to Make a Proper Cup of Tea

A correct "cuppa" is by no means an accident. The brewing method follows certain ground rules that result in a lovely cup of tea. Please note: If you drink your tea with milk, pour the milk into the teacup before adding the tea.

1~Fill a tea kettle with fresh, cold tap water. Bring to a boil over high heat.

2~Meanwhile, choose a ceramic or silver teapot. Pour in hot water and swirl to warm the pot. Pour out the water. Measure good-quality tea into the pot, allotting 1 teaspoon per cup plus 1 teaspoon for the pot.

3~When the kettle of water is approaching a boil, watch carefully. As soon as it reaches a full, rolling boil, pour the water into the pot. (Do not let the water sit, boiling, on stovetop; use it at once.) Cover the pot and let the tea steep for 3 to 8 minutes, depending on the variety of tea used. Pour the tea through a strainer into teacups.

Make this not-too-sweet quick bread ahead of time to allow the flavors to develop. And to make sure it slices neatly for your party, chill well and cut with a serrated knife.

2 CUPS ALL-PURPOSE FLOUR
2 TEASPOONS BAKING POWDER
¼ TEASPOON SALT
4 TABLESPOONS COLD UNSALTED BUTTER, CUT INTO SMALL PIECES
¾ CUP PLUS 1 TABLESPOON SUGAR
4 OUNCES CHOPPED WALNUTS (1 SCANT CUP)
1 TABLESPOON GRATED ORANGE ZEST
1 EGG
⅔ CUP ORANGE JUICE, PREFERABLY FRESH
2 CUPS FRESH CRANBERRIES OR FROZEN (NOT THAWED)
1 TABLESPOON MILK

1~ Preheat the oven to 350°. Butter a 9-by-5-inch loaf pan and line the bottom with waxed paper; butter the paper.

2~ In a large bowl, mix together the flour, baking powder and salt. Cut in the butter until the mixture resembles fine bread crumbs. Add ¾ cup of the sugar, the walnuts and the orange zest and toss to blend.

3~ In a small bowl, beat the egg with a fork until frothy. Beat in the orange juice. Pour this liquid over the dry ingredients and stir just until the dough begins to mass together. Before all of the flour is thoroughly incorporated, add the cranberries and stir them into the dough until evenly distributed.

4~ Scrape the batter into the prepared pan and spread evenly with a spatula. Brush the milk evenly over the surface of the batter and sprinkle the remaining 1 tablespoon sugar on top.

5~ Bake the bread in the middle of the oven for about 1 hour and 15 minutes, or until the loaf is well risen, golden brown and crusty and a tester inserted in the center comes out clean. Transfer the loaf to a rack to cool for 20 minutes.

6~ Run a thin knife around the inside of the pan and invert the loaf onto the rack. Peel off the waxed paper and turn the loaf right-side up; let cool completely. Put the loaf in a tin with a tight-fitting lid and set aside overnight.

SERVES 8 TO 10
RECIPE BY DIANA STURGIS

POPPY SEED TANTE CAKE

CREAM CHEESE ICING

63

The stark whiteness of this cake creates a dramatic contrast to the blue-black poppy seeds. Though this cake is lovely for an afternoon tea, it can be dessert after any dinner—simple or sophisticated.

1 VANILLA BEAN
⅔ CUP MILK
⅔ CUP POPPY SEEDS
1⅔ CUPS CAKE FLOUR
2 TEASPOONS BAKING POWDER
½ TEASPOON SALT
6 OUNCES (1½ STICKS) UNSALTED BUTTER, SOFTENED
1¼ CUPS SUPERFINE SUGAR
4 EGG WHITES, AT ROOM TEMPERATURE
CREAM CHEESE ICING (AT RIGHT)

1~ Slit the vanilla bean lengthwise and cut off the tips. In a small saucepan, scald the milk with the vanilla bean.

2~ In a small bowl, combine the scalded milk, vanilla bean and poppy seeds. Let cool to room temperature. Scrape the inside of the vanilla bean into the milk mixture; discard the pod.

3~ Preheat the oven to 325°. Butter a 9-by-2-inch round cake pan.

4~ Sift together the flour, baking powder and salt into a medium bowl.

5~ In a large mixer bowl, beat the butter on high speed until light and fluffy, about 2 minutes. Gradually add 1 cup of the sugar and continue to beat until very light and creamy, about 5 minutes. Sift in one-third of the flour mixture; stir to combine. Beat in half of the milk-poppy seed mixture. Repeat 2 more times with the remaining dry ingredients and milk.

6~ In a medium bowl, beat the egg whites at medium speed until frothy. Add a pinch of salt and continue beating until soft peaks form, about 2 minutes. Beat in the remaining ¼ cup sugar, 1 teaspoon at a time, increasing the speed to high before adding the last 2 teaspoons. Beat until the meringue is stiff and shiny, about 1 minute. Fold one-fourth of the meringue into the cake batter to lighten it. Fold in the remaining meringue.

7~ Scrape the batter into the prepared pan. Bake for 50 to 55 minutes, or until a tester inserted into the center comes out clean. Let cool in the pan on a rack for 10 minutes.

8~ Remove the cake from the pan and let cool, right-side up, on the rack. *(The cake can be baked up to 1 day in advance, wrapped in plastic and stored at room temperature, or frozen for up to 1 month.)*

9~ Using a long serrated knife, trim off the crusty top of the cake. Slice the cake horizontally into 3 even layers; set aside the middle layer to use as the top. Place the bottom layer on the inverted cake pan. Spread ¾ cup of the Cream Cheese Icing over the bottom cake layer. Repeat with the second cake layer. Top the cake with the middle layer. Frost the sides of the cake with a thin layer of icing. Refrigerate for 10 minutes, then refrost the sides with enough icing to cover completely.

10~ If desired, use a pastry bag fitted with a #2 star tip to pipe a decorative border of icing around the top edge of the cake.

SERVES 10 TO 12
RECIPE BY PEGGY CULLEN

Keep this rich recipe handy for spreading on other cakes or cookies as well.

11 OUNCES CREAM CHEESE, AT ROOM TEMPERATURE
½ POUND (2 STICKS) UNSALTED BUTTER, AT ROOM TEMPERATURE
1 VANILLA BEAN, SPLIT LENGTHWISE
¾ CUP CONFECTIONERS' SUGAR, SIFTED

1~ In a medium mixer bowl, beat the cream cheese until light and fluffy. With the mixer on low speed, gradually beat in the butter until well blended, about 4 minutes.

2~ Scrape the seeds from the inside of the vanilla bean into the mixture; discard the pod. Sift in the confectioners' sugar and continue to beat on low speed, scraping the bowl frequently, until well blended, about 2 minutes.

3~ Cover and refrigerate until ready to use, but do not let harden.

MAKES ABOUT 2½ CUPS
RECIPE BY PEGGY CULLEN

■ ■ ■

THE
ANNE MORROW
LINDBERGH
MEMORIAL LUNCH

"By and large, mothers and housewives are the only workers who do not have regular time off. They are the great vacationless class."

—*ANNE MORROW LINDBERGH*, GIFT FROM THE SEA

Give that lady a round of applause. And while you're at it, take a look at this summertime lunch – it awards a day off to whoever usually does the cooking, woman or man. ～ What we have here is a simple but appealing menu that's easy to prepare, even for children, non-cooks or the most absent-minded professor. The recipes use widely available store-bought ingredients; only the green beans and ice cream sandwiches need be prepared in advance. And though this luncheon is in no way elaborate, its normalcy doesn't mean it's not delicious. Think of it – a table set by the grill in the backyard, you with your feet up, feeling totally unpressured, sipping pink lemonade (did someone spike it with tequila?). A big, juicy sesame-Cheddar burger is just about ready to come off the grill. Anne would love it.

■ ■ ■

*Sesame-Cheddar
Burgers*

*Green Beans in
Mustard-Sherry
Vinaigrette*

*Boston Lettuce
Salad*

SESAME-CHEDDAR BURGERS

THE ANNE MORROW LINDBERGH MEMORIAL LUNCH

Serves 4

PINK LEMONADE

Sesame-Cheddar Burgers

Boston Lettuce Salad

*Green Beans
in Mustard-Sherry Vinaigrette*

Mocha Ice Cream Sandwiches

These cheeseburgers topped with sesame seeds are mouthwateringly juicy whether you cook them outdoors or in.

1 POUND LEAN GROUND ROUND
1 TEASPOON COARSE (KOSHER) SALT
½ TEASPOON FRESHLY GROUND PEPPER
¼ CUP GRATED EXTRA-SHARP CHEDDAR
    CHEESE
4 TEASPOONS TOASTED SESAME SEEDS
8 SLICES TOASTED BREAD, OR 4
    HAMBURGER BUNS

1~ Pat the meat dry with paper towels to absorb any excess moisture. Divide into 4 equal portions. Quickly shape each portion into a patty.

2~ *To grill the burgers:* Cook the patties until almost to the desired degree of doneness. Sprinkle on the salt and pepper and mound 1 tablespoon of the cheese over each burger. Cover and grill until the cheese melts. Sprinkle 1 teaspoon of the toasted sesame seeds over each cheeseburger and serve at once on toasted bread or buns.

To cook the burgers on stovetop: Evenly sprinkle the salt over the bottom of a large heavy skillet. Warm the skillet over high heat until the salt smokes, about 3 minutes. Add the patties and cook for 2 minutes. Reduce the heat to moderate and cook until crusted on the bottom, about 3 minutes longer.

Turn the burgers and sprinkle on the pepper. Mound 1 tablespoon of the cheese on top of each burger. Cover and cook for 2 minutes for rare, 3 minutes for medium rare or 4 minutes for well done. Sprinkle 1 teaspoon of the toasted sesame seeds over each burger and serve hot on toasted bread or buns.

SERVES 4
RECIPE BY FOOD & WINE

BOSTON LETTUCE SALAD

Here's a simple and cooling salad that can be made at any time of year.

1 LARGE HEAD OF BOSTON LETTUCE—LEAVES
    SEPARATED, RINSED AND DRIED
¼ CUP OLIVE OIL
2 TEASPOONS RED WINE VINEGAR
⅛ TEASPOON SALT
FRESHLY GROUND PEPPER
2 CHILLED NAVEL ORANGES, PEELED AND
    SECTIONED, WITH THE MEMBRANE
    REMOVED

1~ Place the lettuce leaves in a medium bowl.
2~ In a small bowl, whisk the olive oil, vinegar, salt
   and pepper to taste until blended.
3~ Pour the dressing over the lettuce and toss
   gently until coated. Divide the salad among
   4 plates and arrange the orange slices on one
   side of each plate.

SERVES 4
RECIPE BY SHIRLEY SARVIS

GREEN BEANS IN MUSTARD-SHERRY VINAIGRETTE

These beans are so tasty it's worth keeping a supply of them in the refrigerator ready to serve any old time.

1¼ POUNDS SMALL TENDER GREEN BEANS
1 TABLESPOON DIJON-STYLE MUSTARD
1½ TABLESPOONS DRY SHERRY
1 TABLESPOON SHERRY WINE VINEGAR OR
    WHITE WINE VINEGAR
1 TABLESPOON WALNUT OR OLIVE OIL
¼ CUP VERY THINLY SLICED SCALLION
    GREENS
SALT AND FRESHLY GROUND PEPPER

1~ Steam the beans until crisp-tender, 6 to 8 minutes. Remove the rack from the steamer and let
   the beans cool while you prepare the dressing.
2~ In a small bowl, combine the mustard and
   sherry and blend. Add the vinegar and oil and
   mix well.
3~ Transfer the beans to a serving dish. Pour the
   dressing over the beans, add the scallions and
   toss to coat well. Season with salt and pepper
   to taste.
4~ Let the beans cool to room temperature. Cover
   and refrigerate until serving time—at least
   several hours, or overnight.

SERVES 4
RECIPE BY ELIZABETH SCHNEIDER

MOCHA ICE CREAM SANDWICHES

This is a fun dessert you can put together in a hurry. The flavors of coffee and chocolate are particularly pleasing, but these cold crunchy sandwiches can be made with any flavor of ice cream and any kind of cookie—choose your favorites.

1 PINT COFFEE ICE CREAM
24 GOOD-QUALITY CHOCOLATE-NUT
    COOKIES, ABOUT 2 INCHES IN DIAMETER
    (SUCH AS PEPPERIDGE FARM BROWNIE
    CHOCOLATE NUT)

1~ Scoop out 1 tablespoon of ice cream and center
   it on the flat side of a cookie. Top with flat side
   of another cookie and press gently to flatten
   the ice cream. Continue making more ice
   cream sandwiches.
2~ Wrap the ice cream sandwiches in plastic.
   Freeze the sandwiches for at least 2 hours, or
   until the ice cream is firm.

SERVES 12
RECIPE BY FOOD & WINE

67

FULL MOON DINNER
FOR TWO

What makes a dinner romantic? That's a tough one. There doesn't seem to be a precise recipe. A full moon helps. A balmy summer night certainly can contribute, although a roaring fire in the hearth at midwinter isn't half-bad either. The atmosphere of a romantic evening should appeal to all of the senses. There should be soft music, a great view or pretty things to look at, comfortable surroundings with pleasantly tactile textures. And definitely, without a doubt, there must be the aroma and flavors of magnificent food. ∼ This menu can please all of the senses but one – you provide your own favorite music. Start the meal off with a rich shrimp bisque, made from roasted red bell peppers and strewn with homemade thyme croutons. The main course is pasta – fettuccine flecked with bits of chive – tossed with lobster and yellow squash. A summery salad is served alongside. Dessert is a two-part affair. First, finish your wine and relish the slight sweetness of the rosé Champagne sorbet. Later, when you're hungry again, treasure each bite of Chocolate Black Walnut Cake.

■ ■ ■

*Chive Fettuccine
with Lobster*

SHRIMP AND RED PEPPER BISQUE

70

***

FULL MOON DINNER FOR TWO

ROSÉ CHAMPAGNE
Shrimp and Red Pepper Bisque
Thyme Croutons

Chive Fettuccine with Lobster and Yellow Squash
Mixed Summer Salad

Rosé Champagne Sorbet

ESPRESSO OR CAPPUCCINO
Chocolate Black Walnut Cake

***

This rich seafood soup can be prepared up to four days in advance, but the shrimp and cream should be added just before serving. Halve the recipe if you don't want leftovers.

4 LARGE RED BELL PEPPERS
2½ POUNDS MEDIUM SHRIMP—PEELED, DEVEINED AND CUT CROSSWISE IN HALF, SHELLS RESERVED
3 TABLESPOONS VEGETABLE OIL
1 LARGE ONION, FINELY CHOPPED
1 LARGE CARROT, FINELY CHOPPED
1 LARGE CELERY RIB, FINELY CHOPPED
¼ CUP ALL-PURPOSE FLOUR
¼ CUP TOMATO PASTE
⅓ CUP BRANDY
4 SPRIGS OF FRESH THYME PLUS ½ TEASPOON FRESH THYME LEAVES OR 1¼ TEASPOONS DRIED
1 IMPORTED BAY LEAF
1½ CUPS HEAVY CREAM, AT ROOM TEMPERATURE
1 TEASPOON SALT
¾ TEASPOON FRESHLY GROUND PEPPER

1~ Roast the peppers directly over a gas flame or under a broiler as close to the heat as possible, turning occasionally, until they are charred all over, 15 to 20 minutes. Seal the peppers in a paper bag and let stand for 10 minutes. Remove the blackened skin, stems, seeds and ribs and puree the peppers in a food processor until smooth. Place the pepper puree in a small bowl and set aside.

2~ Rinse the bowl of the food processor and add the shrimp shells. Chop into small pieces. In a large heavy saucepan or stovetop casserole, heat the oil over high heat. Add the chopped shrimp shells and sauté, stirring occasionally, until lightly browned, about 3 minutes. Add the onion, carrot and celery. Reduce the heat to low and cook, stirring occasionally, until the vegetables are softened and golden brown, about 10 minutes.

3~ Stir in the flour. Add the tomato paste and cook 1 minute. Increase the heat to moderately high and whisk in the brandy, scraping up any browned bits from the bottom of the pan. Cook for 3 minutes, then whisk in 7 cups of water. Add the thyme sprigs or 1 teaspoon of the dried thyme and bay leaf and return to a boil, whisking frequently. Simmer the soup over low heat for 45 minutes.

4~ Meanwhile, in a large saucepan, heat the cream over moderately high heat. Add the shrimp and cook, stirring occasionally, until they are pink and loosely curled, about 8 minutes. Pour the shrimp and cream into a large bowl and set aside.

5~ Strain the soup through a fine-mesh sieve into a large bowl, pressing to extract all the liquid. Return the soup to the pan and stir in the red pepper puree.

6~ Just before serving, stir in the shrimp and cream and season with the salt, pepper and remaining thyme.

SERVES 8 TO 10
RECIPE BY MARCIA KIESEL

THYME CROUTONS

The thyme in these little croutons will echo and complement the thyme in the soup.

3 TABLESPOONS OLIVE OIL
3 CUPS DICED (⅜ INCH) FRENCH OR
    OTHER FIRM-TEXTURED WHITE BREAD
½ TEASPOON FRESHLY GROUND PEPPER
½ TEASPOON DRIED THYME

1~ Preheat the oven to 375°.
2~ In a large ovenproof skillet, heat the olive oil over low heat. Add the bread and season with the pepper and thyme. Toss to mix.
3~ Place the skillet in the oven and bake until the croutons are crisp and nicely browned, 10 to 12 minutes. Drain on paper towels. *(The croutons can be made up to 2 days in advance. Store in an airtight container at room temperature.)*

MAKES ABOUT 3 CUPS
RECIPE BY BOB CHAMBERS

CHIVE FETTUCCINE WITH LOBSTER AND YELLOW SQUASH

If you don't want to bother making the fettuccine, buy 8 ounces of fresh pasta at a local specialty food store.

PASTA:
⅔ CUP MINCED CHIVES
1 EGG
½ TEASPOON SALT
2 TEASPOONS OLIVE OIL
1¼ CUPS ALL-PURPOSE FLOUR

LOBSTER AND SQUASH:
1½-POUND LIVE LOBSTER, OR ¾ POUND
    COOKED LOBSTER MEAT
3½ TABLESPOONS UNSALTED BUTTER
1 SMALL YELLOW (SUMMER) SQUASH, CUT
    INTO QUARTERS AND SLICED LENGTH-
    WISE ¼ INCH THICK (1 CUP)
1½ TABLESPOONS SOUR CREAM
½ TEASPOON SALT
½ TEASPOON FRESHLY GROUND PEPPER
1 TABLESPOON MINCED CHIVES

1~ *Make the Pasta dough:* In a food processor, combine the chives, egg, salt, olive oil, flour and 2 teaspoons of water. Process until the mixture resembles wet sand, about 30 seconds. Remove the dough from the processor and knead until it forms a smooth ball, about 1 minute. Cover with plastic wrap and refrigerate for at least 30 minutes.
2~ *Cook the Lobster:* Meanwhile, plunge the lobster into a large pot of boiling water, cover and cook over high heat for exactly 8 minutes. Transfer the lobster to a large bowl and let

stand until cool enough to handle, about 10 minutes. Crack the lobster claws, the knuckles and tail and remove all of the meat. Remove the large intestine from the tail and cut the meat crosswise into ¼-inch-thick slices. Coarsely chop the knuckle meat, leave the claws whole and set aside.
3~ *Roll out and cut the Pasta:* Cut the pasta into quarters. Roll each piece through a pasta machine set on the widest notch. Continue to roll the dough through the machine on consecutively narrower settings, ending with the second-to-thinnest setting.
4~ Run the pasta through the fettuccine cutter on the machine or cut by hand and hang to dry, about 30 minutes.
5~ *Finish the dish:* In a large skillet, melt the butter over moderately high heat. Add the squash, reduce the heat to low and cook until the squash is tender, about 3 minutes. Set aside.
6~ Bring a large pot of salted water to a boil. Add the fettuccine and cook until tender but still firm, about 4 minutes; drain.
7~ Add the chopped lobster meat to the skillet, increase the heat to high and cook, tossing, until the lobster is warmed through, about 30 seconds. Set the claw meat aside. Add the hot fettuccine; toss to combine. Turn off the heat and sir in the sour cream. Season with the salt and pepper. Garnish with the minced chives and set a claw on top of each serving.

SERVES 2 AS AN ENTRÉE, 4 AS A FIRST COURSE
RECIPE BY MARCIA KIESEL

71

Mixed Summer Salad

72

Pansies or nasturtiums make a colorful addition to this tossed salad of mild and sharp greens, though it's really tasty without them. Prepare the dressing and greens ahead, adjusting the quantities to serve more or fewer people.

1 GARLIC CLOVE, CRUSHED THROUGH
  A PRESS
½ TEASPOON SALT
2 TABLESPOONS FRESH LEMON JUICE
¼ TEASPOON FRESHLY GROUND PEPPER
½ CUP EXTRA-VIRGIN OLIVE OIL
1 HEAD OF RED LEAF LETTUCE, TORN INTO
  BITE-SIZE PIECES
1 HEAD OF BIBB LETTUCE, TORN INTO
  BITE-SIZE PIECES
1 BUNCH OF ARUGULA, LARGE STEMS
  REMOVED
1 BUNCH OF WATERCRESS, LARGE STEMS
  REMOVED
2 TABLESPOONS CHERVIL LEAVES
2 TABLESPOONS CHOPPED FRESH TARRAGON
3 TABLESPOONS CHOPPED CHIVES
¼ CUP CHOPPED PARSLEY
10 PANSIES OR NASTURTIUMS (OPTIONAL)

1~ In a small bowl, blend the garlic with the salt. Whisk in the lemon juice and pepper, then whisk in the olive oil in a thin stream. Pour half of the dressing into a large salad bowl.
2~ Add the red leaf lettuce, Bibb lettuce, arugula, watercress, chervil, tarragon, chives, parsley and pansies or nasturtiums to the salad bowl. Pour the remaining dressing over the salad and toss well.

SERVES 6
RECIPE BY MARY MARSHALL HYNSON

Rosé Champagne Sorbet

Whether the moon is full or new, this palest pink sorbet will give you romantic notions. Use top-quality wine to achieve the most flavorful results.

1 CUP SUGAR
¼ CUP FRESH LEMON JUICE
1 BOTTLE (750 ML) OF GOOD-QUALITY
  ROSÉ CHAMPAGNE OR SPARKLING WINE

1~ In a small nonreactive saucepan, combine the sugar with 1 cup of water. Bring to a boil, stirring constantly until the sugar dissolves. Add the lemon juice. Remove the syrup from the heat and let cool. Refrigerate until chilled.
2~ Combine the Champagne with the chilled syrup. Pour the mixture into an ice cream maker and freeze according to the manufacturer's instructions. Transfer the sorbet to a covered container and freeze at least overnight and for up to 3 days before serving. Serve in chilled glasses or bowls.

SERVES 12
RECIPE BY BOB CHAMBERS

CHOCOLATE BLACK WALNUT CAKE

Black walnuts give this mousse cake an unusual earthy flavor, but if you can't find any in your market, ordinary walnuts will work well.

1 POUND SEMISWEET CHOCOLATE,
  CHOPPED
6 EGGS, AT ROOM TEMPERATURE
2 TABLESPOONS SUGAR
1½ TABLESPOONS DARK RUM
1 TABLESPOON VANILLA EXTRACT
PINCH OF SALT
½ CUP HEAVY CREAM
1 CUP WALNUTS (ABOUT 4 OUNCES),
  PREFERABLY BLACK, TOASTED AND
  FINELY GROUND
WHIPPED CREAM, AS ACCOMPANIMENT

1~ Preheat the oven to 325°. Butter a 9-by-5-by-3-inch loaf pan. Line the bottom and sides of the pan with parchment or waxed paper.
2~ Place the chocolate in a metal bowl over simmering water and stir just until melted. Remove from the heat and let cool slightly.
3~ In a large metal bowl, whisk together the eggs, sugar, rum, vanilla and salt until blended. Set over a pan of simmering water and beat with an electric hand mixer until the egg mixture forms a slowly dissolving ribbon when the beaters are lifted, about 3 minutes. Remove from the heat and beat until cooled to room temperature.

4~ In a medium bowl, beat the cream until soft peaks form. With a rubber spatula, fold the melted chocolate into the egg mixture until blended. Fold in the whipped cream and ground nuts until mixed. Pour into the prepared loaf pan.
5~ Set the loaf pan in a larger pan in the oven and add enough hot water to reach halfway up the loaf. Reduce the oven temperature to 300° and bake for about 1¼ hours, or until set. Remove from the oven and let cool on a rack before unmolding.
6~ Slice the cake about ½ inch thick and pass a bowl of whipped cream on the side.

SERVES 8 TO 10
RECIPE BY BRENDAN WALSH

---

7 3

Adding Spice to a Romantic Dinner

A moonlit dinner for two seems a fitting place to include an aphrodisiac dish or two, and indeed, we do—the pasta has lobster in it. But who would have thought that all of these herbs and spices would be considered aphrodisiacs as well?

allspice	*coriander*	*nutmeg*
aniseed	*cumin*	*paprika*
basil	*curry powder*	*pepper*
bay leaf	*dill*	*pimiento*
capers	*ginger*	*rosemary*
caraway	*hyssop*	*saffron*
cardamom	*licorice*	*sage*
chervil	*marjoram*	*tarragon*
cinnamon	*mint*	*thyme*
clove	*mustard*	*turmeric*

...

BASTILLE DAY CELEBRATION

Summertime holidays and the parties they generate are so predictable – the Memorial Day barbecue followed by the Fourth of July wienie roast followed by the Labor Day barbecue. Enough. This year, consider something revolutionary: Celebrate Bastille Day. And, if you're truly brave, risk two radical steps, more: Have the party indoors, where it's cool and clean, and don't serve any grilled foods at all. ~ Bastille Day is a good time for a party because it falls almost exactly at midsummer, a full ten days after July 4th and a good six weeks before Labor Day. We start our Bastille Day celebration with a range of raw and cooked shellfish. Depending on how many people you invite, quantities can be expanded or decreased at will, or you can simply serve wedges of the *pissaladière*, a savory French onion tart. After the hors d'oeuvre come hearty French main courses – a thick, rich monkfish bourride and a rustic lamb ragout with white beans. And for dessert, is there any question? Let them eat cake! A big cake, in fact, and some madeleines, as well as a peach-raspberry pie and a smooth, tangy raspberry satin sorbet.

Pissaladière

*Cold Shrimp with
Four-Herb
Mayonnaise*

*Broiled Clams
with Tarragon-
Pernod Butter and
Bacon*

*Baked Shellfish
with Red Pepper
and Herb Butter*

*Oysters with
Balsamic Vinegar
Mignonette
Sauce*

■ ■ ■

PISSALADIÈRE

BASTILLE DAY CELEBRATION

Serves 20

FRENCH RED, WHITE AND ROSÉ WINES
Pissaladière
oysters and clams on the half shell
boiled shrimp
Balsamic Vinegar Mignonette Sauce
Cold Shrimp with Four-Herb Mayonnaise
Baked Shellfish with Red Pepper and Herb Butter
Broiled Clams with Tarragon-Pernod Butter and Bacon

Ragout of Lamb with White Beans Provençale
Monkfish Bourride with Garlic Cream
Tossed Salad with Sherry Wine Vinaigrette

Orange Chiffon Cake
Madeleines
Peach-Raspberry Pie
Raspberry Satin Sorbet

Nearly every bakery in Provence sells this substantial pizzalike bread. Cut into smaller portions, it makes an excellent hors d'oeuvre.

2 TABLESPOONS EXTRA-VIRGIN OLIVE OIL
4 MEDIUM ONIONS, THINLY SLICED
2 LARGE GARLIC CLOVES, THINLY SLICED
1 LARGE SPRIG OF FRESH THYME OR
  ½ TEASPOON DRIED
2 LARGE TOMATOES—PEELED, SEEDED AND
  CHOPPED
½ POUND BREAD DOUGH
8 FLAT ANCHOVY FILLETS, RINSED AND
  DRAINED
12 OIL-CURED BLACK OLIVES, PREFERABLY
  FROM NYONS, PITTED AND HALVED

1~ In a large skillet, heat the oil over moderately low heat. Add the onions, garlic and thyme and toss to coat with the oil. Cover and cook, stirring occasionally, until the onions turn a light golden color, about 20 minutes.
2~ Stir in the tomatoes and cook until their liquid has evaporated and the mixture is thick, about 5 minutes. Discard the thyme sprig.
3~ On a lightly floured surface, roll out the dough into an 11-by-14-inch rectangle. Transfer to a baking sheet, cover and let rest for 15 minutes.
4~ Preheat the oven to 450°. Spread the onion-tomato sauce evenly over the dough. Arrange the anchovies in a spoke-like pattern on top and sprinkle with the olives. Let stand for 15 minutes.
5~ Bake the pissaladière until the crust is crisp, 15 to 20 minutes. Slice and serve warm or at room temperature.

SERVES 6 TO 8
RECIPE BY PATRICIA WELLS

BALSAMIC VINEGAR MIGNONETTE SAUCE

Dollops of this tangy sauce are superlative over raw oysters and quite delectable on raw clams. Spoon some of the sauce into a bowl and use as a dip for cold boiled shrimp. Double or triple the recipe as needed.

2 TABLESPOONS MINCED SHALLOT
1 TABLESPOON MINCED CARROT
1 TABLESPOON MINCED PARSLEY
½ TABLESPOON COARSELY CRACKED BLACK
    PEPPER
¼ CUP DRY WHITE WINE
¼ CUP BALSAMIC VINEGAR

In a small bowl, combine the shallot, carrot, parsley, pepper, wine and vinegar. Serve immediately, or cover and refrigerate for up to 3 hours.

MAKES ABOUT ⅔ CUP
RECIPE BY FOOD & WINE

COLD SHRIMP WITH FOUR-HERB MAYONNAISE

This herb mayonnaise makes a splendid cocktail sauce for raw oysters or clams and can be used as a sauce for all sorts of roasted shellfish. Feel free to substitute other fresh herbs if you desire.

2¼ TEASPOONS SALT
3½ POUNDS LARGE SHRIMP—SHELLED,
    WITH THE LAST SECTION OF THE TAIL
    SHELL LEFT INTACT, AND DEVEINED
1 EGG YOLK
¼ TEASPOON DIJON-STYLE MUSTARD
1½ TABLESPOONS FRESH LEMON JUICE
1 TABLESPOON DRY WHITE WINE
5 TO 6 DROPS OF HOT PEPPER SAUCE
PINCH OF SUGAR
1 TEASPOON ANCHOVY PASTE
¾ CUP SAFFLOWER OR OTHER BLAND
    VEGETABLE OIL
¼ CUP EXTRA-VIRGIN OLIVE OIL
1 TABLESPOON WARM WATER
3 TABLESPOONS MINCED CHIVES
2 TABLESPOONS MINCED PARSLEY
3 TABLESPOONS MINCED FRESH TARRAGON
    OR 2 TEASPOONS DRIED
2 TABLESPOONS MINCED FRESH BASIL

1 ~ Bring a large pot of water to a boil with 2 teaspoons of the salt. Add the shrimp, let the water return to a boil and cook until the shrimp are loosely curled and just opaque throughout, 1 to 2 minutes for medium shrimp, 2 to 3 minutes for large and 3 to 4 minutes for jumbo. Drain under cold running water, pat dry with paper towels. Cover with a damp cloth and refrigerate until serving time. *(The shrimp can be prepared up to 5 hours ahead.)*

2 ~ In a medium bowl, combine the egg yolk, mustard, lemon juice, wine, hot sauce, sugar, anchovy paste and the remaining ¼ teaspoon salt. Whisk until thoroughly blended.

3 ~ Gradually whisk in the safflower and olive oils, drop by drop at first, then in a thin stream. When all of the oil has been incorporated, whisk in the warm water. Stir in the minced fresh herbs. Cover and refrigerate for up to 6 hours. Serve with the shrimp.

MAKES ABOUT 5 DOZEN
RECIPE BY FOOD & WINE

BAKED SHELLFISH WITH RED PEPPER AND HERB BUTTER

Keep this butter on hand as an almost "instant" sauce for grilled fish.

½ RED BELL PEPPER, CUT INTO SMALL PIECES
2 SCALLIONS, CHOPPED
1 TABLESPOON CHOPPED GARLIC
½ TEASPOON THYME
1 TABLESPOON CHOPPED PARSLEY
PINCH OF CAYENNE PEPPER
¼ POUND (1 STICK) UNSALTED BUTTER,
    CUT INTO PIECES
24 OYSTERS OR CHERRYSTONE OR LITTLE-
    NECK CLAMS, ON THE HALF SHELL

1~ *Make the Red Pepper and Herb Butter:* Combine the bell pepper, scallions, garlic, thyme, parsley and cayenne in a food processor. Pulse on and off until the ingredients are minced but not pureed. Add the butter pieces and process until blended. Transfer the butter to a sheet of plastic wrap and roll into a log shape about 1½ inches in diameter; twist the ends closed. Freeze the butter until firm, about 1½ hours.

2~ *Bake the Shellfish:* Cover a large ovenproof platter or baking sheet with rock salt and place it in the oven. Preheat the oven to 500°, about 30 minutes.

3~ Set the shellfish on top of the hot rock salt. Top each clam or oyster with ½ teaspoon of the red pepper and herb butter. Bake for 3 to 5 minutes, or until the shellfish is warm or hot, to your taste. Serve immediately.

MAKES 2 DOZEN
RECIPE BY FOOD & WINE

BROILED CLAMS WITH TARRAGON-PERNOD BUTTER AND BACON

Feel free to substitute the Red Pepper and Herb Butter (recipe at left) if you find it more appealing.

1½ TABLESPOONS CHOPPED SHALLOT
1½ TABLESPOONS CHOPPED FRESH TARRA-
    GON OR 2 TEASPOONS DRIED
½ TABLESPOON TARRAGON VINEGAR
1 TEASPOON PERNOD
½ TEASPOON COARSELY CRACKED PEPPER
¼ POUND (1 STICK) UNSALTED BUTTER,
    CUT INTO PIECES
24 CHERRYSTONE OR LITTLENECK CLAMS,
    ON THE HALF SHELL
3 SLICES OF BACON, CUT INTO 8 PIECES EACH

1~ *Make the Tarragon-Pernod Butter:* Combine the shallot, tarragon, vinegar, Pernod and pepper in a food processor. Pulse on and off until the ingredients are minced but not pureed. Add the butter and process until blended. Transfer the butter to a sheet of plastic wrap and roll into a log about 1½ inches in diameter. Roll in plastic; twist the ends closed. Freeze until firm, about 1½ hours.

2~ *Broil the Clams:* Preheat the broiler.

3~ Cover a large ovenproof platter or baking sheet with rock salt. Set the clams in the salt. Top each clam with ½ teaspoon of the tarragon-Pernod butter and a piece of the bacon.

4~ Broil as close to the heat as possible for 4 to 6 minutes, or until the clams are cooked and the bacon is crisp. Serve immediately.

MAKES 2 DOZEN
RECIPE BY FOOD & WINE

RAGOUT OF LAMB WITH WHITE BEANS PROVENÇALE

After cooking, the lamb should rest overnight, so plan your time accordingly. You'll need to double this recipe for a crowd.

5 TO 6 TABLESPOONS UNSALTED BUTTER
5 TO 7 TABLESPOONS OLIVE OIL,
    PREFERABLY EXTRA-VIRGIN
⅓ CUP MINCED SHALLOTS
4 LARGE GARLIC CLOVES, MINCED
1 CAN (35 OUNCES) ITALIAN PEELED
    TOMATOES, DRAINED AND CUT
    CROSSWISE INTO SLICES
½ TEASPOON DRIED THYME
¾ TEASPOON SALT
½ TEASPOON FRESHLY GROUND BLACK
    PEPPER
3 TO 4 POUNDS BONELESS LAMB
    SHOULDER, TRIMMED AND CUT INTO
    1½-INCH CUBES
LARGE PINCH OF SUGAR
1 TABLESPOON ALL-PURPOSE FLOUR
¾ CUP DRY WHITE WINE
BOUQUET GARNI: 1 LARGE SPRIG OF
    PARSLEY, 1 TEASPOON DRIED THYME
    AND 1 BAY LEAF TIED IN A DOUBLE
    THICKNESS OF CHEESECLOTH
2 CUPS BEEF STOCK OR CANNED BROTH
1 LARGE RED BELL PEPPER, CUT INTO
    ½-INCH DICE
WHITE BEANS (AT RIGHT)
½ CUP MINCED FRESH PARSLEY
6 ANCHOVY FILLETS, MINCED

1~ In a medium saucepan, melt 2 tablespoons of the butter in 2 tablespoons of the oil over moderate heat. Add the shallots and half of the garlic and cook for 1 minute without browning. Add the tomatoes and cook, stirring frequently, for 5 minutes. Add the thyme, salt and black pepper.

2~ Reduce the heat to low, partially cover and simmer, stirring frequently, until the juices evaporate and the tomato mixture thickens, 20 to 30 minutes. Remove from the heat and set aside.

3~ Preheat the oven to 350°. Dry the lamb thoroughly on paper towels.

4~ In a large heavy skillet, melt 1 tablespoon of the butter in 2 tablespoons of the oil over high heat. Working in batches, add the lamb cubes without crowding and sauté, turning, until browned on all sides, about 10 minutes. Remove the lamb with a slotted spoon to a side dish. Season with salt and pepper. Add additional butter and oil with the second or third batch if the meat begins to stick.

5~ Discard the fat from the skillet. Add 2 tablespoons of the butter and melt over moderate heat. Return the lamb to the skillet. Sprinkle the lamb with the sugar and flour. Cook for 1 to 2 minutes, tossing, until the lamb is glazed and well browned. With a slotted spoon, transfer the lamb to a large casserole that can be used on stovetop.

6~ Add the wine to the skillet and increase the heat to high. Bring to a boil and cook, scraping up any brown bits from the bottom of the pan, until the wine is reduced to about 3 tablespoons, 3 to 5 minutes.

7~ Add the reserved tomato mixture, the bouquet garni and the beef stock. Bring to a boil and pour over the lamb. Cover the casserole tightly and bake in the center of the oven for 1½ hours, or until the lamb is tender when pierced with a fork. Remove from the oven. Let cool. Cover and refrigerate overnight.

8~ Scrape off any congealed fat from the top of the lamb ragout. Remove and discard the bouquet garni. Place the casserole, covered, on top of the stove and warm over moderately low heat.

9~ In a medium skillet, heat 1 tablespoon of the olive oil over moderately low heat. Add the bell pepper and cook, stirring frequently, until just tender, 6 to 8 minutes.

10~ Add the bell pepper and the white beans to the ragout. Cook over moderately low heat for 15 minutes. Add the remaining garlic, the parsley and anchovies. Season with additional salt and pepper to taste and serve at once.

SERVES 6 TO 8
RECIPE BY PERLA MEYERS

WHITE BEANS

You'll want to double this recipe to satisfy the appetites of a Bastille Day–size crowd.

1 CUP DRIED GREAT NORTHERN WHITE
    BEANS
1 MEDIUM ONION, PEELED AND STUCK
    WITH 1 WHOLE CLOVE
1 MEDIUM CARROT, CUT IN HALF
1 MEDIUM CELERY RIB WITH LEAVES, CUT
    IN HALF
3 PEPPERCORNS
BOUQUET GARNI: 1 LARGE SPRIG OF PARS-
    LEY, ¼ TEASPOON DRIED THYME AND
    1 SMALL BAY LEAF TIED IN A DOUBLE
    THICKNESS OF CHEESECLOTH
½ TEASPOON SALT

1~ Place the beans in a large stovetop-to-oven casserole and cover with 2 inches of cold water. Bring to a boil and remove from the heat. Cover and let stand for 1 hour.

2~ Preheat the oven to 325°.

3~ Drain the beans, return them to the casserole and add cold water to cover by 2 to 3 inches. Add the onion, carrot, celery, peppercorns and bouquet garni. Bring to a boil and immediately remove from the heat.

4~ Cover tightly and cook in the oven for 1½ hours, or until the beans are tender. Remove the bouquet garni. Season with the salt. If not using the beans immediately, let them cool in their cooking liquid. Drain before using. (*The cooked beans will keep in their liquid stored in the refrigerator for up to 10 days.*)

SERVES 6 TO 8
RECIPE BY PERLA MEYERS

79

MONKFISH BOURRIDE WITH GARLIC CREAM

80

Monkfish—known as *lotte* in Provence—is a popular and plentiful Mediterranean fish, one that stands up well in flavorful soups such as this bourride. With the addition of the garlic-rich mayonnaise known as aïoli, the soup is a meal all on its own. We suggest you double this recipe; it will be popular with your friends.

1 POUND BAKING POTATOES, PEELED AND
   THINLY SLICED
1 LEEK (WHITE PART ONLY), SLICED
1 FENNEL BULB, TRIMMED AND THINLY
   SLICED
1 MEDIUM CARROT, SLICED
1 GARLIC CLOVE, MINCED
1 TEASPOON GRATED ORANGE ZEST
3 IMPORTED BAY LEAVES
1 CUP DRY WHITE WINE
4 CUPS FISH STOCK (AT RIGHT)
2 POUNDS MONKFISH, MEMBRANE
   REMOVED, CUT CROSSWISE INTO
   ½-INCH SLICES
AÏOLI (PAGE 115)
2 EGG YOLKS
¼ CUP CRÈME FRAÎCHE OR HEAVY CREAM
½ TEASPOON SALT
¼ TEASPOON FRESHLY GROUND PEPPER
TOASTED SLICES OF PEASANT OR FRENCH
   BREAD, AS ACCOMPANIMENT

1~ In a large nonreactive saucepan or stovetop casserole, combine the potatoes, leek, fennel, carrot, garlic, orange zest, bay leaves, wine and fish stock. Bring to a boil over high heat. Reduce the heat to moderately low and simmer until the vegetables are just tender, 12 to 15 minutes.

2~ Add the monkfish to the vegetables and cook, skimming frequently, until the fish is opaque throughout, about 5 minutes. Discard the bay leaves.

3~ With a slotted spoon, transfer the fish and vegetables to a warmed soup tureen. Cover to keep warm. Boil the soup over high heat until reduced to 3 cups, 5 to 10 minutes.

4~ Meanwhile, in a medium bowl, combine ¾ cup of the aïoli with the egg yolks and crème fraîche; whisk to blend. Gradually stir ½ cup of the hot soup into the aïoli mixture, or garlic cream. Over low heat, whisk the aïoli mixture into the remaining soup until blended. Cook, stirring, for 1 to 2 minutes to thicken slightly; do not let boil. Season with the salt and pepper and pour the soup over the fish and vegetables.

5~ To serve, ladle the soup into warmed bowls, making sure everyone gets some fish and an assortment of vegetables. Pass the remaining aïoli and toasted bread separately.

SERVES 6
RECIPE BY PATRICIA WELLS

FISH STOCK

4 POUNDS NON-OILY FISH BONES, HEADS
   AND TRIMMINGS, GILLS REMOVED, WELL
   RINSED AND CUT UP
1 MEDIUM ONION, CHOPPED
1 TOMATO, COARSELY CHOPPED
BOUQUET GARNI: 12 PARSLEY STEMS,
   8 PEPPERCORNS, ¼ TEASPOON THYME,
   ¼ TEASPOON FENNEL SEEDS AND
   1 IMPORTED BAY LEAF TIED IN A DOUBLE
   THICKNESS OF CHEESECLOTH
PINCH OF SAFFRON THREADS
1 CUP DRY WHITE WINE

1~ In a large nonreactive saucepan, combine the fish bones, heads and trimmings, the onion, tomato, bouquet garni, saffron and white wine. Add 6 cups of water.

2~ Bring to a simmer over moderately low heat, skimming frequently. Simmer uncovered, skimming frequently, for 20 minutes.

3~ Strain the stock through a sieve lined with a double layer of dampened cheesecloth. Measure the fish stock and, if necessary, boil until it is reduced to 4 cups.

MAKES 4 CUPS
RECIPE BY PATRICIA WELLS

TOSSED SALAD WITH SHERRY WINE VINAIGRETTE

A simple salad that can go a long way—you'll want to halve or quarter this recipe if you aren't serving a mob.

1 LARGE HEAD OF ROMAINE LETTUCE, TORN
   INTO BITE-SIZE PIECES
1 LARGE HEAD OF BOSTON LETTUCE, TORN
   INTO BITE-SIZE PIECES
4 HEADS OF RADICCHIO, TORN INTO BITE-
   SIZE PIECES
1 LARGE HEAD OF CURLY ENDIVE, TORN
   INTO BITE-SIZE PIECES
3 TABLESPOONS PLUS 1 TEASPOON SHERRY
   WINE VINEGAR
½ CUP PLUS 2 TABLESPOONS EXTRA-VIRGIN
   OLIVE OIL
1 TEASPOON SALT
1 TEASPOON FRESHLY GROUND PEPPER
2 MEDIUM RED ONIONS, THINLY SLICED
1 CUP NIÇOISE OLIVES

1~ In a large bowl, combine the romaine, Boston lettuce, radicchio and curly endive. (The lettuce can be prepared up to 1 day in advance. Store in airtight bags in the refrigerator.)
2~ In a bowl, whisk the vinegar, olive oil, salt and pepper. Set aside.
3~ When ready to serve the salad, toss one-fourth of the lettuce mixture, half of one sliced red onion and ¼ cup of the olives. Toss with one-fourth of the dressing. Refresh as necessary with more lettuce, onion, dressing and olives.

SERVES 50
RECIPE BY SUSAN WYLER

ORANGE CHIFFON CAKE

Because the oil used in the batter does not harden on chilling, this cake can be served slightly chilled or at room temperature. The cake can also be wrapped and refrigerated for up to one week.

2¼ CUPS SIFTED CAKE FLOUR
1½ CUPS SUGAR
1 TABLESPOON BAKING POWDER
1 TEASPOON SALT
½ CUP SAFFLOWER OIL
6 EGG YOLKS, AT ROOM TEMPERATURE
¾ CUP FRESH ORANGE JUICE
1 TEASPOON VANILLA EXTRACT
2 TABLESPOONS GRATED ORANGE ZEST
8 EGG WHITES, AT ROOM TEMPERATURE
½ TEASPOON CREAM OF TARTAR
CONFECTIONERS' SUGAR, FOR GARNISH

1~ Preheat the oven to 325°.
2~ In the large bowl of an electric mixer, combine the flour, all but 2 tablespoons of the sugar, the baking powder and the salt; blend well. Make a well in the center. Add the oil, egg yolks, orange juice, vanilla and orange zest; beat on medium speed until the batter is smooth, about 1 minute.
3~ In a large bowl, beat the egg whites until frothy. Add the cream of tartar and continue beating until soft peaks form. Beat in the remaining 2 tablespoons sugar and continue beating until the whites are stiff but not dry. Gently fold the beaten egg whites into the batter until just blended. (A large balloon wire whisk or slotted skimmer is ideal for this.)
4~ Pour into an ungreased 10-inch tube pan with removable bottom and bake for 55 minutes, or until a cake tester inserted in the center comes out clean and the cake springs back when pressed lightly in the center.
5~ Invert the pan and let the cake cool completely in the pan; this takes about 1½ hours. When cool, loosen the sides of the cake with a long metal spatula and lift out the center of the pan with the cake on it. Carefully loosen the bottom of the cake and central core with a spatula or thin, sharp knife. (A wire cake tester works well around the center core.) Invert onto a greased wire rack and invert right-side up onto a serving plate.
6~ Sprinkle with confectioners' sugar. To serve, cut with a serrated knife.

SERVES 12 TO 16
RECIPE BY ROSE LEVY BERANBAUM

MADELEINES

PEACH-RASPBERRY PIE

82

These absolutely wonderful "cakes" may well be America's second-best gift from the French —right after the Statue of Liberty.

3 EGGS, AT ROOM TEMPERATURE
¾ CUP SUGAR
1 TEASPOON VANILLA EXTRACT
2 TEASPOONS GRATED LEMON ZEST
¼ TEASPOON FRESH LEMON JUICE
1⅓ CUPS SIFTED ALL-PURPOSE FLOUR
¾ CUP CLARIFIED UNSALTED BUTTER

1~ In a large bowl, whisk the eggs with the sugar until light colored and thick enough to fall in ribbons. Beat in the vanilla, lemon zest and lemon juice.

2~ Using a rubber spatula, fold the flour into the eggs. Fold in ½ cup of the butter until just incorporated; do not overfold. Tightly cover the bowl with plastic wrap and refrigerate for at least 1 hour until chilled through. *(The recipe can be prepared to this point up to 24 hours ahead.)*

3~ Preheat the oven to 425°.

4~ Using a small pastry brush, coat two 12-form madeleine molds of 3-inch-long forms with 2 tablespoons of the butter. Place the molds upside-down over a baking sheet to catch drips so that the butter will evenly coat the molds and won't pool in the bottom; refrigerate until the butter is set, about 10 minutes. Brush again with 2 tablespoons butter and chill until set.

5~ Spoon rounded tablespoons of the batter into the mold; do not smooth the batter. Bake in the center of the oven for 5 minutes; then reduce the heat to 375° and bake for 7 to 10 minutes, until the madeleines are golden in the center and browned around the edges.

6~ Remove from the oven. Sharply rap the mold against a flat surface to loosen the madeleines. Turn out and let cool slightly on a wire rack. Serve warm, if possible. *(The madeleines can be loosely wrapped in waxed paper and stored in a loosely covered container for up to 24 hours.)*

MAKES ABOUT 3 DOZEN
RECIPE BY JOHN ROBERT MASSIE

You can make this pie with a latticed crust if you don't want to hide the peaches and raspberries inside. On the other hand, a decorated solid top might make the filling a delightful surprise.

2 CUPS ALL-PURPOSE FLOUR
PINCH OF SALT
¼ POUND (1 STICK) UNSALTED BUTTER, CUT INTO SMALL PIECES
¼ CUP VEGETABLE SHORTENING, CHILLED
5 TABLESPOONS ICE WATER
6 CUPS PEELED RIPE PEACHES, SLICED ABOUT ⅜ INCH THICK
½ CUP PLUS 1 TABLESPOON SUGAR
2 TEASPOONS FRESH LEMON JUICE
2 TABLESPOONS INSTANT TAPIOCA
1 CUP FRESH RASPBERRIES
1 EGG, BEATEN

1~ In a large bowl, combine the flour and salt. Cut in the butter until the mixture resembles coarse crumbs. Work in the shortening and add the ice water. Gather the dough into a ball. Divide the dough in half and flatten each piece into a 6-inch disk. Wrap in plastic wrap and refrigerate for at least 30 minutes.

2~ Preheat the oven to 450°.

3~ In a large bowl, combine the peaches, ½ cup of the sugar, the lemon juice and tapioca.

4~ On a lightly floured surface, roll out one piece of dough into a 14-inch circle. Fit into a 9-inch pie pan without stretching; trim the edge, leaving about a ¼-inch overhang; reserve the scraps. Roll out the second piece of dough to a 14-inch circle.

5~ Add the raspberries to the peaches. Using a slotted spoon, scoop the filling into the pie shell, leaving most of the accumulated juices behind. Brush the rim of the dough lightly with some of the beaten egg. Place the second dough circle on top or cut it into strips and make a latticed top crust. Press the edges gently to seal. Trim the edges, leaving ½ inch over the rim; fold the dough under and flute it, if desired.

6~ If you made a solid top crust, cut out some decorative shapes from the scraps of dough for the top of the pie. Using a sharp knife, cut at least several steam vents into the top crust. Brush the crust with the beaten egg and arrange the pastry cutouts on top. Brush again with the beaten egg and sprinkle the pie with the remaining 1 tablespoon sugar. If you made a lattice top, brush the pastry with the beaten egg and sprinkle on the sugar.

7~ Bake the pie for 15 minutes. Reduce the oven temperature to 350° and continue to bake for 40 to 45 minutes longer, or until bubbling and golden brown on top. Let the pie cool for at least 3 hours before serving.

SERVES 6 TO 8
RECIPE BY MARCIA KIESEL

RASPBERRY SATIN SORBET

The addition of egg white lends a particularly satiny texture to sorbets. Without it, the results will be flavorful, but not as smooth.

⅔ CUP PLUS 1 TABLESPOON SUGAR
4 CUPS (2 PINTS) RASPBERRIES
1 TABLESPOON FRAMBOISE (RASPBERRY BRANDY) OR VODKA
1 EGG WHITE

1~ In a medium nonreactive saucepan, combine ⅔ cup of the sugar with 1 cup water. Cook over moderate heat, stirring, until the sugar dissolves, about 2 minutes. Bring to a boil, add the raspberries and toss with the syrup. Return to a boil and simmer for 2 minutes.

2~ Pour the berries and syrup into a fine-mesh sieve set over a medium bowl. Using a rubber spatula, press the mixture through the sieve; or puree in a blender or food processor and strain. Discard the solids.

3~ Stir the framboise into the raspberry liquid and refrigerate until chilled, about 30 minutes. Scrape the sorbet mixture into an ice cream maker and freeze according to the manufacturer's instructions, until the sorbet is light colored, thickened and partially frozen, about 25 minutes.

4~ Meanwhile, beat the egg white until soft peaks form. Gradually beat in the remaining 1 tablespoon sugar until stiff peaks form. Add the beaten egg white to the ice cream maker and churn the sorbet until it freezes into a smooth, satiny mass, about 15 minutes.

5~ Transfer the sorbet to a chilled bowl, cover and freeze or serve at once.

MAKES ABOUT 1 QUART
RECIPE BY DIANA STURGIS

■ ■ ■

A Lunch
for the Hottest Day
of the Year

Anyone will tell you that it's extra-important to take good care of yourself during the hottest days of the year. You should wear a hat, stay out of the sun, drink plenty of liquids and eat light but nutritious foods. Here's the way we recommend doing just that. ∽ Gather your friends under the shade of an umbrella next to a beautiful swimming pool. Alternate sips of mineral water with sips of frozen piña coladas. When you think appetites are piqued, show off your culinary handiwork from the night before. Start off lunch with a cup of chilled avocado soup topped with papaya-pepper relish. At the same time, bring out the chicken salad and potato salad so guests can help themselves as they please. Though you baked the pastry and filling for the Hawaiian pineapple tart ahead of time, adding the pineapple and glaze takes just minutes before serving. Cut it into wedges and serve with a scoop of toasted coconut ice cream for a cooling dessert on summer's hottest day.

■ ■ ■

*Avocado Soup
with Papaya-Pepper
Relish*

*Triple-Mustard
Chicken Salad*

AVOCADO SOUP WITH PAPAYA-PEPPER RELISH

A LUNCH FOR THE HOTTEST DAY OF THE YEAR

Serves 6

PIÑA COLADAS

Avocado Soup with Papaya-Pepper Relish

Triple-Mustard Chicken Salad
Lightened Potato Salad

Toasted Coconut Ice Cream
Hawaiian Pineapple Tart

Cold soup is just what you need on a hot summer day or night. This one is great.

2 TEASPOONS UNSALTED BUTTER
1 SMALL ONION, MINCED
1 CARROT, MINCED
2 SMALL CELERY RIBS, MINCED
1 GARLIC CLOVE, MINCED
4 CUPS CHICKEN STOCK OR CANNED BROTH
1 CUP HEAVY CREAM, CHILLED
1 SMALL RED BELL PEPPER
1 POBLANO PEPPER
2 LARGE RIPE AVOCADOS (PREFERABLY HASS), CUT INTO ¼-INCH DICE
2 TABLESPOONS FRESH LIME JUICE
5 TABLESPOONS MINCED FRESH CORIANDER
¼ TEASPOON SALT
¼ TEASPOON FRESHLY GROUND BLACK PEPPER
1 SMALL RIPE PAPAYA—PEELED, SEEDED AND CUT INTO ¼-INCH DICE
1 TEASPOON WALNUT OIL
3 JALAPEÑO PEPPERS, SEEDED AND MINCED

1~ In a large saucepan or stovetop casserole, melt the butter over moderate heat. Add the onion, carrot, celery and garlic and cook, stirring, until softened but not browned, about 6 minutes. Add the chicken stock and bring to a boil. Remove from the heat and let cool to room temperature. Stir in the cream and refrigerate until well chilled, about 2 hours or overnight.

2~ Roast the red bell pepper and poblano over a gas flame or under the broiler, turning, until charred all over. Put the peppers in a paper bag and let them steam for 10 minutes. Peel and seed the peppers and discard the cores. Cut the peppers into ¼-inch dice.

3~ Whisk the diced avocados into the chilled soup until they begin to break up and thicken it slightly. Stir in 1 tablespoon of the lime juice, 2½ tablespoons of the coriander, ⅛ teaspoon of the salt and ⅛ teaspoon of the black pepper. Refrigerate until the flavors are well blended.

4~ In a small bowl, combine the papaya and the roasted red pepper and poblano with the remaining 1 tablespoon lime juice and 2½ tablespoons coriander. Stir in the walnut oil and the remaining ⅛ teaspoon each of salt and black pepper.

5~ Serve the soup chilled, with a dollop of the papaya relish and a sprinkling of the minced jalapeños.

SERVES 8 TO 10
RECIPE BY ROBERT DEL GRANDE

TRIPLE-MUSTARD CHICKEN SALAD

Toasted mustard seeds make this chicken salad extra special. This dish will feed large crowds or can be halved for fewer servings.

8 POUNDS SKINLESS, BONELESS CHICKEN
    BREASTS

2 CUPS MAYONNAISE

¼ CUP POMMERY MUSTARD

½ CUP EXTRA-SHARP DIJON MUSTARD

½ CUP FRESH LEMON JUICE

½ TEASPOON SALT

1 TEASPOON FRESHLY GROUND PEPPER

12 LARGE CELERY RIBS, PEELED AND THINLY
    SLICED ON THE DIAGONAL

¾ CUP MUSTARD SEEDS

¼ CUP EXTRA-VIRGIN OLIVE OIL

4 LARGE BUNCHES OF WATERCRESS, TOUGH
    STEMS REMOVED, OR 3 LARGE HEADS OF
    LEAF LETTUCE

1~ Put the chicken in a large heavy pot and add enough cold salted water to cover by at least 1 inch. Bring to a simmer over moderate heat. Reduce the heat to low and simmer until the chicken is juicy but no longer pink in the center, about 20 minutes. Cut the chicken into 1-inch dice. *(The recipe can be prepared to this point up to 1 day in advance. Cover and refrigerate.)*

2~ In a medium bowl, combine the mayonnaise, Pommery and Dijon mustards, lemon juice and salt and pepper; whisk to blend well.

3~ In a large bowl, combine the chicken, celery and mustard mayonnaise. Toss to coat well.

4~ In a medium skillet, combine the mustard seeds and olive oil. Cook, covered, over moderate heat, shaking the pan, until the seeds begin to pop, 1 to 2 minutes. Immediately remove from the heat and continue shaking the pan until the seeds are toasted and fragrant and have stopped popping. Scrape the seeds and oil over the salad and fold to combine.

5~ Transfer the salad to a serving platter or individual plates and surround with the greens. Serve slightly chilled or at room temperature.

SERVES 36
RECIPE BY SUSAN WYLER

LIGHTENED POTATO SALAD

Use one, two or a mixture of the vegetables listed below to lighten this mayonnaise-dressed potato salad, but use a total of six cups. For a less traditional flavor, add a good handful of any minced fresh herb, such as basil, tarragon or coriander.

3 POUNDS WAXY POTATOES, PEELED AND
    CUT INTO ½-INCH DICE

½ CUP DRY WHITE WINE

3 TABLESPOONS CIDER VINEGAR

1½ TEASPOONS SALT

½ TEASPOON FRESHLY GROUND PEPPER

4 JUMBO EGGS—HARD COOKED, PEELED
    AND CHOPPED

¾ CUP MAYONNAISE, PREFERABLY
    HOMEMADE

2 CUPS JULIENNED ZUCCHINI
    (1 BY ⅛ INCH)

1 CUP JULIENNED JICAMA (1 BY ⅛ INCH)

1 CUP JULIENNED DAIKON RADISH
    (1 BY ⅛ INCH)

1 CUP PACKED WATERCRESS LEAVES AND
    SMALL STEMS

1 CUP SLIVERED FRESH WATER CHESTNUTS

⅓ CUP MINCED BASIL, TARRAGON OR
    CORIANDER (OPTIONAL)

RECIPE CONTINUES ON THE NEXT PAGE

LIGHTENED POTATO SALAD CONTINUED

88

1~ Bring a large pot of salted water to a boil. Add the potatoes and cook, stirring occasionally, until easily pierced with a fork, about 10 minutes. Drain well and place in a large bowl.

2~ In a small nonreactive saucepan, combine the wine, vinegar, ½ teaspoon of the salt and ¼ teaspoon of the pepper. Bring just to a boil. Pour the hot dressing over the potatoes and toss to coat. Let the potatoes cool in the liquid, tossing occasionally.

3~ Add the chopped hard-cooked eggs and the mayonnaise to the potatoes and toss to coat. Just before serving, add the vegetables, remaining 1 teaspoon salt, ¼ teaspoon pepper and the herbs. Season with additional salt and pepper to taste.

SERVES 6 TO 8
RECIPE BY ANNE DISRUDE

TOASTED COCONUT ICE CREAM

Toasted coconut makes a big difference in the depth of flavor of this cooling ice cream.

1 CUP SWEETENED SHREDDED OR FLAKED COCONUT
2 CUPS HEAVY CREAM
1 CUP MILK
2 TABLESPOONS SUGAR
PINCH OF SALT
3 EGG YOLKS
½ TEASPOON VANILLA EXTRACT
½ CUP CREAM OF COCONUT, SUCH AS COCO LOPEZ

1~ Preheat the oven to 325°.

2~ Spread the coconut on a baking sheet in a thin layer and toast in the oven, tossing frequently, for 10 minutes, or until golden. Let cool.

3~ In a heavy medium saucepan, combine the cream, milk, sugar and salt. Cook over moderate heat, stirring frequently, until the sugar dissolves and the mixture is hot, 6 to 8 minutes.

4~ In a large bowl, beat the egg yolks lightly. Gradually whisk in the hot liquid in a thin stream. Return to the saucepan and cook over moderately low heat, stirring constantly, until the custard thickens enough to coat the back of a spoon lightly, 5 to 7 minutes; do not let the custard boil.

5~ Strain the custard into a metal bowl. Set the bowl in a basin of cold water and ice and let stand, stirring occasionally, until cooled to room temperature, about 20 minutes. Stir in the vanilla, cream of coconut and the toasted coconut. Mix well. Cover and refrigerate for at least 6 hours, or overnight.

6~ Pour the custard into an ice cream maker and freeze according to the manufacturer's instructions. Transfer to a covered container and freeze.

7~ Remove the ice cream from the freezer about 10 minutes before serving.

MAKES ABOUT 1 QUART
RECIPE BY LESLIE NEWMAN

HAWAIIAN PINEAPPLE TART

Serve this tart with a scoop of the Toasted Coconut Ice Cream on the side, and you'll have the equivalent flavors of a piña colada, but without the liquor.

TART SHELL:
1 EGG YOLK
1 TEASPOON SUGAR
¼ TEASPOON SALT
1 TABLESPOON FLAVORLESS VEGETABLE OIL
1½ CUPS ALL-PURPOSE FLOUR
¼ POUND (1 STICK) CHILLED UNSALTED
    BUTTER, CUT INTO ½-INCH CUBES

FILLING AND ASSEMBLY:
¼ POUND (1 STICK) UNSALTED BUTTER,
    AT ROOM TEMPERATURE
⅓ CUP SUGAR
2 EGGS, AT ROOM TEMPERATURE
½ CUP CAKE FLOUR, SIFTED
1 RIPE PINEAPPLE
¼ CUP APRICOT PRESERVES

1~ *Make the Tart Shell:* Blend the egg yolk, sugar and salt in a 1-cup liquid measure. Add enough cold water to measure ¼ cup. Blend in the oil.

2~ Put the flour in a mixer fitted with the dough paddle. Scatter the butter on top. Blend on low speed until the mixture is the texture of coarse meal. Stir the liquids, beat into the bowl in a thin stream and continue to mix until the dough masses together. (This dough can also be made by hand or in a food processor.)

3~ Gather the dough into a ball, press into a 6-inch disk; wrap and refrigerate for 30 to 60 minutes, until cold but still malleable.

4~ Roll out the dough ⅛ inch thick. Fit the dough into a loose-bottomed 11-inch tart pan. Trim the overhang to 1 inch. Fold the dough in and press to reinforce the sides. Refrigerate the crust for 30 minutes.

5~ Preheat the oven to 375°. Line the tart shell with foil and add aluminum baking weights or dried beans. Blind bake for 20 to 25 minutes. Remove the foil and bake for 10 minutes, until the pastry is lightly browned. Set the shell aside to cool on a rack. Leave the oven on.

6~ *Make the Filling and assemble the tart:* In a bowl, cream the butter and sugar until light. Beat in 1 of the eggs and then half the flour; add the remaining egg and flour, beating until the mixture is smooth and well blended. Scrape the batter into the cooled tart shell and slide it onto a baking sheet.

7~ Bake the tart in the center of the oven until the top is golden, about 20 minutes.

8~ Slide the tart from the baking sheet onto a rack. Pierce with a fork every ½ inch over the entire surface. Let stand until cool before unmolding.

9~ No more than 2 hours before serving, peel, core and slice the pineapple into ¼-inch-thick wedges, working over a bowl to catch the juices. Brush some of the juices over the sponge filling. Arrange the pineapple in a pretty flower pattern, overlapping the slices and working from the outside to the center of the tart.

10~ In a small nonreactive saucepan, melt the apricot preserves with 2 tablespoons of the reserved pineapple juice over low heat, stirring until smooth. Simmer for 1 minute. Strain through a sieve. With a pastry brush, paint a thin glaze over the top and exposed sides of the fruit and along the rim of the shell.

SERVES 8 TO 10
RECIPE BY JIM DODGE

SUMMER HARVEST LUNCH

Everyone has a different reaction to the end of summer. Some people cheer it as a time to "get back to business"; others are saddened because their activities will be curtailed by shorter days and colder temperatures. There is no one, though, who won't miss the lush, ripe, utterly delicious foods of summer–homegrown tomatoes, basil, sweet corn, cucumbers, green beans, lettuce and peaches. Is it possible to get too much of them when they're at their best? We don't think so. ∽ This menu is designed to take advantage of what's left in the garden just before autumn arrives. All of the dishes are vegetarian; if you miss the meat or want to enlarge the party, feel free to add the catch of the day, grilled steaks or chicken. Or you might want to spoon the chili over chunks of barbecued beef or lamb. ∽ If you don't have a garden, drive outside of town to find fresh-picked fruits and vegetables at roadside farm stands. You might select some extra tomatoes and peaches or whatever looks particularly good so you can make a doggie bag for each of your guests to take home.

■ ■ ■

Tomatoes on
Basil Chiffonnade

Focaccia

Sugar Snap Peas
in Toasted Sesame

92

SUMMER HARVEST LUNCH

Serves 8

WHITE WINES: ORVIETO OR VINHO VERDE
RED WINES: CHIANTI OR MERLOT

Focaccia

Eggplant Cookies with Goat Cheese and Tomato-Basil Sauce

Corn and Avocado Torta

Vegetarian Chili

Sugar Snap Peas in Toasted Sesame Seed Vinaigrette

Calabrese Potato Salad

Tomatoes on Basil Chiffonnade

Peach Parfait Cake

FOCACCIA

Many pizzerias will be very happy to sell you uncooked pizza dough. If there's no pizzeria around, defrosted supermarket bread or pizza dough works very nicely. Or use Basic Pizza Dough (page 106).

½ CUP SLICED SHALLOTS (ABOUT 8 MEDIUM)
3 TO 4 SMALL SPRIGS OF FRESH ROSEMARY OR ½ TEASPOON DRIED
½ TEASPOON COARSE (KOSHER) SALT
½ TEASPOON COARSELY GROUND PEPPER
5 TABLESPOONS EXTRA-VIRGIN OLIVE OIL
1 POUND UNCOOKED PIZZA DOUGH

1~ Preheat the oven to 425°.
2~ In a small bowl, toss the shallots, rosemary, salt and pepper with 3½ tablespoons of the olive oil; set aside.
3~ On a lightly floured surface, roll out the dough to form a 10-inch circle about ½ inch thick.
4~ Place a heavy ovenproof 12-inch skillet over high heat for 1 minute. Add the remaining 1½ tablespoons oil. When the oil is shimmering, remove from the heat and carefully lay the rolled-out dough in the pan.
5~ Using your fingertips, make indentations all over the dough. Spread the shallot mixture on top. Bake the focaccia in the upper third of the oven for about 25 minutes, until browned on top. Let cool on a rack for 15 minutes before cutting into wedges.

SERVES 4 TO 8
RECIPE BY ANNE DISRUDE

EGGPLANT COOKIES WITH GOAT CHEESE AND TOMATO-BASIL SAUCE

These savory "cookies" are topped with a tequila-spiked, perfect end-of-summer sauce.

6 TABLESPOONS PLUS 2 TEASPOONS OLIVE OIL
1 LARGE GARLIC CLOVE, MINCED
1 SMALL SHALLOT, MINCED
1 TABLESPOON TEQUILA, PREFERABLY GOLDEN
1½ TABLESPOONS DRY RED WINE
2 LARGE TOMATOES—PEELED, SEEDED AND CHOPPED
PINCH OF SALT AND FRESHLY GROUND PEPPER
2 TABLESPOONS JULIENNED FRESH BASIL
½ CUP ALL-PURPOSE FLOUR, SIFTED
1 EGG, LIGHTLY BEATEN
½ CUP FRESH BREAD CRUMBS
2 LONG, NARROW ORIENTAL EGGPLANTS, PEELED AND CUT INTO ½-INCH ROUNDS
4 OUNCES CYLINDRICAL GOAT CHEESE, CUT INTO 12 ROUNDS

1~ In a medium saucepan, heat 2 teaspoons of the oil. Add the garlic and shallot and cook over moderate heat, stirring, until softened but not browned, about 1 minute. Add the tequila and red wine and cook until almost completely absorbed, about 1 minute. Stir in the tomatoes, salt and pepper and cook until slightly thickened, about 5 minutes. Stir in the basil and keep warm.

2~ Put the flour, egg and bread crumbs in 3 separate shallow bowls. Dip the eggplant rounds in the flour until completely coated. Next, coat with the egg and then roll in the bread crumbs.

3~ In a large heavy skillet, heat 2 tablespoons of the olive oil over moderately high heat. Add one-third of the eggplant slices and sauté, turning once, until crisp and golden brown, about 4 minutes on each side. Drain on paper towels. Repeat 2 more times with the remaining oil and eggplant.

4~ Sandwich 1 slice of the goat cheese in between 2 slices of hot fried eggplant. Spoon the tomato-basil sauce onto heated plates or a platter and arrange the eggplant "cookies" over it. Serve warm.

Serves 4
Recipe by Robert McGrath

Corn and Avocado Torta

End-of-summer corn mixes brilliantly with rich avocados to make this overstuffed torta really tasty and colorful.

1 EAR OF CORN, OR ¾ CUP CORN KERNELS
2 TABLESPOONS UNSALTED BUTTER
1 RED BELL PEPPER, CUT INTO ¼-INCH DICE
1 JALAPEÑO PEPPER, SEEDED AND MINCED
3 SCALLIONS, CHOPPED
1 RIPE AVOCADO (PREFERABLY HASS), CUT INTO ¼-INCH DICE
¼ CUP CHOPPED FRESH CORIANDER
1 OUNCE GOAT CHEESE, CRUMBLED
2 TEASPOONS WALNUT OIL
1 TEASPOON FRESH LIME JUICE
½ TEASPOON SALT
¼ TEASPOON FRESHLY GROUND BLACK PEPPER
2 FLOUR TORTILLAS (7 INCHES IN DIAMETER)
½ CUP SOUR CREAM
SPRIGS OF CORIANDER, AS GARNISH

1~ Cut the kernels from the corn cob. In a large skillet, melt 1 tablespoon of the butter over moderate heat. Add the corn and cook, stirring, until golden brown, about 10 minutes. Stir in the red pepper, jalapeño and scallions and cook until softened, about 5 minutes. Remove from the heat and let cool slightly. Stir in the avocado, coriander, goat cheese, walnut oil and lime juice. Lightly mash the avocado to bind the ingredients. Season with the salt and pepper.

2~ Spread the avocado mixture over one of the tortillas. Cover with the second tortilla to make a sandwich, or torta.

3~ In a large skillet, melt the remaining 1 tablespoon butter over moderate heat. Add the avocado torta and cook until golden brown on the bottom, about 2 minutes. Using a large spatula, carefully turn the torta and cook the other side until browned, about 2 minutes longer.

4~ Using a sharp knife, cut the torta into quarters. Garnish each wedge with 2 tablespoons of the sour cream and a sprig of fresh coriander.

Makes 4 side-dish or appetizer servings
Recipe by Robert Del Grande

93

VEGETARIAN CHILI

Rich, tasty and nutritious, too, this chili is terra-cotta color, accented with a topping of Cheddar cheese, sliced scallions and sour cream. Make the chili a day before you want to serve it. It improves upon standing. Use a food processor to do the vegetable chopping.

8 OUNCES DRIED SMALL RED BEANS, RINSED AND PICKED OVER, OR 3 CUPS DRAINED AND RINSED CANNED RED BEANS
1 TABLESPOON VEGETABLE OIL
3 MEDIUM ONIONS, CHOPPED
3 LARGE CELERY RIBS, CUT INTO ¼-INCH DICE
¼ CUP MINCED GARLIC
3 LARGE CARROTS, FINELY CHOPPED
2 CUPS PACKED FINELY CHOPPED CABBAGE
½ POUND MUSHROOMS, FINELY CHOPPED
2 MEDIUM RED BELL PEPPERS (8 OUNCES TOTAL), FINELY CHOPPED
2 MEDIUM GREEN BELL PEPPERS (8 OUNCES TOTAL), FINELY CHOPPED
⅓ CUP CHILI POWDER (1½ OUNCES)
1 TABLESPOON UNSWEETENED COCOA POWDER
1 TABLESPOON SUGAR
1 TABLESPOON CUMIN SEEDS
1 TABLESPOON PLUS ¼ TEASPOON OREGANO
2 TEASPOONS FENNEL SEEDS
1 TEASPOON THYME
½ TEASPOON CAYENNE PEPPER
½ TEASPOON GROUND CINNAMON
1 TABLESPOON SALT
½ TEASPOON FRESHLY GROUND BLACK PEPPER
1 CAN (28 OUNCES) ITALIAN PEELED TOMATOES, WITH THEIR LIQUID
2 TABLESPOONS SOY SAUCE
2 TABLESPOONS DRY SHERRY
1 TEASPOON HOT PEPPER SAUCE
¾ CUP SOUR CREAM
1½ CUPS SLICED SCALLIONS
¼ POUND CHEDDAR CHEESE, SHREDDED

1~ If using dried beans, put the beans in a medium bowl and add enough water to cover by 3 inches. Let soak overnight; drain. (Alternatively, place the beans in a medium saucepan and add enough cold water to cover by 2 inches. Bring to a boil and cook for 1 minute. Remove from the heat, cover and let stand for 1 hour; drain.) Place the beans in a medium saucepan, add enough cold water to cover by 3 inches and bring to a boil over high heat. Reduce the heat and simmer until tender, about 1 hour; drain.

2~ In a large stovetop casserole, heat the oil over moderate heat. Add the onions and celery and sauté until the onions are softened and translucent, 6 to 8 minutes. Add the garlic and cook for 1 minute longer.

3~ Add the carrots, cabbage and mushrooms to the casserole and cook, stirring occasionally, until the vegetables are tender, about 10 minutes. Add the red and green peppers and cook until softened, 5 to 8 minutes.

4~ Stir in the chili powder, cocoa, sugar, cumin seeds, 1 tablespoon of the oregano, the fennel seeds, thyme, cayenne, cinnamon, salt and ¼ teaspoon of the black pepper. Stir in the tomatoes; break them up with a spoon. Add the beans (see *Note*), the tomato liquid and 4 cups of water. Simmer over low heat, stirring occasionally, until thick and rich tasting, about 2 hours. Remove from the heat and let cool to room temperature. Cover and refrigerate overnight.

5~ Reheat the chili over low heat. Add the reserved ¼ teaspoon each oregano and black pepper. Remove from the heat and stir in the soy sauce, sherry and hot sauce. Serve the chili hot in 1½-cup portions, topped with 1 heaping tablespoon sour cream, 3 tablespoons sliced scallions and 2 tablespoons shredded Cheddar cheese.

Note: If using canned beans, add when the chili is removed from the heat.

SERVES 8
RECIPE BY JIM FOBEL

SUGAR SNAP PEAS IN TOASTED SESAME SEED VINAIGRETTE

You can blanch the peas for this dish and make the dressing ahead of time. But don't combine them until just before it's time to eat. You might want to double this recipe.

1 POUND SUGAR SNAP PEAS, STEM ENDS
    AND STRINGS REMOVED
¼ CUP SESAME SEEDS
1 SMALL GARLIC CLOVE, CRUSHED
    THROUGH A PRESS
1 TEASPOON DIJON-STYLE MUSTARD
1 TABLESPOON FRESH LEMON JUICE
¼ TEASPOON SALT
¼ TEASPOON FRESHLY GROUND PEPPER
1 TABLESPOON RED WINE VINEGAR
¼ CUP OLIVE OIL
1½ TEASPOONS ORIENTAL SESAME OIL

1~ In a large saucepan of boiling salted water, cook the sugar snap peas until crisp-tender, about 30 seconds. Drain, rinse under cold running water and then drain well.
2~ In a dry heavy skillet, toast the sesame seeds over moderate heat, stirring, until nut brown, about 3 minutes. Pour onto a plate to cool.
3~ In a medium bowl, combine the garlic, mustard, lemon juice, salt and pepper. Blend in the vinegar. Whisk in the olive oil and sesame oil. Add the sugar snap peas and toasted sesame seeds and toss. Serve at room temperature or slightly chilled.

SERVES 4
RECIPE BY PHILLIP STEPHEN SCHULZ

CALABRESE POTATO SALAD

Make this potato salad ahead of time, but don't refrigerate it. It's meant to be served at room temperature.

1 MEDIUM RED ONION, SLICED PAPER THIN
3 POUNDS MEDIUM RED POTATOES, PEELED
    AND SLICED ¼ INCH THICK
1½ TEASPOONS SALT
FRESHLY GROUND PEPPER
½ CUP PLUS 1 TABLESPOON EXTRA-VIRGIN
    OLIVE OIL
3 TABLESPOONS RED WINE VINEGAR
½ CUP FINELY CHOPPED FRESH MINT
¼ CUP FINELY CHOPPED PARSLEY

1~ Put the onion slices in a bowl with cold water to cover and soak for at least 1 hour, changing the water 3 times. Drain well and pat dry.
2~ Put the potatoes in a bowl and rinse with cold water until the water runs clear. Place in a pot of cold salted water to cover, bring to a boil and cook until tender, 10 to 12 minutes. Drain well.
3~ Scatter one-third of the onions over a serving platter. Cover with one-third of the hot potatoes. Season with ½ teaspoon of the salt and a generous grinding of pepper. Sprinkle with 3 tablespoons of the oil, 1 tablespoon of the vinegar and one-third of the mint and parsley. Repeat with half the remaining onions, potatoes and dressing and seasoning ingredients and top with the remainder. Let cool.
4~ Serve at room temperature; do not refrigerate.

SERVES 6 TO 8
RECIPE BY NANCY VERDE BARR

TOMATOES ON BASIL CHIFFONNADE

When tomatoes are in season, it's shocking how many can be eaten at a single sitting. Double or triple this recipe—even then, you won't have leftovers.

2 CUPS PACKED FRESH BASIL LEAVES
1 POUND RIPE TOMATOES, CUT INTO
    1-INCH WEDGES
4 GARLIC CLOVES, BRUISED
2 TEASPOONS CAPERS, CHOPPED
1 CUP EXTRA-VIRGIN OLIVE OIL
½ TEASPOON FRESHLY GROUND PEPPER
⅛ TEASPOON SALT
2 TEASPOONS WHITE WINE VINEGAR
3 CUPS CURLY ENDIVE, TORN INTO
    BITE-SIZE PIECES

1~ Chop 1 cup of the basil. In a medium bowl, combine the tomatoes, garlic, capers, olive oil, pepper and chopped basil. Toss to coat the tomatoes with oil. Cover with plastic wrap and refrigerate overnight.
2~ Pour off and reserve the marinade from the tomato-basil mixture. Measure out ¼ cup of the marinade. Stir in the salt and vinegar. (Extra marinade may be reserved and used in a salad dressing or to marinate more tomatoes.)
3~ Just before serving, spread the endive leaves over a platter. With a sharp knife, finely shred the remaining 1 cup basil and distribute evenly over the endive. Arrange the tomato wedges on top of the basil. Drizzle on the dressing.

SERVES 4
RECIPE BY MARCIA KIESEL

PEACH PARFAIT CAKE

Whether or not you've ever done it before, it's fun to bake a cake in a bowl. This one makes a lovely presentation.

CAKE:

6 EGGS
⅔ CUP GRANULATED SUGAR
1 TEASPOON VANILLA EXTRACT
1⅓ CUPS SIFTED ALL-PURPOSE FLOUR
3 TABLESPOONS UNSALTED BUTTER,
    MELTED AND COOLED SLIGHTLY

FILLING AND DECORATION:

10 MEDIUM-SIZE PEACHES, PREFERABLY
    FREESTONE (ABOUT 3½ POUNDS)
¼ CUP FRESH LEMON JUICE
4 OR 5 CUPS HEAVY CREAM
1½ TEASPOONS ALMOND EXTRACT
1 CUP SIFTED CONFECTIONERS' SUGAR

GLAZE:

1 JAR (12 OUNCES) PEACH PRESERVES
3 TABLESPOONS BRANDY

1~ Preheat the oven to 350°. Lightly butter a 4-quart stainless-steel bowl and dust it with a little flour, shaking out the excess; set aside. Chill a bowl and beaters for whipping the cream later.

2~ *Prepare the Cake:* In a double boiler, over simmering water, beat the eggs with a whisk until frothy, about 1 minute. Whisk in the granulated sugar, beating until it has dissolved and the eggs are just warm to the touch. Transfer the mixture to a bowl and beat until tripled in volume, 3 to 5 minutes. The mixture should be cool, light in color and should run off in a ribbon when the whisk is lifted. Beat in the vanilla.

3~ Sift the flour over the egg mixture a third at a time, quickly folding it in with a rubber spatula. Fold in the melted butter and pour the batter into the prepared bowl. Bake the cake in the center of the oven for 45 to 50 minutes, or until the center springs back when lightly touched. Cool for about 5 minutes. Then place a rack over the bowl and invert both, unmolding the cake onto the rack; cool completely.

4~ *Prepare the Filling:* Peel the peaches, halve them lengthwise, pit and cut into slices about ½ inch thick. Place in a bowl and toss with the lemon juice.

5~ If you are going to pipe designs on the cake, you will need to whip 5 cups of the cream; otherwise 4 cups will be enough. Using the chilled bowl and beaters and working in two batches, whip the cream until soft peaks form. Add the almond extract and confectioners' sugar and beat until the cream is very stiff. Cover and refrigerate.

6~ *Prepare the Glaze:* Place the preserves in a small saucepan and bring to a boil over moderate heat. Using a wooden spoon, force the preserves through a strainer into a bowl. Stir in the brandy.

7~ *Assemble the Cake:* Using a long serrated knife, split the cake horizontally into four equal layers, using toothpicks to mark out the layers before cutting if necessary. Place the bottom layer on a cake plate and brush the top of it with one-third of the glaze. Spread ¼ inch of whipped cream over the glaze and arrange 1½ cups of the peach slices over the cream. Top the peaches with another ¼ inch of the whipped cream and add the next layer of cake. Brush the second layer with half the remaining glaze and top it with ¼ inch of whipped cream, 1 cup of peach slices and another ¼ inch of whipped cream. Add the third layer of cake, brush with the remaining glaze, spread with ¼ inch of whipped cream, add 1 cup of the peach slices and ¼ inch more of the whipped cream. Top with the remaining cake layer.

8~ *Decorate the Cake:* Reserving about 2 cups of the whipped cream if you wish to pipe designs on the cake, frost the cake evenly with whipped cream. To decorate, fit a pastry bag with a ¼-inch star tip and fill it with the reserved whipped cream. Arrange 8 of the remaining peach slices on the top of the cake in a spoke design; pipe a shell design between each two. Pipe heart designs around the side of the cake and then evenly space 10 or 11 peach slices around the base, piping a swirl between each two.

9~ Chill the cake, uncovered, until serving time or up to 12 hours. Serve cold.

SERVES 12
RECIPE BY JIM FOBEL

AUTUMN

■ ■ ■

A
NOTHING TO IT
DINNER

If you are the cook of the family, then you are familiar with those times when you just can't bear the thought of preparing yet another meal. Sometimes it's a Friday after a particularly grueling week, sometimes it's Saturday evening after a day of too much sun and sport, sometimes it's just a matter of being tired and wholly uninspired. That's when this dinner is a winner. Mostly, you assemble it from grocery-store ingredients; very little is cooked. ~ Start off with hearts of palm wrapped up in thin slices of prosciutto. These are best when marinated for a few hours, but aren't at all bad if merely coated with the sauce. The main course is a stunning sandwich and salad double-header. We don't know which part is better, the warm Caesar salad or smoked turkey and Cheddar stacked between slices of sourdough bread that's coated with hot pepper jelly and grilled until the bread is toasted and the cheese melts. For dessert, it's do-it-yourself banana splits, concocted individually and served with quick sauces that can be made on stovetop or in a microwave oven.

*Warm
Caesar Salad*

*Grilled Smoked
Turkey
and Cheddar
Sandwich*

*Prosciutto-
Wrapped Hearts
of Palm*

■ ■ ■

100

A NOTHING TO IT DINNER

Serves 2 to 4

BEER, SAUVIGNON BLANC OR
A CÔTES DU RHÔNE
Prosciutto-Wrapped Hearts of Palm

*Grilled Smoked Turkey and Cheddar
Sandwiches*
Warm Caesar Salad

Mr. Jennings's Banana Split
Hot Chocolate Sauce
Butterscotch Sauce
Nesselrode Sauce

PROSCIUTTO-WRAPPED HEARTS OF PALM

Halve this recipe for a Nothing to It dinner unless everyone's starving and you want to give yourself dawdling time before preparing the rest of the meal. Since they're marinated anyway, these hearts of palm can be prepared a whole day ahead, if you like.

¼ CUP WHITE WINE VINEGAR
½ CUP EXTRA-VIRGIN OLIVE OIL
4 SPRIGS OF FRESH THYME OR ½ TEA-
    SPOON DRIED
¼ TEASPOON FRESHLY GROUND PEPPER
2 CANS (14 OUNCES EACH) HEARTS OF
    PALM, DRAINED AND RINSED
½ POUND THINLY SLICED PROSCIUTTO,
    HALVED LENGTHWISE
2 BUNCHES OF ARUGULA, LARGE STEMS
    REMOVED

1~ In a nonreactive bowl, combine the vinegar, oil, thyme and pepper.
2~ Cut the hearts of palm in half crosswise. (If some are very thick, halve them lengthwise first. Use only the tender stalks.) Wrap each piece in a slice of prosciutto and secure with a toothpick. Place the hearts of palm in the marinade, cover with plastic wrap and refrigerate for 3 hours or overnight.
3~ Remove the prosciutto-wrapped hearts of palm from the marinade. Place the arugula leaves on a serving platter and arrange the wrapped hearts of palm on top. Sprinkle with a grinding of pepper and serve at room temperature.

SERVES 8
RECIPE BY JIM BROWN

GRILLED SMOKED TURKEY AND CHEDDAR SANDWICH

This grilled combination is particularly appealing. If you're not making Warm Caesar Salad, a crunchy coleslaw might be the perfect mate. Double or quadruple the recipe to serve more people.

4 TABLESPOONS UNSALTED BUTTER
2 SLICES OF SOURDOUGH OR COUNTRY-
    STYLE WHITE BREAD, SLICED ½ INCH
    THICK, FROM AN OVAL LOAF ABOUT
    7 INCHES ACROSS
4 TABLESPOONS HOT PEPPER JELLY
4 OUNCES SHARP WHITE CHEDDAR
    CHEESE, THINLY SLICED
½ POUND SLICED SMOKED TURKEY, SKIN
    AND FAT REMOVED

1~ In a small saucepan, melt the butter over low heat. Set aside.
2~ Spread one side of each bread slice with 2 tablespoons of the pepper jelly. Lay the sliced cheese over the jelly, dividing evenly between the two slices of bread. Fold each slice of turkey in half and arrange the slices, overlapping slightly, over the cheese on one slice of bread. Invert the remaining cheese-covered bread slice on top of the turkey.

Warm Caesar Salad

3~ Heat a medium griddle or cast-iron skillet over moderate heat until just warm. Generously brush half the melted butter over the top surface of the sandwich. Invert the sandwich butter-side down onto the heated griddle. Brush the remaining butter over the top of the sandwich.

4~ Cook, covered, until the bread is crisp and golden brown on the bottom and the cheese is beginning to melt, about 5 minutes. With a wide spatula, turn and brown the other side.

5~ Transfer the sandwich to a cutting board and cut in half with a serrated knife. Serve at once.

MAKES 1 LARGE SANDWICH
RECIPE BY MICHAEL MCLAUGHLIN

All the elements of a classic Caesar salad—anchovy, garlic, Parmesan cheese and Worcestershire sauce—are even zestier when the salad is served warm. Guests are always delighted with this adaptation of an old favorite.

2 MEDIUM HEADS OF ROMAINE LETTUCE
2 TABLESPOONS UNSALTED BUTTER
¾ CUP OLIVE OIL
8-OUNCE LOAF OF ITALIAN OR VIENNESE BREAD, CUT INTO ¾-INCH CUBES
2 HARD-COOKED EGGS
1½ TABLESPOONS ANCHOVY PASTE
1 TABLESPOON WORCESTERSHIRE SAUCE
1 GARLIC CLOVE, CRUSHED THROUGH A PRESS
3 TABLESPOONS WHITE WINE VINEGAR
¼ CUP FRESHLY GRATED PARMESAN CHEESE
FRESHLY GROUND PEPPER

1~ Trim away the ends and any wilted outer leaves from the romaine. Separate the leaves, wash them well and dry. Tear the leaves into bite-size pieces; wrap and refrigerate. *(The romaine can be prepared to this point up to a day ahead.)*

2~ In a medium skillet, melt the butter in 2 tablespoons of the oil over moderate heat. When the foam subsides, add the bread cubes and toss to coat. Reduce the heat to moderately low and sauté the bread cubes, stirring often, until crisp and golden brown, 5 to 7 minutes. Set aside.

3~ Meanwhile, coarsely chop the eggs; then force them through a sieve into a small bowl. Put the prepared romaine in a large salad bowl.

4~ In a small nonreactive saucepan, combine the anchovy paste, Worcestershire sauce, garlic and vinegar. Whisk to blend well. Whisk in the remaining olive oil. Set the pan over moderate heat and bring just to a boil.

5~ Remove from the heat and immediately pour the hot dressing over the lettuce; toss well. Add the Parmesan to the bowl and toss again.

6~ Serve from the bowl, or divide the salad among 6 plates. Sprinkle the croutons on top and mound the sieved egg in the center. Season generously with pepper and serve at once.

SERVES 6
RECIPE BY MICHAEL MCLAUGHLIN

102

Toppings and Mix-Ins for Ice Cream Concoctions

Whether you mash them into slabs of ice cream or merely sprinkle them over the top of a sundae, parfait or banana split, consider using bits of the ingredients that follow to enliven your favorite ice cream concoctions. Chances are, you already have some on hand.

M & Ms
peanut brittle
chocolate chips
dried apricots
Junior Mints
shredded pineapple
granola
honey-roasted peanuts
chocolate-covered graham crackers
miniature Reese's Peanut Butter Cups
chocolate-covered raisins
toasted macadamias

sugared almonds
salted pecans
salted pistachios
brandied cherries
frozen brownies
caramels
toasted coconut

MR. JENNINGS'S BANANA SPLIT

Barbara Kafka made one change to Mr. Jennings's Banana Split recipe—she cuts the banana lengthwise instead of crosswise into rounds. You, of course, can do as you please.

½ CUP HEAVY CREAM
1 BANANA, SPLIT LENGTHWISE IN HALF
6 TO 8 SCOOPS (ACCORDING TO THE CAPACITY OF THE EATER) OF ICE CREAM: CHOCOLATE, VANILLA, COFFEE, STRAWBERRY, BUTTER PECAN AND/OR MINT CHOCOLATE CHIP
1 PERFECT STRAWBERRY
HOT CHOCOLATE SAUCE (AT RIGHT), ABOUT 1 TABLESPOON FOR EVERY 2 SCOOPS OF ICE CREAM
BUTTERSCOTCH SAUCE (AT RIGHT), ABOUT 1 TABLESPOON FOR EVERY 2 SCOOPS OF ICE CREAM
1 TABLESPOON CRÈME DE MENTHE, WHITE OR GREEN

1~ In a chilled metal bowl, beat the cream with a balloon whisk until it stands in soft peaks. Set the banana halves along the edges of a boat dish. Pile the ice cream scoops over the banana in as neat a pyramid as possible. Dollop the whipped cream over the ice cream, mounding it high in the center. Place the strawberry dead center in the whipped cream.

2~ Drizzle the chocolate and butterscotch sauces in a lacy fashion over all and trickle the crème de menthe down through the banana split so that it percolates all the way to the bottom.

SERVES 1
RECIPE BY BARBARA KAFKA

HOT CHOCOLATE SAUCE

This is a wonderfully rich, thick and glossy chocolate sauce that can be used hot on ice cream. If there is any left over, refrigerate it in a glass jar, for a week or more. Reheat for one minute, uncovered, in a microwave oven or over hot water.

4 OUNCES GOOD-QUALITY SEMISWEET CHOCOLATE, BROKEN INTO 1½-INCH PIECES
¼ CUP STRONG BREWED COFFEE
2 TABLESPOONS UNSALTED BUTTER
2 TABLESPOONS HEAVY CREAM
2 TABLESPOONS DARK RUM

To prepare on stovetop: In a small heavy nonreactive saucepan, melt the chocolate in the coffee over moderately low heat, stirring, until the chocolate is almost melted and smooth, about 2 minutes. Remove from the heat and stir in the butter until melted and smooth. Stir in the cream and rum. Serve warm or at room temperature.

To prepare in a microwave oven: In an 8-cup glass measuring cup or bowl, combine the chocolate, coffee, butter and cream. Cover tightly with microwave plastic wrap. Cook at high power (100 percent) for 1½ minutes, or until the chocolate is just melted. Using a pot holder, remove the bowl from the microwave and pierce the plastic wrap with the tip of a sharp knife to let the steam escape. Remove the plastic wrap. Whisk the sauce until smooth. Blend in the rum. Serve warm or at room temperature.

MAKES ABOUT ¾ CUP
RECIPE BY BARBARA KAFKA

BUTTERSCOTCH SAUCE

Now this is the stuff that should have been sitting in those heated pots at the end of the soda fountain, ready to puddle alluringly over and around rich, creamy ice cream. Even in the heyday of soda fountains, the butterscotch sauces were seldom this wonderful. Extra sauce will keep in a covered jar in the refrigerator for up to 4 months. To reheat, remove the lid and microwave the sauce on high power (100 percent) for one minute.

1 CUP PACKED LIGHT BROWN SUGAR
¼ POUND (1 STICK) UNSALTED BUTTER
½ CUP LIGHT CORN SYRUP
2 TABLESPOONS HEAVY CREAM
½ TEASPOON VANILLA EXTRACT
⅛ TEASPOON SALT

To prepare on stovetop: In a small heavy nonreactive saucepan, bring the brown sugar and 4 tablespoons of the butter to a boil over moderate heat. Whisk in the corn syrup, cream, vanilla and salt. Reduce the heat to moderately low and boil until the mixture registers 235° on a candy thermometer, about 3 minutes. Immediately remove from the heat and whisk in the remaining 4 tablespoons butter. Serve warm or at room temperature.

To prepare in a microwave oven: In an 8-cup microwave glass bowl, combine the brown sugar, 4 tablespoons of the butter, the corn syrup, cream and salt. Cover tightly with microwave plastic wrap and cook at high power (100 percent) for 5 minutes.

Using a pot holder, remove the bowl from the oven. Pierce the plastic with the tip of a sharp knife to allow the steam to escape. Remove the plastic wrap. Whisk in the remaining 4 tablespoons butter and the vanilla. Serve warm or at room temperature.

MAKES ABOUT 1⅔ CUPS
RECIPE BY BARBARA KAFKA

NESSELRODE SAUCE

Here's a grown-up ice cream sauce that uses a wee dram of rum to soften its sweet and savory edges.

1 JAR (6 OUNCES) MARASCHINO CHERRIES, COARSELY CHOPPED, ¼ CUP OF JUICE RESERVED
1 CONTAINER (3½ OUNCES) CANDIED MIXED FRUITS
1 CUP ORANGE MARMALADE
½ CUP (3 OUNCES) COARSELY CHOPPED CRYSTALLIZED GINGER
1 CUP ROASTED UNSALTED MIXED NUTS, COARSELY CHOPPED
½ CUP DARK RUM

1~ In a medium bowl, combine all of the ingredients. Stir to mix well.
2~ Transfer the sauce to a jar and cover very securely. Refrigerate, stirring occasionally, for at least 2 days or up to 2 months before serving, to allow the flavors to ripen.

MAKES 3½ CUPS
RECIPE BY BARBARA KAFKA

103

Chanterelle and
Chèvre Pizza

Duck Pizza with
Leeks and Garlic

PIZZA PARTY

There was a time when pizza was something you bought on Friday or Saturday nights, usually with "everything but anchovies." It was basically the same wherever you went, good but not great. And then, in the Eighties, pizza came into its own; it blossomed. Restaurant chefs started creating "designer" pizzas, and the craze took hold. Pizzas got smaller and more individual. Virtually no ingredient was exempt as a topping; pizzas were strewn with smoked fish, caviar, wild mushrooms, duck breast. And, in some cases at least, it was very, very good. ~ Is there any reason the pizza party of the early Sixties should disappear? Absolutely not. Bring it back, but serve a collection of pizzas that are simple, interesting, surprising and wonderfully tasty. Or gather a variety of ingredients and let your guests assemble their own. ~ We give you a reliable all-purpose pizza dough and six excellent pizza recipes (even one that's low in calories, cholesterol and sodium). Add some other savory ingredients – say, sweet onions, sun-dried tomatoes, fresh oregano, anchovies, smoked mozzarella and prosciutto – and you'll end up with the pizza party that has everything, including anchovies.

BASIC PIZZA DOUGH

■ ■

PIZZA PARTY

Serves 10 to 12 or more

RED WINE, WHITE WINE AND BEER
Zucchini and Sausage Pizza
Olive and Roasted Red Pepper Pizza
Duck Pizza with Leeks and Garlic
Seafood Pizza
Three Mushroom and Cheese Pizza
Chanterelle and Chèvre Pizza
tossed green salad

■ ■

Add this recipe to your collection of all-time favorite basics, and feel free to double it so you'll always have frozen dough ready and waiting for a pizza emergency.

1 ENVELOPE (¼ OUNCE) ACTIVE DRY YEAST
1 TABLESPOON SUGAR
1½ CUPS LUKEWARM WATER (105° TO 115°)
3¼ CUPS UNBLEACHED FLOUR, PREFERABLY
  BREAD FLOUR
½ TEASPOON SALT
¼ CUP OLIVE OIL, PREFERABLY
  EXTRA VIRGIN

1~ In a small bowl, combine the yeast and sugar. Add the water and stir to mix. If the yeast is not active and bubbling within 5 minutes, discard it and repeat the procedure with a new envelope of yeast.
2~ Measure 3 cups of flour into a large bowl. Stir in the salt, then form a well in the center of the flour.
3~ Pour the yeast mixture into the well and add the oil. Stir in the flour, beginning in the center and working toward the sides of the bowl. When all of the flour is incorporated and the dough is still soft but begins to mass together, turn out onto a lightly floured work surface.
4~ Using a dough scraper to lift any fragments that cling to the work surface, knead the dough, adding just enough of the remaining ¼ cup flour so that the dough is no longer sticky. (It is better that the dough be too soft than too stiff.) Continue to knead until the dough is smooth, shiny and elastic, 10 to 15 minutes.

5~ Shape the dough into a ball and place it in a large, oiled bowl; turn the dough over to coat with the oil. Cover with plastic wrap, set in a warm draft-free place and let rise until doubled in bulk, 1 to 1½ hours. Punch down the dough and reshape into a ball. Cover and refrigerate until doubled in bulk, 20 minutes to 1 hour.
6~ If making deep-dish pizza, divide the dough in half. If making flat pizza, divide the dough into 7 balls of equal weight (4 ounces) and use one for each flat pizza. To freeze, wrap each ball well in plastic; let thaw before proceeding.

MAKES 1¾ POUNDS OF DOUGH, ENOUGH FOR
  SEVEN 7-INCH FLAT PIZZAS OR TWO 9-INCH
  DEEP-DISH PIZZAS
RECIPE BY FOOD & WINE

ZUCCHINI AND SAUSAGE PIZZA

For tradition's sake, every party should include a pizza dotted with sweet Italian sausage. The addition of zucchini makes this one unexpectedly pretty.

½ POUND SWEET ITALIAN SAUSAGE
6 TABLESPOONS OLIVE OIL
2 MEDIUM ZUCCHINI, CUT LENGTHWISE INTO ¼-INCH SLICES AND TRIMMED TO 4½ INCHES
14 OUNCES (½ RECIPE) BASIC PIZZA DOUGH (AT LEFT)
¼ CUP FRESHLY GRATED PARMESAN CHEESE
6 OUNCES MONTEREY JACK CHEESE, SHREDDED (1¼ CUPS)
½ CUP CHUNKY TOMATO SAUCE (AT RIGHT)
¼ TEASPOON SALT
⅛ TEASPOON FRESHLY GROUND PEPPER

1~ Preheat the oven to 450°. Remove the sausage from its casing and crumble into a medium skillet. Fry over moderate heat until browned. Drain on paper towels.
2~ Lightly brush the bottom of a large heavy well-seasoned skillet with some of the olive oil and warm over moderate heat until the oil is hot enough to evaporate a drop of water upon contact. Working in batches, lay as many zucchini strips into the skillet as will easily fit in a single layer. Lightly brush the tops of the strips with oil and cook, turning once, until lightly browned, about 2 minutes on each side. Remove to a plate. Lightly oil the skillet and repeat with the remaining slices.

3~ To assemble the pizza, oil a predarkened 9-inch deep-dish pizza pan with sides about 2 inches high. On a lightly floured surface, roll out the dough and place the deep-dish pizza pan in the center of it. Cut out a round of dough that will comfortably line the pan with 1 inch of overlap. Drape the dough loosely over the pan and ease it in and against the bottom and sides.
4~ Brush the dough with about 1 tablespoon of oil. Sprinkle with the Parmesan and 1 cup of the Monterey Jack. Dot with the sausage, then spoon the Chunky Tomato Sauce on top. Lay the zucchini slices on top in an overlapping pinwheel pattern. Drizzle with the remaining oil and sprinkle with the salt and pepper.
5~ Bake for 25 minutes, or until the crust is golden. Remove from the oven and sprinkle the remaining ¼ cup of Monterey Jack over the pizza. Bake for 5 minutes until melted.
6~ Remove the pizza from the pan. Let stand on a rack for 10 minutes before slicing to allow the filling to set.

MAKES ONE 9-INCH DEEP-DISH PIZZA
RECIPE BY ANNE DISRUDE

CHUNKY TOMATO SAUCE

Use this sauce with zucchini deep-dish pizza, as a base for other toppings or even as an all-purpose sauce for your favorite pasta.

2 TABLESPOONS OLIVE OIL
3 MEDIUM ONIONS, THINLY SLICED
4 LARGE GARLIC CLOVES, MINCED
½ CUP CANNED TOMATO PUREE
1 CAN (16 OUNCES) ITALIAN PLUM TOMATOES WITH THEIR JUICE, CRUSHED
5 SPRIGS OF PARSLEY
12 FRESH PLUM TOMATOES (ABOUT 1½ POUNDS)—PEELED, SEEDED AND COARSELY CHOPPED
½ TEASPOON SALT
¼ TEASPOON FRESHLY GROUND PEPPER
2 TABLESPOONS MINCED FRESH BASIL

1~ In a heavy medium nonreactive saucepan over moderate heat, heat the olive oil until shimmering. Add the onions and garlic, cover and cook over low heat until softened and translucent, about 10 minutes.
2~ Add the tomato puree, crushed canned tomatoes with their juice and parsley. Simmer, uncovered, for 30 minutes.
3~ Pass the sauce through a food mill or fine-mesh sieve to remove the solids. Return to low heat and simmer until very thick (there will be about 2 cups).
4~ Add the fresh tomatoes and cook for 2 minutes. Season with the salt, pepper and basil.

MAKES ABOUT 3 CUPS
RECIPE BY ANNE DISRUDE

OLIVE AND ROASTED RED PEPPER PIZZA

108

Simple ingredients on a simple pizza can deliver a big punch. This is one pie to include in every pizza party—no matter how big or small.

3 FLAT ANCHOVY FILLETS, RINSED AND PAT-
   TED DRY
1 LARGE GARLIC CLOVE, CRUSHED
   THROUGH A PRESS
¼ TEASPOON FRESHLY GROUND BLACK
   PEPPER
¼ CUP OLIVE OIL
1 CAN (6 OUNCES) PITTED BLACK OLIVES,
   RINSED AND DRAINED
12 OUNCES (3 BALLS) BASIC PIZZA DOUGH
   (PAGE 106)
CORNMEAL
4 OUNCES MOZZARELLA CHEESE, CUT
   INTO 9 THIN SLICES
1 RED BELL PEPPER—ROASTED, PEELED,
   SEEDED AND MINCED

1~ Preheat the oven to 500°. If you have one, place a pizza stone (available in housewares stores) or unglazed stone tiles in the oven to preheat along with the oven. (Either of these will help promote a crisp pizza crust, but neither is vital to home pizza baking. If you don't use them, make sure your pizza pan or baking sheet is well-made and very heavy.)
2~ Combine the anchovies, garlic, black pepper, and 2 tablespoons of the oil in a food processor or blender and puree until almost liquefied. Add the olives and process until chopped but not pureed.

3~ On a lightly floured surface, roll out each ball of dough into a 7-inch round that is ¼ inch thick. Dust a pizza peel or baking sheet with cornmeal; lay each round of dough on top. Lightly brush each crust with 1 teaspoon of the oil. Divide the olive mixture among the pizzas and spread out evenly. Drizzle the remaining 1 tablespoon oil over all.
4~ Slide the pizza onto the hot stone or place the baking sheet in the oven. Bake for 6 to 8 minutes, or until the bottom of the crust is lightly browned. Remove from the oven and place 3 slices of mozzarella on each pizza. Sprinkle with the roasted pepper. Bake for about 5 minutes more, or until the cheese is melted.

MAKES 3 SMALL PIZZAS
RECIPE BY ANNE DISRUDE

DUCK PIZZA WITH LEEKS AND GARLIC

Don't dismiss this pizza merely because you've never encountered anything like it—it's scrumptious.

1 HEAD OF GARLIC, SEPARATED INTO CLOVES
¼ CUP PLUS 1 TABLESPOON OLIVE OIL
1 BONELESS WHOLE DUCK BREAST, CUT IN
   HALF AND TRIMMED OF EXCESS FAT
SALT AND COARSELY CRACKED PEPPER
2 MEDIUM LEEKS (WHITE AND TENDER
   GREEN), CUT INTO 2-INCH JULIENNE
8 OUNCES (2 BALLS) BASIC PIZZA DOUGH
   (PAGE 106)
CORNMEAL

1~ Preheat the oven and a pizza stone or tiles to 500° 1 hour before use.
2~ Combine the garlic cloves and ¼ cup of the olive oil in a small saucepan. Cover and cook over moderate heat until the garlic is soft, 20 to 30 minutes. Pass through a food mill or fine-mesh sieve. Discard the skins; reserve the puree.
3~ In a medium skillet, sauté the duck breasts, skin-side down, over moderately high heat until the skin is browned, about 8 minutes. Pour off the excess fat. Turn the breasts and sauté until lightly browned on the bottom, about 3 minutes.
4~ Remove the duck from the skillet and, when cool enough to handle, remove and reserve the skin. Slice the duck breasts into thin strips. Season lightly with salt and pepper. Cover loosely and set aside.

SEAFOOD PIZZA

5~ Cut the duck skin into thin strips and return to the skillet. Cook over moderate heat until the fat is rendered and the skin is crisp, about 20 minutes. Drain the cracklings on paper towels.

6~ Toss the leeks with the remaining 1 tablespoon olive oil; season lightly with salt and pepper.

7~ On a lightly floured surface, roll out each ball of dough into a 7-inch round that is ¼ inch thick. Dust a pizza peel or baking sheet with cornmeal; lay each round of dough on top. Spread half of the garlic puree over each pizza crust.

8~ Reserve 2 tablespoons of the cracklings for garnish; sprinkle the remainder over the garlic puree. Reserve 2 tablespoons of the leeks for garnish; divide the remainder between the pizzas.

9~ Slide the pizza onto the hot stone or place the baking sheet in the oven. Bake for 5 to 7 minutes or until the bottom of the crust is lightly browned. Remove from the oven and arrange the duck strips on top. Continue baking for about 3 minutes, until the duck is warmed through and the bottom of the crust is browned. Garnish with the reserved cracklings and leeks.

MAKES 2 SMALL PIZZAS
RECIPE BY ANNE DISRUDE

This recipe was inspired by Vincenzo Buonassisi's Four Seasons Pizza from his book *Pizza* (Little, Brown). His is big-league, real Italian inspiration.

1 POUND MUSSELS, SCRUBBED AND
   DEBEARDED
¼ CUP DRY WHITE WINE
1 LARGE SHALLOT, COARSELY CHOPPED
2 TABLESPOONS OLIVE OIL
1 TABLESPOON MINCED FRESH BASIL
SALT AND FRESHLY GROUND PEPPER
8 MEDIUM SHRIMP, SHELLED AND DEVEINED
1 LARGE GARLIC CLOVE, MINCED
½ TO 1 TEASPOON CHINESE CHILI PASTE
6 OUNCES (1½ BALLS) BASIC
   PIZZA DOUGH (PAGE 106)
CORNMEAL
SPRIGS OF PARSLEY, FOR GARNISH

1~ Preheat the oven and a pizza stone or tiles to 500° 1 hour before use.

2~ In a large nonreactive saucepan, combine the mussels, wine and shallot. Bring to a boil over high heat and cook, covered, tossing occasionally, until the mussels open, about 5 minutes; discard any mussels that do not open. Drain and remove from the shells. Toss with 2 teaspoons of the olive oil and the basil and season with salt and pepper to taste. (*This can be done a day ahead. Cover and refrigerate. Let the mussels return to room temperature before continuing.*)

3~ In a small skillet, heat 2 teaspoons of the oil. Add the shrimp and toss over high heat for 1 minute. Add the garlic and chili paste and toss to coat. Cook, until the shrimp start to lose their translucency, 1 to 2 more minutes. Remove from the heat.

4~ On a lightly floured surface, roll out the whole ball of dough into a 7-inch round that is ¼ inch thick. Divide the remaining half-ball of dough in two; roll each half into a 12-inch-long rope. Fold each rope in half and twist together. Lay the twists on top of the pizza to divide it into quadrants; moisten the ends of the twists and press to seal.

5~ Dust a pizza peel or a baking sheet with cornmeal and lay the dough on top. Brush with the remaining 2 teaspoons of oil. Prick the surface to prevent the dough from bubbling.

6~ Slide the pizza onto the hot stone or place the baking sheet in the oven. Bake for 8 to 10 minutes, until the top of the crust is golden. Remove from the oven and arrange the mussels and shrimp on alternating quadrants. Garnish with the parsley sprigs in the center.

MAKES 1 SMALL PIZZA
RECIPE BY ANNE DISRUDE

THREE MUSHROOM AND CHEESE PIZZA

110

Yes, this looks like a ton of ingredients, but it really amounts to an easy preparation that produces a comely, rich pizza.

1 ENVELOPE (¼ OUNCE) ACTIVE DRY YEAST
⅓ CUP LUKEWARM MILK (105° TO 115°)
⅔ CUP LUKEWARM WATER (105° TO 115°)
1½ TABLESPOONS PLUS 1 TEASPOON
    OLIVE OIL
PINCH OF SUGAR
2 CUPS UNBLEACHED ALL-PURPOSE FLOUR
3 TABLESPOONS WHOLE WHEAT FLOUR
1½ TEASPOONS SALT
1½ OUNCES DRIED PORCINI MUSHROOMS
1½ OUNCES DRIED SHIITAKE MUSHROOMS
4 CUPS BOILING WATER
1 TABLESPOON UNSALTED BUTTER
3 POUNDS FRESH MUSHROOMS, SLICED
½ TEASPOON FRESHLY GROUND PEPPER
1½ CUPS DRY RED WINE
2 TO 3 TEASPOONS CRUSHED GARLIC
1 TEASPOON DRIED THYME
1 TEASPOON DRIED OREGANO
1 TEASPOON DRIED MARJORAM
1 TEASPOON DRIED SAGE
6 OUNCES PROVOLONE CHEESE, SHREDDED
6 OUNCES ITALIAN FONTINA CHEESE,
    SHREDDED
1 TO 2 TABLESPOONS FRESHLY GRATED
    PARMESAN CHEESE
3 TABLESPOONS MIXED FRESH HERBS,
    PREFERABLY A COMBINATION OF CHOPPED
    PARSLEY, CHIVES, MARJORAM AND
    OREGANO

1~ Dissolve the yeast in the warm milk and stir in the warm water, olive oil and sugar. Let stand for 5 minutes.

2~ In a large bowl, mix together the all-purpose and whole wheat flours and ½ teaspoon of the salt. Add the yeast mixture and stir well to form a soft workable dough. (If the dough is too sticky, add small amounts of all-purpose flour.)

3~ Turn the dough out onto a lightly floured surface and knead for 10 minutes by hand (or for 5 minutes in a mixer with a dough hook), until the dough is smooth and elastic.

4~ Place the dough in a large bowl, cover with a damp cloth and let rise in a warm place until doubled, about 1 hour.

5~ Meanwhile, soak the porcini and shiitake mushrooms in the boiling water until they are very soft and the water has cooled to room temperature, 30 to 45 minutes. Remove the mushrooms with a slotted spoon and set aside. Strain the soaking liquid through a sieve lined with several layers of dampened cheesecloth and reserve. Trim the tough stems from the shiitake mushrooms and the sandy root areas from the porcini. Thinly slice the mushrooms.

6~ In a large skillet, melt the butter over moderately high heat. Add the fresh mushrooms and sauté, tossing, until slightly wilted, 3 to 5 minutes. Season with the remaining 1 teaspoon salt and the pepper.

7~ In a small nonreactive saucepan, combine the reserved mushroom liquid with the wine. Boil over moderate heat until the liquid is reduced to ⅓ cup, 15 to 20 minutes.

8~ In a bowl, toss together the sautéed and dried mushrooms, the garlic, the dried thyme, oregano, marjoram and sage and the reduced wine-mushroom liquid.

9~ Preheat the oven to 500°. Punch down the dough and divide it into 3 equal parts, about 6 ounces each. Form each piece of dough into a ball and roll it out on a floured surface to form a pizza round, 8 to 9 inches in diameter. Place each pizza round on a small baking sheet and set aside to rise for 10 minutes.

10~ Top each round of dough with about ⅔ cup of the mushroom mixture, spreading to cover evenly, but leaving a ½- to ¾-inch border. Combine the provolone and Fontina cheeses and sprinkle over the mushrooms.

11~ Bake the pizzas for 7 minutes; switch the pizzas on the bottom rack to the top and continue to bake until the crusts are crisp and golden brown, 3 to 5 minutes longer. Remove from the oven and sprinkle with the Parmesan cheese and fresh herbs. Serve hot.

MAKES 3 SMALL PIZZAS
RECIPE BY ANNIE SOMERVILLE
GREENS, SAN FRANCISCO

CHANTERELLE AND CHÈVRE PIZZA

This pizza from the spa at the Sonoma Mission Inn is low in calories (261 per serving), cholesterol and sodium. To simplify the preparation, use canned low-sodium tomato sauce and substitute lightly toasted whole wheat pita halves for the dough made in Steps 1, 2 and 5.

2 TEASPOONS HONEY

½ CUP LUKEWARM WATER (105° TO 110°)

1¼ TEASPOONS ACTIVE DRY YEAST

1 CUP WHOLE WHEAT PASTRY FLOUR

⅓ CUP UNBLEACHED ALL-PURPOSE FLOUR

¼ TEASPOON SALT (OPTIONAL)

2 TABLESPOONS OLIVE OIL

1½ POUNDS FRESH CHANTERELLES OR
    CULTIVATED MUSHROOMS

2 TABLESPOONS DRY SHERRY

2 TABLESPOONS DRY WHITE WINE

1 LARGE SHALLOT, MINCED

1 CUP LOW-FAT COTTAGE CHEESE

6 TABLESPOONS LOW-SODIUM FRESH GOAT
    CHEESE

1 TABLESPOON CHOPPED FRESH DILL

1¾ TEASPOONS CHOPPED FRESH THYME
    OR ¾ TEASPOON DRIED

⅛ TEASPOON CHOPPED FRESH ROSEMARY
    OR A PINCH OF DRIED, CRUMBLED

1 TABLESPOON CORNMEAL

1½ CUPS LOW-SODIUM TOMATO SAUCE

¼ CUP MINCED FRESH PARSLEY

¼ CUP MINCED FRESH CHIVES

1~ In a small bowl, dissolve the honey in the warm water. Sprinkle the yeast over the top and let stand for 5 minutes.

2~ In a medium bowl, combine the whole wheat flour, all-purpose flour and salt. Make a well in the center, pour in the yeast mixture and 1 tablespoon plus 1 teaspoon of the olive oil. Stir until blended. Turn out the dough onto a lightly floured surface and knead for about 2 minutes, until it forms a smooth mass. Put in a lightly oiled bowl, turn to coat with the oil, cover with a towel and set in a warm place to rise until doubled in bulk, 1 to 1½ hours.

3~ Cut the chanterelles into large pieces or thickly slice the mushrooms. Put in a large skillet. Sprinkle the sherry, white wine and shallot over the mushrooms. Cover and cook over moderate heat for 10 minutes. Drain off any liquid in the pan; set the chanterelles aside.

4~ In a medium bowl, combine the cottage cheese, goat cheese, dill, thyme and rosemary. Mix to blend well.

5~ Preheat the oven to 450°. When the dough has risen once, punch it down and knead for 30 seconds. Form into a 6-inch log and cut into 6 equal pieces. Roll each piece into a 5½-inch circle about ⅛ inch thick. Turn under about ½ inch of dough and pinch to form a raised border. Sprinkle the cornmeal over a heavy baking sheet. Place the dough rounds on the sheet. Cover the rounds lightly and let rise for 20 minutes.

6~ Paint the dough rounds lightly with the remaining 2 teaspoons olive oil. Spread a generous 2 tablespoons of the tomato sauce over each pizza. Spoon about 2 tablespoons of the cheese mixture over the sauce. Divide the mushrooms among the pizzas.

7~ Bake the pizzas on the lowest rack of the oven for 15 to 20 minutes, until the crust is well browned and cooked through.

8~ Sprinkle with the parsley and chives. Serve hot.

SERVES 6
RECIPE BY CHRISTIAN CHAVANNE
SONOMA MISSION INN AND SPA
BOYES HOT SPRINGS, CALIFORNIA

■ ■ ■

DINNER TO CELEBRATE THE NOUVEAUX BEAUJOLAIS

By tradition in the French wine trade, the nouveaux Beaujolais wines are released on November 15 every year. Cases and cases of the wines arrive here almost immediately thereafter. If you're interested in setting traditions of your own, then weigh the advantages of hosting a weekend dinner party to celebrate the arrival of these very drinkable, fruity wines. Falling just one or two weekends before Thanksgiving, your party can open the holiday season. ∼ The menu calls for soothing, typically French food. To start, guests will be tasting the slightly chilled young wines from a variety of shippers and munching vegetables dipped in the garlicky aïoli. When the time is right, invite your guests for a sit-down or buffet-style dinner of braised turkey breast (turkey is excellent with nouveaux Beaujolais, so keep it in mind too for a Thanksgiving dinner wine), roasted garlic potatoes and a green salad. For dessert, guests will drink to your health when they taste your delicious, authentic French apple tart with rich almond custard.

■ ■ ■

Tapenade

Grand Aïoli

Anchoïade

Aïoli

GRAND AÏOLI

DINNER TO CELEBRATE THE NOUVEAUX BEAUJOLAIS

Serves 16 to 20

NOUVEAUX BEAUJOLAIS
THROUGHOUT

Grand Aïoli

Tapenade

Anchoïade

Braised Turkey Breast with Cider Sauce

Roasted Garlic Potatoes

endive and arugula salad with vinaigrette

Apple Tart with Almond Custard

Aïoli gives its name to the pungent garlic mayonnaise as well as to this Provençal dish in which the mayonnaise stars.

2 POUNDS SALT COD

2 POUNDS SMALL POTATOES, SCRUBBED

1 POUND THIN GREEN BEANS

1 POUND MEDIUM CARROTS

1 HEAD OF CAULIFLOWER, CUT INTO FLORETS

1 POUND MEDIUM BEETS

8 HARD-COOKED EGGS

AÏOLI (AT RIGHT), RECIPE TRIPLED

1~ One to two days before preparing the aïoli, depending on the saltiness of the fish, soak the salt cod in a large bowl of cold water. Change the water 3 or 4 times during the soaking period to remove excess salt. Drain and rinse the fish.

2~ Put the cod in a large saucepan. Add fresh cold water to cover and bring just to a simmer over moderate heat. Immediately remove the pan from the heat. Cover and let stand for at least 15 minutes. Drain well. Scrape off any fatty skin and remove any bones. Tear the fish into large pieces.

3~ Steam or boil the vegetables until tender, about 20 minutes for the potatoes, 4 minutes for the beans, 20 minutes for the carrots, 7 minutes for the cauliflower and 40 minutes for the beets. Let cool, then peel the beets. Halve the beets, carrots and eggs. Arrange the vegetables, cod and eggs on a large heated platter. Pass the aïoli separately.

SERVES 12 TO 16
RECIPE BY PATRICIA WELLS

AÏOLI

This is an authentic Provençal aïoli, which needs fresh, juicy garlic cloves. If you do not have a large mortar and pestle, you can crush the garlic and salt together to a paste with the flat side of a knife and make the aïoli with a whisk or an electric hand mixer.

6 GARLIC CLOVES, HALVED LENGTHWISE
½ TEASPOON SALT
2 EGG YOLKS, AT ROOM TEMPERATURE
1 CUP EXTRA-VIRGIN OLIVE OIL

1~ Remove the green sprouting "germ" that runs through the center of the garlic if there is one. Coarsely chop the garlic.
2~ Pour boiling water into a large mortar to warm it; discard the water and dry the mortar. Add the garlic and salt and mash together to form a paste. Slowly add the egg yolks one at a time, stirring and pressing slowly and evenly with the pestle in the same direction to thoroughly blend the garlic and egg yolks.
3~ Very slowly work in the oil, drop by drop, until the mixture thickens. Gradually whisk in the remaining oil in a slow, thin stream until the sauce is thickened to a mayonnaise consistency.

MAKES ABOUT 1¼ CUPS
RECIPE BY PATRICIA WELLS

TAPENADE

Unlike most tapenades, which are blended to a puree, this version of the Provençal black olive, caper, anchovy and herb spread is only very lightly mixed in a food processor until chunky. If your olives are very salty, you may want to rinse or soak them before assembling the tapenade.

2 TABLESPOONS DRAINED CAPERS
4 FLAT ANCHOVY FILLETS
2 TABLESPOONS EXTRA-VIRGIN OLIVE OIL
1 TEASPOON CHOPPED FRESH THYME
1 TABLESPOON AMBER RUM
2 CUPS (8 OUNCES) OIL-CURED BLACK OLIVES, PREFERABLY FROM NYONS, PITTED

1~ In a food processor, combine the capers, anchovies, olive oil, thyme and rum. Process until just blended.
2~ Add the olives and turn the machine on and off about 10 times, until the tapenade is blended but still quite coarse.

MAKES ABOUT 1 CUP
RECIPE BY PATRICIA WELLS

ANCHOÏADE

This delicious anchovy, garlic and olive oil spread, also known as *quichet*, is served on tiny toast rounds with drinks at Chez Gilbert, a Provençal bistro set along the sun-kissed port of Cassis. You'll want to double this recipe to serve a crowd.

16 SLICES OF LONG, NARROW FRENCH BREAD, CUT ½ INCH THICK
2 CANS (2 OUNCES EACH) FLAT ANCHOVY FILLETS IN OLIVE OIL, DRAINED, OIL RESERVED
2½ TEASPOONS RED WINE VINEGAR
4 GARLIC CLOVES, COARSELY CHOPPED
⅓ CUP CHOPPED FRESH PARSLEY

1~ Preheat the broiler. Arrange the bread slices on a baking sheet and broil about 4 inches from the heat, turning once, until browned on both sides, about 1½ minutes.
2~ (If you find anchovies too salty, proceed with this step. If you like their saltiness, skip it.) In a small bowl, cover the anchovies with 1 cup of cold water. Soak for 10 minutes. Drain the anchovies and pat dry on paper towels.
3~ Finely chop the anchovies with their reserved oil. Add the vinegar, garlic and parsley and chop together; the mixture should be rather coarse. Spread the anchoïade over the toasts and broil for about 1 minute, just until warm. Serve immediately.

SERVES 6 TO 8
RECIPE BY PATRICIA WELLS

BRAISED TURKEY BREAST WITH CIDER SAUCE

When serving a number of guests, it's wise to do as much as possible ahead of time. This turkey breast is perfect, since it is completely prepared before guests arrive and then served at room temperature.

TURKEY:
3 TABLESPOONS BUTTER
2 TABLESPOONS VEGETABLE OIL
6 MEDIUM CARROTS, CUT INTO ½-INCH SLICES (ABOUT 3 CUPS)
3 MEDIUM ONIONS, COARSELY CHOPPED (ABOUT 3 CUPS)
2 GARLIC CLOVES, CRUSHED
1 WHOLE TURKEY BREAST, BONE IN (ABOUT 10 POUNDS)
6 CUPS HARD APPLE CIDER, PREFERABLY FRENCH
2 TABLESPOONS SALT
1 LARGE BOUQUET GARNI: 8 SPRIGS OF PARSLEY, 1 TABLESPOON DRIED THYME, 1 TABLESPOON DRIED ROSEMARY, 1 BAY LEAF AND 6 PEPPERCORNS TIED IN A DOUBLE THICKNESS OF CHEESECLOTH

SAUCE:
2½ CUPS MAYONNAISE, PREFERABLY HOMEMADE
¼ CUP DRY WHITE WINE
2 TABLESPOONS BRANDY
2 TABLESPOONS DIJON-STYLE MUSTARD
3 TABLESPOONS MINCED PARSLEY, FOR GARNISH

1~ *Make the Turkey:* Preheat the oven to 375°.
2~ In a large skillet, heat the butter and oil. Add the carrots, onions and garlic; cover the skillet and cook over low heat until the vegetables soften, about 10 minutes. Transfer the vegetables to an ovenproof casserole or deep roasting pan that will hold the turkey breast snugly. Place the turkey on top of the vegetables.
3~ Add the cider, salt and bouquet garni to the casserole. Cover with aluminum foil or a tight lid and bake for 2 to 2½ hours, or until a thermometer inserted in the thickest part of the breast registers 160°. Remove from the oven, uncover and let rest until the turkey is cool enough to handle.
4~ Remove and discard the turkey skin. Using a long, sharp knife and working close to the breast bone, remove the meat in 2 solid pieces (one from each side of the breast) and place in a deep bowl. Strain the broth from the casserole over the turkey; cover and let cool to room temperature. Discard the breast bone and the solids in the sieve.
5~ Remove the turkey from the broth and reserve the broth for the sauce. Slice the turkey thinly across the grain. Arrange the slices on a large platter. Cover tightly with plastic wrap and refrigerate until chilled.
6~ *Prepare the Sauce and assemble the dish:* Degrease the reserved broth; there will be about 8 cups. Pour the broth into a medium saucepan and bring to a boil. Cook over moderately high heat until reduced to 1 cup, about 45 minutes. (The broth will reduce to a thick syrup; watch carefully during the last 15 minutes to prevent scorching.) Remove from the heat and let cool to room temperature, stirring occasionally.
7~ Place the mayonnaise in a medium bowl and whisk in the reduced broth, wine, brandy and mustard until blended. Spoon the sauce over the turkey and garnish with the parsley. If not serving immediately, cover the turkey and refrigerate. Let stand at room temperature for ½ hour before serving.

SERVES 20
RECIPE BY W. PETER PRESTCOTT

ROASTED GARLIC POTATOES

Crisp, crusty and crunchy, these potatoes are almost no work at all. They make a remarkably tasty accompaniment to the Braised Turkey Breast.

5 POUNDS (ABOUT 10) BAKING POTATOES, PEELED AND EACH CUT LENGTHWISE INTO 8 WEDGES
½ POUND (2 STICKS) BUTTER
6 GARLIC CLOVES, MINCED (ABOUT 3 TABLESPOONS)
1 TABLESPOON COARSE (KOSHER) SALT
1 TEASPOON FRESHLY GROUND PEPPER

1~ Preheat the oven to 500°.
2~ Bring a large pot of water to a boil. Add the potatoes, return the water to a boil and cook for 5 minutes. Drain thoroughly.
3~ Melt the butter in a large skillet. Add the garlic and cook over low heat until it is softened but not browned, about 3 minutes. Add the potatoes and stir gently to coat them with the garlic butter.
4~ Transfer the potatoes and garlic butter to enough baking dishes or roasting pans to hold the potatoes in a single layer. Sprinkle with the salt and pepper. (*At this point, the potatoes can be set aside, uncovered, at room temperature until 1 hour before you plan to serve them.*)
5~ Bake the potatoes for 1 hour, stirring gently every 10 minutes, until they are golden brown and very crisp on the outside. Serve hot.

SERVES 20
RECIPE BY W. PETER PRESTCOTT

APPLE TART WITH ALMOND CUSTARD

The apples for this tasty tart will caramelize faster if sautéed in a cast-iron skillet.

4 TABLESPOONS UNSALTED BUTTER
¼ CUP DARK RUM
2¼ POUNDS FIRM COOKING APPLES, SUCH AS JONATHAN, GOLDEN DELICIOUS OR GOLDEN RUSSET—PEELED, CORED AND CUT INTO 1-INCH CUBES
⅓ CUP PLUS ½ CUP SUGAR
PREBAKED BUTTER-CRUST TART SHELL (AT RIGHT)
½ CUP CRÈME FRAÎCHE
2 EGGS
¾ CUP GROUND ALMONDS
CRÈME FRAÎCHE OR WHIPPED CREAM, AS ACCOMPANIMENT

1~ In a large nonreactive heavy skillet, combine the butter, rum, apples and ⅓ cup of the sugar. Cook over moderate heat, tossing, until the apples are golden brown, 10 to 15 minutes. Let cool slightly. Pour the apple mixture into the baked tart shell.
2~ Preheat the oven to 400°.
3~ In a medium bowl, stir together the crème fraîche, eggs, almonds and remaining ½ cup sugar. Pour the mixture over the apples in the tart shell.
4~ Set the tart on a cookie sheet and bake for 25 to 30 minutes, or until golden brown. Serve warm, with additional crème fraîche, if desired.

SERVES 8 TO 10
RECIPE BY LYDIE MARSHALL

PREBAKED BUTTER-CRUST TART SHELL

117

1½ CUPS UNBLEACHED ALL-PURPOSE FLOUR
6 OUNCES (1½ STICKS) COLD UNSALTED BUTTER, CUT INTO SMALL PIECES
1 TABLESPOON SUGAR
⅛ TEASPOON SALT

1~ In a food processor, combine the flour, butter, sugar and salt. Process until the mixture resembles coarse meal, about 10 seconds. Add 3 to 4 tablespoons of cold water and pulse on and off, until the mixture resembles small peas, about 5 seconds; do not mix until it forms a ball. Turn the dough out onto a lightly floured surface and knead lightly, just until the dough holds together. Flatten into a 6-inch disk, wrap in plastic and refrigerate for at least 15 minutes.
2~ On a generously floured surface, roll out the dough into a 15-inch circle. Fit into an 11-inch tart pan without stretching. Press the pastry against the fluted side of the pan and trim off any excess. Prick the bottom, cover with plastic wrap and freeze for about 30 minutes before baking.
3~ Meanwhile, preheat the oven to 400°.
4~ Remove the plastic wrap from the pie shell. Line the pastry with foil and fill it with pie weights or dried beans, making sure they are pushed well against the sides.
5~ Bake for 20 minutes, or until the pastry is almost dry. Remove the foil and weights and bake for 5 to 8 minutes longer, or until the crust is lightly browned.

MAKES ONE 11-INCH TART SHELL
RECIPE BY LYDIE MARSHALL

118

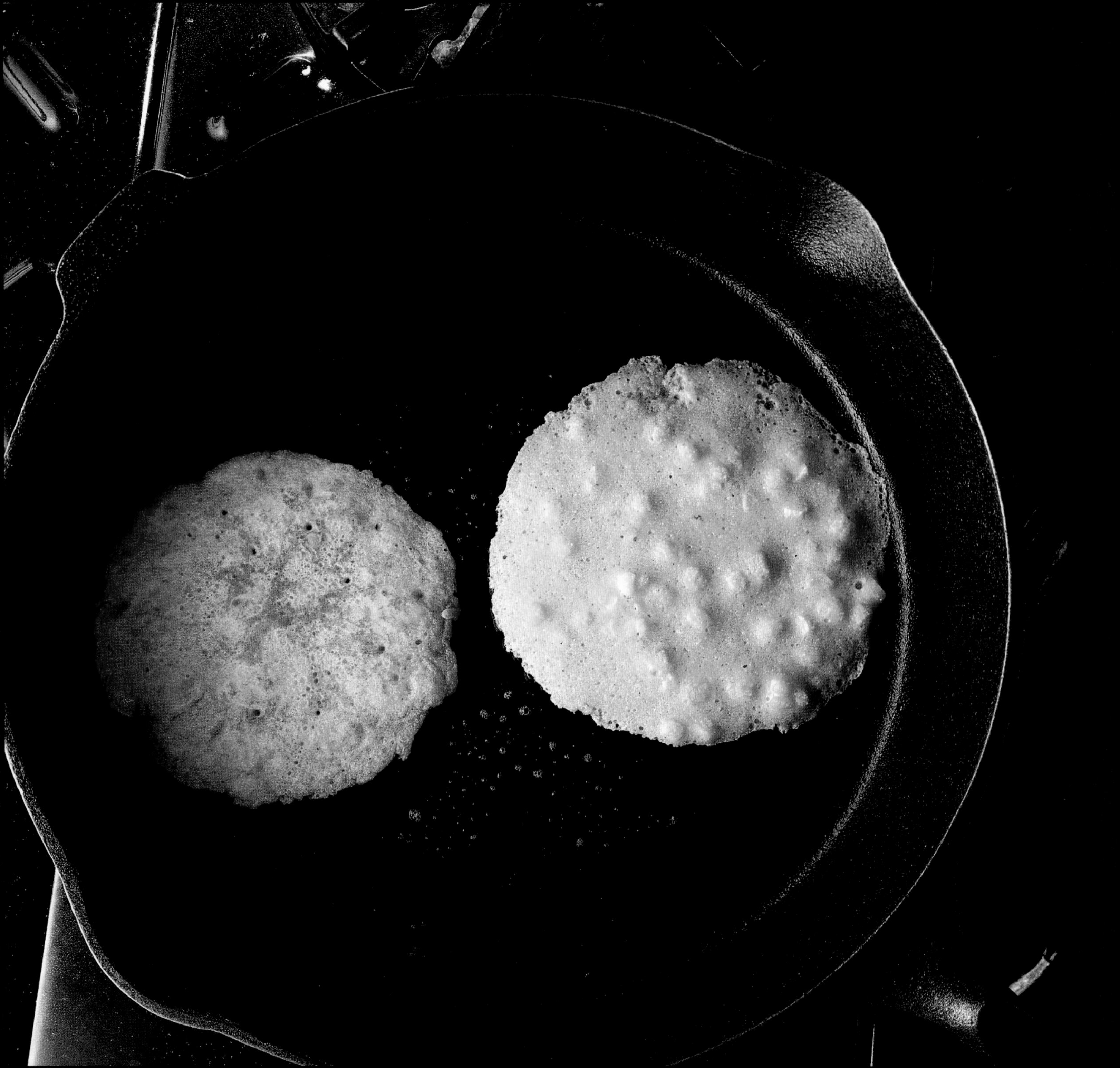

■ ■ ■

GRIDDLECAKE
BREAKFAST

There seems to be some sort of link between pancakes and weekends. Seldom do we mix up a batch of
flapjacks on a Tuesday or Wednesday morning, grill
them quickly, eat them and rush off to the office.
There's something about pancakes that requires a
more leisurely setting for their enjoyment: fully
awake people, a nicely set table, whipped sweet butter, warmed maple syrup and perhaps a jam or two
for those who like it. And even then, we don't want
plain pancakes. No, only something slightly different will do. ∼ The cornmeal pancakes in our menu
will melt in your mouth. They're best made with
fresh sweet corn, but we often substitute frozen
corn kernels and use this recipe year-round. The
buckwheat and almond pancakes are an unexpected
touch that will be much appreciated at the weekend
breakfast table. ∼ If the breakfast you're making
will be fuel for a whole day outdoors, you'll want to
make up a skillet full of the all-American Corned
Beef Hash to provide protein for extra energy.

119

■ ■ ■

*Cornmeal
Breakfast Pancakes*

CORNMEAL BREAKFAST PANCAKES

GRIDDLECAKE BREAKFAST

Serves 6 to 8

MIXED VEGETABLE JUICE
COFFEE AND TEA
Cornmeal Breakfast Pancakes
Buckwheat and Almond Pancakes
whipped butter
warm maple syrup
rye toast
Corned Beef Hash

Though these pancakes are terrific when made with fresh corn kernels, substituting frozen corn works very, very well.

1½ CUPS YELLOW CORNMEAL
¼ CUP UNBLEACHED ALL-PURPOSE FLOUR
2 TABLESPOONS SUGAR
1 TEASPOON BAKING SODA
½ TEASPOON SALT
2 CUPS BUTTERMILK
2 TABLESPOONS UNSALTED BUTTER, MELTED
1 EGG, SEPARATED
1¼ CUPS FRESH CORN KERNELS (FROM 3 TO 4 EARS OF CORN) OR FROZEN CORN KERNELS
1 TEASPOON VEGETABLE OIL

1~ In a medium bowl, combine the cornmeal, flour, sugar, baking soda and salt. Make a well in the center and pour in the buttermilk, butter and egg yolk. Working quickly, stir just until the ingredients are moistened. Add the corn kernels and stir until just combined (the batter should not be perfectly smooth).
2~ Beat the egg white until stiff but not dry. Fold the beaten white into the cornmeal batter.

3~ On a griddle or in a large heavy skillet, heat the oil over moderate heat. Working in batches, spoon about 3 tablespoons of the batter for each pancake onto the griddle; space the pancakes about 1 inch apart to allow for spreading. Cook until bubbles form on the surface of the pancakes, about 2 minutes. Turn with a spatula and cook until golden brown on the second side, about 2 minutes longer. Transfer the pancakes to a platter; cover to keep warm while cooking the remaining batches.
4~ Serve with butter, warm maple syrup and crisp, thick-sliced bacon.

MAKES ABOUT 18 PANCAKES
RECIPE BY RICHARD SAX

BUCKWHEAT AND ALMOND PANCAKES

The ground almonds in these pancakes add flavor and texture that make them a nice counterpoint to the cornmeal pancakes.

½ CUP BUCKWHEAT FLOUR
½ CUP ALL-PURPOSE FLOUR
¼ CUP WHOLE WHEAT FLOUR
¼ CUP GROUND ALMONDS
2 TABLESPOONS SUGAR
1½ TEASPOONS BAKING POWDER
½ TEASPOON SALT
2 EGGS, SEPARATED
1 CUP MILK
2 TABLESPOONS MELTED BUTTER
OIL, FOR THE GRIDDLE

1~ In a medium bowl, stir together the buckwheat flour, all-purpose flour, whole wheat flour, almonds, sugar, baking powder and salt.
2~ In a small bowl, whisk the egg yolks, milk and butter until blended; pour into the dry ingredients. Stir just until blended.
3~ Beat the egg whites until stiff but not dry. Quickly fold them into the batter.
4~ Lightly oil a large griddle or skillet. Place over moderately low heat until hot. Pour the batter by quarter-cupfuls onto the griddle and cook for 2½ to 3 minutes on one side, until lightly browned; turn and cook for about 1 minute on the second side, until speckled with brown. (The remaining batches will take less time because the grill will be hotter.)
5~ Serve on hot plates with warmed wildflower honey and a pat of butter, if desired.

MAKES ABOUT 1 DOZEN
RECIPE BY MICHÈLE URVATER

CORNED BEEF HASH

You'll want to do Steps 1 through 4 on the night before the breakfast. That's good, though—it leaves less for you to do in the bleary-eyed morning.

4 MEDIUM POTATOES
½ POUND LEAN SLAB BACON, SLICED
2 TEASPOONS VEGETABLE OIL
2 POUNDS COLD CORNED BEEF, COARSELY CHOPPED
1 LARGE ONION, MINCED
2 TABLESPOONS BOURBON
2 TEASPOONS WORCESTERSHIRE SAUCE
1 TEASPOON FRESHLY GRATED NUTMEG
SALT AND FRESHLY GROUND PEPPER
1 CUP HEAVY CREAM
3 TABLESPOONS MINCED FRESH PARSLEY
6 POACHED OR FRIED EGGS

1~ In a large saucepan of boiling salted water, cook the potatoes until tender, about 25 minutes; drain. As soon as the potatoes are cool enough to handle, peel and chop coarsely.
2~ In a saucepan of boiling water, blanch the bacon over moderately high heat for 10 minutes; drain. Remove and discard any rind, pat the bacon dry and cut into ⅛-inch dice.
3~ In a medium skillet, sauté the bacon in the oil over moderate heat until the bacon is browned and crisp, about 20 minutes. Drain on paper towels; reserve 4 tablespoons of the drippings and set aside.
4~ In a large bowl, combine the corned beef, potatoes, bacon, onion, bourbon, Worcestershire sauce, nutmeg and salt and pepper to

taste; mix well. Cover and refrigerate for at least 2 hours, or overnight.
5~ Just before preparing the hash, place the cream in a medium saucepan and boil over moderate heat until reduced by half, about 20 minutes.
6~ In a large ovenproof skillet (see Note), preferably nonstick, melt the reserved bacon drippings over moderately high heat until sizzling. Add the hash mixture, pressing down firmly with the back of a wooden spoon, and cook uncovered for 15 minutes.
7~ Add the reduced cream and stir well. Press the mixture down again, reduce the heat to moderate and cook until a dark golden crust forms on the bottom, about 25 minutes. After about 15 minutes, preheat the broiler.
8~ Transfer to a hot broiler and broil 4 inches from the heat until the top is browned, about 10 minutes. Turn the hash out onto a large platter and sprinkle with the parsley. Top each serving with a poached or fried egg.
Note: If you do not have an ovenproof skillet, the hash can be prepared through Step 7 in a regular skillet. Then, instead of broiling, invert the hash onto a cookie sheet and slide it back into the pan to brown the second side.

SERVES 6
RECIPE BY FOOD & WINE

■ ■ ■

A
GAMES NIGHT
DINNER

Whether it's a regularly scheduled event or something that happens just once in a blue moon, everybody likes to get together with friends, play some games and have a casual good time. Whether it's pinochle, poker, Pictionary or all three, most players like to keep the game going. So when people begin to get hungry, serve them olive toasts and set out a crock of tuna and roasted red pepper spread with some vegetables or crackers to take the edge off their appetites. ∼ Later, when there's a break in the action, you can all sit down to dinner: tiny ear-shaped pasta baked with cheese, olives and zucchini plus a colorful salad. Dessert's a big deal: Chocolate Pecan Pudding with Bourbon Sauce. You can be sure no one will pass it up. And if your fellow game players are the staying type, your ace in the hole is the homemade popcorn candy and pecan brittle you made for late-night munchies.

■ ■ ■

*Orecchiette
with Olives,
Vegetables and
Mozzarella*

Tricolor Salad

OLIVE TOASTS

124

Crostini are pieces of toast, often flavored with garlic and olive oil, that serve as a base for many different toppings. The toasts themselves can be made early on the day of serving, and the olive paste spread on one hour before needed.

3 LARGE GARLIC CLOVES, CRUSHED
    THROUGH A PRESS
¼ CUP EXTRA-VIRGIN OLIVE OIL
1 LONG NARROW LOAF OF ITALIAN OR
    FRENCH BREAD
4 OUNCES OLIVADA (OLIVE PASTE),
    AVAILABLE AT ITALIAN MARKETS AND
    SPECIALTY FOOD SHOPS

1~ Preheat the oven to 400°.
2~ In a small bowl, combine the garlic and olive oil.
3~ Cut the bread into 48 slices, ½ inch thick. If all you can find is a wide loaf (about 4 inches around), cut 24 slices and then cut each one in half. Arrange the bread on a couple of large baking sheets and toast in the oven, turning once, until lightly browned, about 5 minutes on each side. Brush the warm toasts on one side only with the garlic oil. *(The recipe can be prepared to this point up to 6 hours ahead. Set aside at room temperature.)*

4~ Up to 1 hour before serving, spread the oiled side of the toasts with olivada and arrange on a serving tray. Cover with plastic wrap before serving at room temperature.
Note: To make Olive-Cheese Toasts: Follow the recipe for Olive Toasts through Step 3, but put them on a baking sheet rather than a serving tray. Top each toast with a thin slice of mozzarella cheese (about ½ pound total). Just before serving, bake in a 400° oven until the cheese melts, about 5 minutes. Serve hot.

MAKES 48 TOASTS
RECIPE BY NANCY VERDE BARR

TUNA AND ROASTED RED PEPPER SPREAD

Here's a year-round favorite that's sure to please your guests. Spread it on breads, toasts, crackers or vegetables.

1 LARGE RED BELL PEPPER
1 CAN (6½ OUNCES) TUNA, PACKED IN
   OLIVE OIL, DRAINED
6 TABLESPOONS UNSALTED BUTTER,
   SOFTENED
1 TABLESPOON FRESH LEMON JUICE
½ TEASPOON SALT
½ TEASPOON FRESHLY GROUND BLACK
   PEPPER

1~ Roast the pepper directly over a gas flame or under the broiler as close to the heat as possible, turning, until charred all over. Place the pepper in a bag and let steam for 10 minutes. Peel the pepper over a bowl. Remove the core, seeds and ribs; coarsely chop the pepper.

2~ In a food processor, combine the tuna, butter, lemon juice, salt, black pepper and half of the roasted pepper. Process until smooth, about 2 minutes. Add the remaining roasted pepper and process until just finely chopped.

3~ Pack the mousse into a crock or a bowl and refrigerate, covered, overnight. Let soften slightly before serving.

MAKES 2 CUPS
RECIPE BY MICHAEL MCLAUGHLIN

ORECCHIETTE WITH OLIVES, VEGETABLES AND MOZZARELLA

Orecchiette, literally "little ears," is a disk-shaped pasta that is fun to eat, but hardly essential to the success of this dish. Feel free to substitute ziti, rigatoni or fusilli. Quick and fresh and light, this pasta can serve as a simple main course or a side dish.

3 TABLESPOONS OLIVE OIL
2 MEDIUM ZUCCHINI—SCRUBBED,
   TRIMMED AND CUT INTO ½-INCH CUBES
¼ TEASPOON SALT
½ TEASPOON FRESHLY GROUND PEPPER
8 OUNCES ORECCHIETTE OR OTHER
   SHAPED PASTA, SUCH AS ZITI OR
   RIGATONI
1 CUP CALAMATA OLIVES, PITTED AND
   COARSELY CHOPPED
3 FIRM, RIPE TOMATOES, PEELED AND
   DICED
1 CUP FRESHLY GRATED PARMESAN CHEESE
8 OUNCES WHOLE-MILK MOZZARELLA,
   CUT INTO ½-INCH DICE, AT ROOM
   TEMPERATURE

1~ In a large skillet, preferably nonstick, heat the olive oil. Add the zucchini and cook over moderately high heat, stirring occasionally, until lightly browned, about 5 minutes. Season with the salt and ¼ teaspoon of the pepper. Using a slotted spoon, transfer the zucchini to a large bowl.

2~ In a large pot of boiling salted water, cook the orecchiette, stirring occasionally, until tender but still firm, 10 to 12 minutes. Drain immediately, rinse under cold water and drain again. In a bowl, toss the pasta with the zucchini. *(The recipe can be made to this point several hours ahead. Cover with plastic wrap and set aside at room temperature.)*

3~ Preheat the oven to 375°. Butter a large, shallow baking dish.

4~ Add the olives, tomatoes, ½ cup of the Parmesan cheese and the remaining ¼ teaspoon pepper to the pasta and toss well. Spoon the mixture into the prepared dish.

5~ Scatter the mozzarella evenly over the pasta. Bake in the upper third of the oven until the cheese is melted and the pasta is heated through, about 10 minutes. Pass the remaining ½ cup Parmesan cheese at the table.

SERVES 4 AS A MAIN COURSE OR 6 AS A FIRST COURSE
RECIPE BY MICHAEL MCLAUGHLIN

TRICOLOR SALAD

Salads are meant to please the eye as well as the palate. This one does a great job of meeting both criteria.

1 LARGE BUNCH OF ARUGULA
1 LARGE OR 2 SMALL HEADS OF
   RADICCHIO, TORN INTO LARGE PIECES
3 TO 4 BELGIAN ENDIVE, CUT INTO
   ½-INCH LENGTHS
3 TABLESPOONS EXTRA-VIRGIN OLIVE OIL
2 TEASPOONS RED WINE VINEGAR
SALT AND FRESHLY GROUND PEPPER

1~ In a salad bowl, combine the arugula, radicchio and endive.
2~ Just before serving, pour the oil and vinegar over the salad. Season with salt and pepper to taste. Toss well to coat.

SERVES 8
RECIPE BY ARTHUR GOLD AND ROBERT FIZDALE

CHOCOLATE PECAN PUDDING WITH BOURBON SAUCE

Midway between a chocolate cake and a soufflé, this pudding can be served right from the oven or allowed to cool slightly. Although it sinks a bit when fully cooled, it is still delicious and moist.

4 OUNCES SEMISWEET CHOCOLATE,
   CHOPPED
1½ CUPS PECAN PIECES (ABOUT 5½
   OUNCES)
⅓ CUP SUGAR
¼ CUP DRY BREAD CRUMBS
¼ TEASPOON GROUND CINNAMON
¼ POUND (1 STICK) UNSALTED BUTTER,
   SOFTENED
1 TABLESPOON BOURBON
5 EGGS, SEPARATED
PINCH OF SALT
BOURBON SAUCE (AT RIGHT)

1~ Preheat the oven to 350°. Butter a 1½-quart baking dish or 8-inch square baking pan.
2~ Place the chocolate in a small heatproof bowl. Add 3 tablespoons of hot water and set the bowl over a pan of hot but not simmering water. Stir with a whisk until the chocolate is melted and smooth. Remove the bowl from the water and let the chocolate cool to room temperature.
3~ Coarsely chop the pecan pieces in a food processor. Remove ½ cup of the pecans and set aside. Add 1 tablespoon of the sugar to the remaining nuts and grind to a fine powder. Combine the finely ground pecans, bread crumbs and cinnamon in a bowl; mix well and set the ground pecan mixture aside.

4~ In a large mixer bowl, beat the butter with 2 tablespoons plus 1 teaspoon of the sugar until soft and light. Beat in the cooled chocolate and then the bourbon. Add the egg yolks, 1 at a time, beating until smooth. Stir in the ground pecan mixture.
5~ In a large bowl, beat the egg whites with the salt until they form very soft peaks. Gradually beat in the remaining 2 tablespoons sugar and continue beating until the egg whites hold soft peaks. Stir one-fourth of the beaten egg whites into the chocolate batter to lighten it. Gently fold in the remaining egg whites.
6~ Pour the batter into the prepared baking dish. Smooth the top. Scatter the reserved chopped pecans evenly over the surface of the batter. Place the baking dish in a larger pan and pour hot tap water into the larger pan to reach halfway up the side of the baking dish.
7~ Bake the pudding in the middle of the oven for 30 to 35 minutes, until the pudding puffs and feels slightly firm when pressed with the palm of the hand; do not overbake.
8~ To serve, spoon the warm chocolate pecan pudding onto dessert plates. Ladle 2 or 3 tablespoons of the Bourbon Sauce over or around the pudding. Pass the remaining sauce separately.

SERVES 6 TO 8
RECIPE BY NICHOLAS MALGIERI

BOURBON SAUCE

Custard sauces are so versatile that you can flavor them to your taste by substituting a favorite liquor or liqueur. Or omit the alcohol altogether and double the vanilla.

1½ CUPS MILK
⅓ CUP SUGAR
4 EGG YOLKS
2 TABLESPOONS BOURBON
1 TEASPOON VANILLA EXTRACT

1~ In a medium nonreactive saucepan, combine the milk and sugar. Bring to a boil over moderate heat.
2~ Beat the egg yolks in a small bowl until liquefied. When the milk boils, gradually whisk one-third of it into the yolks. Return the remaining milk to a boil over low heat and whisk in the yolk mixture. Cook, whisking constantly, until the sauce thickens, 1 to 1½ minutes; do not let boil. Immediately remove from the heat.
3~ Whisk the sauce constantly for 1 minute to cool. Strain through a fine sieve into a bowl and whisk for 30 seconds. Stir in the bourbon and vanilla. Serve the sauce warm.
Note: If it is necessary to reheat the sauce, pour it into a heatproof bowl and whisk over a pan of simmering water until just warm, about 2 minutes.

MAKES ABOUT 2 CUPS
RECIPE BY NICHOLAS MALGIERI

POPCORN CANDY

Game-playing nights require sweet snacks like this one—eating it won't monopolize your attention during the game.

3 CUPS SUGAR
½ CUP LIGHT CORN SYRUP
¼ CUP VEGETABLE OIL
½ CUP POPPING CORN
1 CUP PECANS
1 CUP ALMONDS
½ CUP WALNUTS
½ CUP MACADAMIA NUTS

1~ Preheat the oven to 350°.
2~ Place the sugar in a medium saucepan and drizzle the corn syrup over it. Cook over moderately low heat until the sugar melts and becomes golden, about 45 minutes.
3~ Meanwhile, pour 3 tablespoons of the oil into a large saucepan. Add the popping corn. Cover and cook over moderate heat, shaking constantly, until all of the corn has popped; set aside.
4~ Spread the pecans, almonds, walnuts and macadamias on a large baking sheet. Bake for about 10 minutes, until lightly toasted. Let cool. Add to the popcorn.
5~ Use the remaining 1 tablespoon of oil to grease two 12-by-18-inch baking sheets. Divide the popcorn mixture between the baking sheets.
6~ Drizzle the hot caramel evenly over both batches of popcorn and nuts. When cool, place the candy on a flat surface and break into pieces. Store in an airtight tin.

MAKES ABOUT 10 CUPS
RECIPE BY DIANA STURGIS

PECAN BRITTLE

127

Pecans add a distinctive Southern taste to this snack, one of the best munchies on earth.

2 CUPS PECANS, BROKEN INTO SMALL PIECES
1 CUP SUGAR
1 CUP LIGHT CORN SYRUP
1 TABLESPOON BAKING SODA, SIFTED

1~ Butter a large baking sheet; set aside.
2~ In a large saucepan, combine the pecans, sugar and corn syrup. Bring to a boil over moderate heat, stirring constantly. Continue to boil without stirring until the syrup reaches the hard-crack stage (300° on a candy thermometer), about 15 minutes. Immediately remove from the heat and quickly stir in the baking soda (the caramel mixture will start to foam). Pour the brittle onto the buttered baking sheet and let stand until cool enough to handle.
3~ With a spatula, stretch the candy out to fill the sheet, making it as thin as possible. Let cool completely until hard; then break into small pieces. *(The brittle can be stored in an airtight container for up to 1 month.)*

MAKES 1¼ POUNDS
RECIPE BY LEE BAILEY

■ ■ ■

GUESS WHO'S COMING TO DINNER

It doesn't happen often, but it does happen. You're faced with planning and cooking a meal for people you've never met. It could be a business associate from out of town, an important client, an exchange student, visiting professor, errant great aunt or the friend of a friend. You have no idea of what they like or dislike. ∼ What do you do? Easy–you take a look at this menu. If your plans include cocktails and hors d'oeuvre, the Prosciutto and Cheese Appetizer Toasts will suit the occasion. If your strangers don't eat pork, skip the hors d'oeuvre altogether. Proceed directly to the table, instead, and sit down to the rich vegetable and cheese soup. Serve the main dishes family-style so guests need take only what they want to eat. Explain what is in each dish: the chicken is marinated with garlic and lemon thyme, sautéed in olive oil and coated with a creamy shallot glaze; the potatoes are layered with sweet marjoram and Parmesan and baked until browned and bubbly. For dessert, go absolutely all-American with Chocolate Fudge Sheba from Commander's Palace in New Orleans or serve scoops of chocolate-cinnamon ice cream in your prettiest stemmed glasses.

■ ■ ■

Chocolate
Fudge Sheba

GUESS WHO'S
COMING TO DINNER

Serves 6 to 8

Prosciutto and Cheese Appetizer Toasts

Broccoli, Onion and Cheese Soup
crusty bread or homemade croutons

Chicken Scallops with Shallots and
Lemon Thyme

Scalloped Potatoes with
Sweet Marjoram
and Parmesan Cheese

Spinach Salad with Warm Balsamic
Dressing

COFFEE
Chocolate Fudge Sheba
Chocolate-Cinnamon Ice Cream

PROSCIUTTO AND
CHEESE APPETIZER
TOASTS

Serve these toasts along with welcoming cocktails before you call your guests to the table.

4 NOT-TOO-THIN SLICES OF PROSCIUTTO
  (ABOUT 3 OUNCES)
8 SLICES OF ITALIAN OR FRENCH BREAD,
  ABOUT 3 INCHES IN DIAMETER, CUT
  ½ INCH THICK
¼ POUND ITALIAN FONTINA OR
  MOZZARELLA CHEESE, SHREDDED
4 FRESH SAGE OR BASIL LEAVES
ABOUT ¼ CUP EXTRA-VIRGIN OLIVE OIL
1 LARGE GARLIC CLOVE, SMASHED AND
  PEELED
1 SMALL FRESH OR DRIED HOT PEPPER
1 LEMON, QUARTERED
SPRIG OF FRESH SAGE OR BASIL, FOR
  GARNISH

1~ Fold a slice of prosciutto over each of 4 slices of the bread. Top each with 1 heaping tablespoon of the shredded cheese and a sage or basil leaf. Sandwich each with a second slice of bread.

2~ In a large heavy skillet, heat ¼ cup olive oil with the garlic and hot pepper over moderate heat. When the garlic sizzles, carefully lay the sandwiches in the oil. Fry until the bottom slice of the bread is golden, about 4 minutes. With a wide spatula, turn the sandwiches over, add a little more oil if needed and reduce the heat slightly. Fry until the second side is golden and the cheese is melted but not runny, about 3 minutes.

3~ Place the sandwiches on a serving plate and cut them in half. If desired, warm the remaining oil in the pan and drizzle a little of the seasoned oil over the sandwiches. Garnish with the lemon quarters and a small sprig of fresh sage or basil. Serve hot.

SERVES 8
RECIPE BY RICHARD SAX

BROCCOLI, ONION AND CHEESE SOUP

A small serving of this rich soup makes a fine opener. Don't use huge bowls, though, or guests will fill up before you want them to.

5 TABLESPOONS UNSALTED BUTTER
2 LARGE BERMUDA ONIONS, THINLY SLICED
¼ TEASPOON FRESHLY GROUND BLACK
   PEPPER
3 SPRIGS OF FRESH THYME OR ½ TEA-
   SPOON DRIED
1 TABLESPOON SUGAR
¾ CUP RIESLING OR OTHER SWEET WHITE
   WINE
3 CUPS CHICKEN STOCK OR CANNED LOW-
   SALT CHICKEN BROTH
3 TABLESPOONS ALL-PURPOSE FLOUR
1½ CUPS MILK
½ CUP HEAVY CREAM
¼ TEASPOON DRY MUSTARD
⅛ TEASPOON FRESHLY GROUND NUTMEG
DASH OF CAYENNE
½ POUND JARLSBERG CHEESE, GRATED
¼ CUP GRUYÈRE CHEESE, GRATED
1 BUNCH OF BROCCOLI, SEPARATED INTO
   1½-INCH FLORETS (ABOUT 4 CUPS)
1 RED BELL PEPPER, CUT INTO ¼-INCH DICE

1~ In a large heavy stovetop casserole, melt 2 tablespoons of the butter over moderately high heat. Add the onions, black pepper, thyme and sugar. Reduce the heat to moderately low, place a circle of waxed paper directly over the top of the onions and cover tightly with a lid. Simmer, stirring occasionally, until the onions are very soft and golden, about 1 hour and 15 minutes.

2~ Remove the cover and the waxed paper and increase the heat to moderate. Cook until the onions are golden brown, about 25 minutes.
3~ Add the wine and boil until it is reduced by half, about 5 minutes. Add the chicken stock and 2 cups of water. Bring to a boil and simmer for 15 minutes.
4~ In a large saucepan, melt the remaining 3 tablespoons butter over moderate heat. Whisk in the flour and cook, stirring, for 2 minutes without browning. Whisk in the milk, cream, dry mustard, nutmeg and cayenne and bring to a boil. Boil, stirring, for 2 minutes. Remove from the heat and stir in the Jarlsberg and Gruyère until smooth.
5~ Scrape the cheese mixture into the hot soup, add the broccoli and cook until crisp-tender, about 8 minutes. Stir in the red pepper and cook until heated through, about 2 minutes. If desired, run each bowl of soup under the broiler for a minute or two, until lightly browned on top. Serve hot.

SERVES 8 TO 10
RECIPE BY MIMI RUTH BRODEUR

SPINACH SALAD WITH WARM BALSAMIC DRESSING

The balanced, mellow flavor of balsamic vinegar makes possible a one-to-one vinegar-to-oil ratio. The warm dressing softens the spinach slightly without wilting it, and the toasted almonds are deliciously crunchy.

½ POUND FRESH SPINACH, TORN INTO
   BITE-SIZE PIECES
1 LARGE RED BELL PEPPER, CUT INTO THIN
   STRIPS
¼ CUP BALSAMIC VINEGAR
¼ CUP FRUITY OLIVE OIL
2 GARLIC CLOVES, MINCED
¼ TEASPOON FRESHLY GROUND BLACK
   PEPPER
½ CUP SLICED TOASTED ALMONDS

1~ In a medium bowl, combine the spinach and bell pepper.
2~ In a small nonreactive saucepan, whisk the vinegar and oil until well blended. Whisk in the garlic and black pepper. Warm the dressing over low heat, stirring, until heated through, about 1 minute.
3~ Pour the warm dressing over the spinach and red pepper and toss until coated. Just before serving, add the almonds and toss to mix.

SERVES 6
RECIPE BY ANNE MONTGOMERY

CHICKEN SCALLOPS WITH SHALLOTS AND LEMON THYME

132

Since these chicken breasts marinate overnight, be sure to do your shopping the day before the dinner.

5 TABLESPOONS FRUITY OLIVE OIL

3 LARGE GARLIC CLOVES, SLIVERED LENGTHWISE

15 SMALL SPRIGS OF LEMON THYME PLUS 1½ TEASPOONS MINCED FRESH LEMON THYME

1¼ POUNDS SKINLESS, BONELESS CHICKEN BREAST HALVES, POUNDED FLAT

3 SHALLOTS, MINCED

½ CUP DRY WHITE WINE OR DRY VERMOUTH

¾ CUP CHICKEN STOCK OR CANNED BROTH

1½ TEASPOONS DIJON-STYLE MUSTARD

¼ TEASPOON FRESHLY GROUND PEPPER

½ CUP CRÈME FRAÎCHE OR HEAVY CREAM

SALT

1~Rub 1 tablespoon of the oil over the bottom of a 9-inch square baking dish. Scatter one-third of the slivered garlic and one-third of the lemon thyme sprigs over the bottom. Top with half of the chicken. Repeat this layering of oil, garlic, thyme and the chicken, ending with a sprinkling of the remaining garlic and thyme sprigs. Cover tightly with plastic wrap and let marinate in the refrigerator overnight.

2~In a large heavy skillet, heat the remaining 2 tablespoons oil over moderately high heat. Add the shallots and minced lemon thyme and stir-fry until golden, about 2 minutes. Using a slotted spoon, transfer the herbed shallots to a small plate.

3~Increase the heat to high, add the chicken in batches and sauté, turning, until browned, about 1 minute per side; transfer to a plate as the pieces are cooked. Add the wine to the skillet and bring to a boil, scraping up any browned bits from the bottom of the pan. Boil until the wine reduces to a rich amber glaze, 2 to 3 minutes.

4~Return the shallots to the skillet, add the chicken stock and blend in the mustard and pepper. Boil, stirring constantly, until the sauce has reduced by about two-thirds, 3 to 4 minutes. Stir in the crème fraîche and boil until reduced by half, about 2 minutes. Season the sauce with salt to taste.

5~Reduce the heat to low, return the chicken to the skillet and warm through, spooning the sauce over the top, about 2 minutes. Serve on heated plates.

SERVES 6
RECIPE BY JEAN ANDERSON

SCALLOPED POTATOES WITH SWEET MARJORAM AND PARMESAN CHEESE

Scalloped potatoes add a warm and felicitous touch to any meal.

4 LARGE BAKING POTATOES, PEELED AND THINLY SLICED

1 TEASPOON SALT

¼ TEASPOON FRESHLY GROUND PEPPER

¼ TEASPOON FRESHLY GRATED NUTMEG

2 MEDIUM GARLIC CLOVES, MINCED

¼ CUP MODERATELY FINELY CHOPPED FRESH SWEET MARJORAM

¼ CUP FRESHLY GRATED PARMESAN CHEESE

2 CUPS HEAVY CREAM

1~Preheat the oven to 350°. Butter a 6-cup gratin dish or shallow casserole.

2~Layer one-fifth of the potato slices in the gratin dish and season with one-quarter each of the salt, pepper, nutmeg, garlic, marjoram and Parmesan. Repeat the layering 3 times. Top with a final layer of potato slices, overlapping them attractively.

3~Combine the cream with ½ cup of water and pour evenly over the potatoes. Cover the dish snugly with aluminum foil.

4~Bake the potatoes for 1½ hours, then uncover and bake for 30 minutes longer, or until lightly browned. Remove from the oven and let stand for 10 minutes before serving.

SERVES 6 TO 8
RECIPE BY JEAN ANDERSON

CHOCOLATE-CINNAMON ICE CREAM

This combination of flavors is unexpected in ice cream, but utterly irresistible. Try it.

3 CUPS HEAVY CREAM
1 CUP MILK
¾ CUP SUGAR
¾ TEASPOON GROUND CINNAMON, OR
   2 CINNAMON STICKS
4 EGG YOLKS
3 OUNCES SEMISWEET CHOCOLATE
1 OUNCE UNSWEETENED CHOCOLATE

1 ~ In a large heavy saucepan, combine the cream, milk, sugar and cinnamon. Cook over moderately high heat, stirring occasionally, until the sugar is dissolved and the mixture is hot.

2 ~ In a medium bowl, whisk the egg yolks briefly. Gradually whisk in 1 cup of the hot cream mixture. Slowly whisk the egg yolk mixture into the remaining hot cream in the saucepan.

3 ~ Cook the custard over moderate heat, stirring constantly, until it thickens enough to coat the back of a spoon lightly, about 8 minutes. Do not let it boil.

4 ~ In a double boiler or heavy saucepan, melt the semisweet and unsweetened chocolate over low heat, stirring occasionally, until smooth.

5 ~ Gradually stir 2 cups of the custard into the chocolate; whisk to blend well. Stir the chocolate mixture into the remaining custard in the saucepan and blend well. Strain into a stainless steel bowl and let cool to room temperature. Chill, if possible, before churning.

6 ~ Freeze in an ice cream maker according to the manufacturer's instructions.

MAKES ABOUT 1 QUART
RECIPE BY JERRIE STROM

CHOCOLATE FUDGE SHEBA

Since all the world loves chocolate, it follows that all of your guests will love this sumptuous indulgence from the esteemed New Orleans restaurant, Commander's Palace. The pecans that top this easy-to-make dessert bespeak its Southern heritage.

1¼ POUNDS SEMISWEET CHOCOLATE,
   BROKEN INTO PIECES
6 EGG YOLKS
6 OUNCES (1½ STICKS) UNSALTED
   BUTTER, AT ROOM TEMPERATURE
7 EGG WHITES
½ CUP SUGAR
1 CUP PECAN HALVES OR PIECES
UNSWEETENED WHIPPED CREAM OR
   VANILLA CUSTARD SAUCE, AS
   ACCOMPANIMENT

1 ~ Butter a 9-inch springform pan.

2 ~ Melt the chocolate in a double boiler over barely simmering water, stirring until smooth. Set aside to cool.

3 ~ In a medium bowl over simmering water, whisk the egg yolks until warmed through and lighter in color, about 2 minutes. Remove from the heat and whisk until cool, about 1 minute.

4 ~ In a large bowl, beat the butter until light and fluffy. Fold in the cooled melted chocolate. Fold in the egg yolks.

5 ~ In a large bowl, beat the egg whites until soft peaks begin to form. Gradually beat in the sugar, 1 tablespoon at a time, until the meringue forms stiff peaks. Fold the meringue into the chocolate mixture; pour into the buttered pan.

6 ~ Arrange or sprinkle the pecans over the top and lightly press them into the chocolate. Cover with plastic wrap. Refrigerate until set, at least 3 hours.

7 ~ To serve, remove the sides of the springform. Cut into wedges and serve with whipped cream or custard sauce.

SERVES 12 TO 16
RECIPE FROM COMMANDER'S PALACE, NEW ORLEANS

133

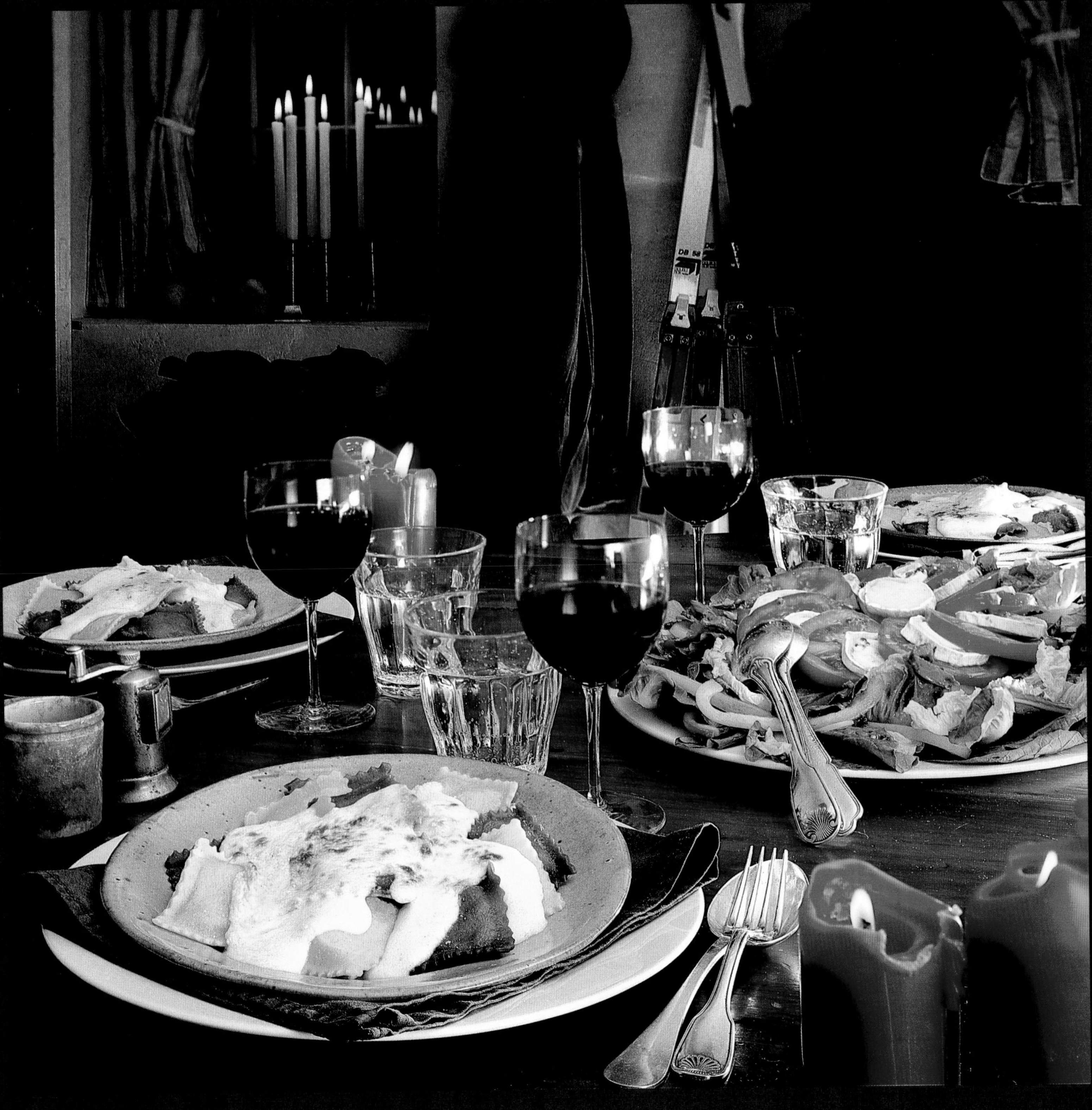

■ ■ ■

THE
CLARENCE BIRDSEYE
MEMORIAL
FRIDAY NIGHT SUPPER

We're all so fortunate to live now: after Thomas Edison discovered electricity, after running water replaced the hand pump and after dear Clarence Birdseye invented a way to deep-freeze foods commercially. Thanks to Clarence, we can buy frozen foods, we can squirrel away a store of seasonal favorites for off-season treats, and we can prepare foods ahead of time so that they're always just about ready to use. Foods prepared in advance and frozen for safekeeping are especially convenient for Friday night entertaining. ∽ Nearly every dish in this menu can be made well ahead of time and refrigerated or frozen until needed; only the pasta sauces and salad are assembled quickly from fresh ingredients. As guests arrive, serve Honey Walnuts along with cocktails. Then bring out one of the pâtés (save the other for a no-work weekend lunch or dinner), some French bread, sharp mustard and cornichons and open a bottle of wine. You'll have all the time you need to prepare the pasta, sauce and salad. And since you're so organized, homemade brown sugar ice cream is in the freezer at the ready for dessert.

■ ■ ■

*Potato, Onion
and Cheese
Ravioli in Cheese
Béchamel*

*Composed Salad
of Tomatoes,
Peppers and
Goat Cheese*

HONEY WALNUTS

THE CLARENCE BIRDSEYE MEMORIAL FRIDAY NIGHT SUPPER

Serves 6

COCKTAILS
Honey Walnuts

HEARTY RED WINE,
SUCH AS CÔTES DU RHÔNE
Pâté de Campagne
with bread, cornichons and sharp mustard

Potato, Onion and Cheese Ravioli in Cheese Béchamel or Creamy Tomato Sauce

Composed Salad of Tomatoes, Peppers and Goat Cheese

COFFEE
Brown Sugar Ice Cream
store-bought cookies

Because these sweet, crisp walnuts are irresistible, we recommend making a generous batch. No one can eat just one, and extras keep well—refrigerated or frozen—for a very long time.

12 OUNCES WALNUT HALVES (ABOUT
   3½ CUPS)
¼ CUP SUGAR
4 CUPS PEANUT OIL

1~ In a medium saucepan, bring 4 to 5 cups of water to a boil over high heat. Add the walnuts and boil for 5 minutes to remove any bitterness. Drain, rinse under cold running water and drain again. Pour 5 cups of fresh cold water into the saucepan and bring to a boil. Again, add the nuts, cook for 5 minutes, drain, rinse and drain well. Let the nuts drain thoroughly on paper towels.

2~ In a wok, bring ¼ cup plus 2 tablespoons of water to a boil over high heat. Add the sugar and cook, stirring constantly to dissolve the sugar. Boil for 1 minute. Add the walnuts. Stir until the walnuts are coated with syrup and the remaining liquid in the wok evaporates, about 4 minutes. Remove the walnuts and set them aside. Rinse the wok out with extremely hot water to remove the sugar. Dry it well.

3~ Heat the oil in the wok over high heat until it begins to smoke, 350° to 375°. Add the walnuts and fry, stirring occasionally with a wooden spoon or chopsticks to keep the nuts separate, until they turn golden brown, 4 to 5 minutes. Drain in a strainer and spread out on a plate to cool completely. Separate, if necessary, as soon as they are cool enough to handle. (*The nuts can be made ahead and kept in a tightly closed container in the refrigerator for up to 10 days or frozen for 3 to 4 weeks. Let return to room temperature before serving.*)

MAKES ABOUT 3½ CUPS
RECIPE BY EILEEN YIN-FEI LO

PÂTÉ DE CAMPAGNE

This pistachio-studded pâté is easy to assemble. The recipe makes two loaf-size pâtés and should be prepared at least two days in advance so that the flavors can mellow.

2 CUPS FRESH BREAD CRUMBS

¾ CUP HEAVY CREAM

½ POUND WELL-CHILLED FRESH PORK FAT, CUT INTO 1-INCH CUBES

¾ POUND CHICKEN LIVERS, TRIMMED

2 EGGS

1 MEDIUM-LARGE ONION, MINCED

2 LARGE GARLIC CLOVES, MINCED

1 TABLESPOON SALT

2 TEASPOONS FRESHLY GROUND PEPPER

1 TEASPOON GROUND THYME

2 TEASPOONS GROUND ALLSPICE

1 TEASPOON GROUND ROSEMARY

1 TEASPOON GROUND GINGER

1 TEASPOON DRY MUSTARD

½ CUP COGNAC OR OTHER BRANDY

½ CUP CALVADOS OR APPLEJACK

1 POUND VEAL, PREFERABLY GROUND TWICE

1 POUND PORK, PREFERABLY GROUND TWICE

1 CUP SHELLED UNSALTED PISTACHIOS

1½ POUNDS THICKLY SLICED BACON

4 LARGE IMPORTED BAY LEAVES

1~ In a small bowl, combine the bread crumbs and heavy cream; set aside. Place the pork fat in a food processor and finely chop. Transfer to a large bowl. Add the chicken livers to the processor and finely chop; add to the pork fat.

2~ In a medium bowl, whisk together the eggs, onion and garlic. Whisk in the salt, pepper, thyme, allspice, rosemary, ginger and mustard. Stir in the Cognac and Calvados.

3~ Add the ground veal and pork to the chopped pork fat and livers. Mix with your hands until well blended. Mix in the bread crumbs and cream, then blend in the egg mixture. Stir in the pistachios until evenly distributed.

4~ Preheat the oven to 350°. Line two 9-by-5-by-3-inch loaf pans crosswise with the sliced bacon, leaving some overhang on each side and reserving 4 strips for the tops.

5~ Fill the pans with the meat mixture, pressing it evenly into the corners. Fold the bacon over the top of each pâté and arrange 2 bay leaves on each. Top with the reserved bacon strips. Cover the pans with a double thickness of foil and set in a deep roasting pan. Pour in enough hot water to reach three-fourths of the way up the pans.

6~ Bake for 1 hour and 45 minutes, or until a knife inserted into the pâtés comes out clean.

7~ Remove the pans from the water bath. Peel off the foil and let cool. Cover the pâtés with plastic wrap and place one on top of the other. Place two 14-ounce cans on the top of the pâté and refrigerate, weighted, for 2 days. (The pâtés can be prepared a week ahead. Remove the weights after 2 days.)

8~ Unmold the pâtés and scrape off all the surrounding fat. Remove the bay leaves, leaving the bacon if desired. Slice and serve slightly chilled.

MAKES 2 PÂTÉS

RECIPE BY W. PETER PRESTCOTT

137

The Father of Frozen Foods

Clarence Birdseye worked for the United States Geographic Service from 1914 to 1917, and that made all the difference. While working in Labrador, Birdseye noticed that fish and caribou meat that froze in the chill Arctic air was fresh-tasting and tender when cooked several months later. He knew that when foods were frozen slowly, by existing methods, large ice crystals formed between the cells. When defrosted, the food became mushy. He reasoned that if foods could be frozen quickly at extremely low temperatures, as they had done naturally in Labrador, crystals couldn't form and the texture of the food wouldn't be affected. And he was right. In 1924, at his home in Gloucester, Massachusetts, he invented a method for fast-freezing foods. This led to the founding of the General Foods Company, which still markets the Birds Eye brand. Next time you open a package of berries or corn or peas, think fondly of dear old Clarence, who made it all possible.

POTATO, ONION AND CHEESE RAVIOLI IN CHEESE BÉCHAMEL

138

This is actually three recipes rolled into one technique that leads to a finished dish. You can use one, two or all three recipes—say, make the pasta and substitute a different filling, or use just the filling recipe and buy sheets of pasta for shaping at home, or just make the béchamel recipe.

EGG PASTA:
ABOUT 2½ CUPS ALL-PURPOSE OR
   BREAD FLOUR
3 WHOLE EGGS
1 EGG YOLK
2 TEASPOONS OLIVE OIL
PINCH OF SALT

POTATO, ONION AND CHEESE FILLING:
2 MEDIUM BAKING POTATOES (ABOUT
   8 OUNCES EACH), PEELED AND
   QUARTERED
1 TABLESPOON OLIVE OIL
2 MEDIUM ONIONS, CHOPPED
½ CUP FRESHLY GRATED PARMESAN CHEESE
8 OUNCES FARMER'S CHEESE
1 EGG
1¼ TEASPOONS SALT
¼ TEASPOON FRESHLY GROUND WHITE
   PEPPER
¼ TEASPOON FRESHLY GRATED NUTMEG

BÉCHAMEL SAUCE WITH CHEESE:
2 CUPS MILK
BOUQUET GARNI: 5 SPRIGS OF PARSLEY,
   ¼ TEASPOON DRIED THYME AND
   ½ BAY LEAF TIED IN A DOUBLE THICK-
   NESS OF CHEESECLOTH
2 TABLESPOONS UNSALTED BUTTER
3 TABLESPOONS ALL-PURPOSE FLOUR
½ TEASPOON SALT
PINCH OF FRESHLY GROUND WHITE PEPPER
PINCH OF FRESHLY GRATED NUTMEG
½ CUP FRESHLY GRATED PARMESAN CHEESE
ADDITIONAL FRESHLY GRATED PARMESAN,
   FOR BROILING (OPTIONAL)

1~ *Make the Egg Pasta:* Place 2½ cups of flour in a medium bowl. Make a well in the center and add the whole eggs, egg yolk, oil and salt. Using your fingers or a fork, mix the wet ingredients, gradually incorporating the flour, until the mixture is blended and begins to mass together. The dough should be soft, pliable and sticky. If the dough is too dry and stiff or will not absorb the flour, add up to 2 tablespoons water, 1 teaspoon at a time. If it is too wet and sticky, add extra flour, 1 tablespoon at a time.

2~ Turn the dough out onto a lightly floured surface and knead for 8 to 10 minutes, until smooth and elastic.

3~ Shape the dough into a ball, dust lightly with flour and cover with plastic wrap. Let rest for at least 1 hour before rolling out. *(Though it is better if used the day it is made, the dough can be made 1 day ahead, tightly wrapped and refrigerated.)*

4~ Meanwhile, *make the Potato, Onion and Cheese Filling:* In a medium saucepan of boiling salted water, cook the potatoes until tender, 15 to 20 minutes. Drain; put through a ricer or the medium disk of a food mill.

5~ While the potatoes cook, heat the oil in a medium skillet over moderate heat. Add the onions and sauté until softened and translucent, about 5 minutes.

6~ Puree the onions in a food processor or pass through the medium disk of a food mill.

7~ In a large bowl, combine the potatoes, onions, Parmesan, farmer's cheese, egg, salt, pepper and nutmeg. Mix until well blended. *(The filling can be made 1 day ahead, covered and refrigerated.)*

8~ *Make and fill the ravioli:* Divide the disk of dough into sixths. Pat out each piece of dough into a rectangle. Fold the dough into thirds. Pass the dough through a pasta machine with the rollers set at the widest setting. Continue rolling the pasta into a sheet, reducing the space between the rollers by one number each time, until the pasta has run through at the thinnest setting. Roll out the remaining pieces of dough in the same fashion.

9~ Cut each long sheet of dough into 2 shorter lengths (each one will be at least 12 inches long).

To make ravioli using a ravioli mold, drape one sheet of the dough over the mold. Set the top of the mold in place and push down to form the pockets for the filling. Spoon the filling into the indentations. Paint all of the exposed dough with water. Cover the mold with another sheet of pasta. Press down the center and crosswise between the ravioli to force out as much air as possible. Press around the outside rim of the mold to seal the dough. Roll a rolling pin over the edges of the mold to seal and cut the ravioli. Pop the ravioli out of the mold; continue making more ravioli until the filling and remaining pasta are used.

To make free-form ravioli, without a mold, place a sheet of dough on a flat surface. Spoon or pipe mounds of filling onto the dough, leaving space between the mounds. Paint the exposed areas with water. Drape a second sheet of pasta over the first. Press down around the mounds of filling to remove the air and to shape the ravioli with your fingers. Press well to seal the edges. Cut out the ravioli with a pastry wheel or ravioli stamp. *(Fresh ravioli freeze beautifully. Simply spread them out on a baking sheet and freeze until hard. Transfer them to a plastic bag and seal well. Cook frozen ravioli just as you would fresh; the cooking time is approximately the same.)*

10~ Meanwhile, preheat the broiler.

11~ Cook the ravioli, 12 at a time, in a large pot of boiling salted water for 6 to 7 minutes, until the pasta is al dente. The filling will be hot and cooked through. Do not overcrowd or the ravioli might stick together. Drain well.

12~ *Make the Béchamel Sauce:* In a heavy medium saucepan, combine the milk and bouquet garni and bring to a boil.

13~ Meanwhile, in another heavy medium saucepan, melt the butter over moderate heat. Add the flour and cook, stirring, for 1 to 2 minutes without browning to make a roux.

14~ Whisking constantly, strain the boiling milk into the roux. Return to a boil and cook, whisking, until the sauce is thickened and smooth, 3 to 4 minutes. Season with the salt, pepper and nutmeg. Stir in the cheese.

15~ *To serve:* coat each portion of ravioli with some of the sauce. Sprinkle on additional Parmesan, if desired. Run under the broiler for 30 seconds, or until lightly browned and bubbly. Serve at once.

MAKES 72 RAVIOLI, ENOUGH FOR 6 MAIN-COURSE SERVINGS OR 10 FIRST-COURSE SERVINGS
RECIPE BY JOHN ROBERT MASSIE

CREAMY TOMATO SAUCE

139

This simple sauce can be an alternative to béchamel or a standby for any other pasta dish.

1 CAN (35 OUNCES) PEELED ITALIAN
  TOMATOES, DRAINED
BOUQUET GARNI: 5 SPRIGS OF PARSLEY, ½
  TEASPOON THYME AND 5 PEPPERCORNS
  TIED IN A DOUBLE THICKNESS OF
  CHEESECLOTH
¾ CUP HEAVY CREAM
½ TEASPOON SALT
FRESHLY GROUND PEPPER

1~ Place the tomatoes in a blender or food processor and puree until smooth. Strain through a coarse mesh sieve to remove the seeds.

2~ In a large nonreactive skillet, bring the tomato puree with the bouquet garni to a boil over moderate heat. Boil, uncovered, for 5 minutes to reduce slightly. Stir in the cream and add the salt. Discard the bouquet garni. Season with additional salt and pepper to taste.

MAKES 1½ CUPS
RECIPE BY JOHN ROBERT MASSIE

Composed Salad of Tomatoes, Peppers and Goat Cheese

140 Make the vinaigrette before you begin to arrange the salad ingredients since it needs some time to develop its flavors.

SHALLOT VINAIGRETTE:
1 LARGE SHALLOT, MINCED
1 SMALL GARLIC CLOVE, MINCED
1 TABLESPOON CHOPPED FRESH PARSLEY
1½ TABLESPOONS RED WINE VINEGAR
1 TEASPOON DIJON-STYLE MUSTARD
½ TEASPOON SALT
½ TEASPOON FRESHLY GROUND PEPPER
¼ CUP EXTRA-VIRGIN OLIVE OIL

SALAD:
11-OUNCE LOG OF MONTRACHET OR
    OTHER MILD GOAT CHEESE, THINLY
    SLICED
2 POUNDS BEEFSTEAK TOMATOES, SLICED
2 BUNCHES OF ARUGULA, TOUGH STEMS
    REMOVED
1 HEAD OF BIBB LETTUCE, TORN INTO
    PIECES
2 RED BELL PEPPERS, CUT INTO THIN STRIPS
2 YELLOW BELL PEPPERS, CUT INTO THIN
    STRIPS

1~ In a small jar, combine the shallot, garlic, parsley, vinegar, mustard, salt and pepper. Cover with a tight lid and shake to blend well. Add the oil, shake again and set aside for at least 30 minutes.

2~ Arrange the goat cheese and tomatoes, overlapping the slices, in the center of a large platter. Drizzle the cheese and tomatoes with half of the Shallot Vinaigrette.

3~ In a large bowl, combine the arugula, lettuce and red and yellow pepper strips. Add the remaining vinaigrette and toss to coat. Arrange the tossed salad around the sliced tomatoes and cheese.

SERVES 8
SALAD RECIPE BY DIANA STURGIS
VINAIGRETTE RECIPE BY MARCIA KIESEL

Brown Sugar Ice Cream

Brown sugar adds a little nitty-gritty, down-home soul to what would otherwise be plain vanilla ice cream. We'd be sure to have cookies on hand to serve with this one.

4 EGG YOLKS
1 CUP PACKED LIGHT BROWN SUGAR
1 CUP HEAVY CREAM
3 CUPS HALF-AND-HALF OR LIGHT CREAM
1½ TEASPOONS VANILLA EXTRACT

1~ In a heavy medium nonreactive saucepan, whisk together the egg yolks and brown sugar until thick.

2~ In another medium saucepan, bring the cream and half-and-half just to a boil over moderate heat. Gradually whisk the hot cream into the egg yolk mixture in a thin stream.

3~ Cook over low heat, stirring constantly, until the custard is thick enough to coat the back of a spoon, about 6 minutes; do not boil.

4~ Immediately strain the custard into a medium bowl. Stir in the vanilla and let cool to room temperature, stirring occasionally, about 30 minutes. Cover with plastic wrap placed directly on the surface and refrigerate until very cold, at least 5 hours.

5~ Pour the cold custard into an ice cream maker and freeze according to the manufacturer's instructions. Let the ice cream soften slightly before serving.

MAKES 5½ CUPS
RECIPE BY MICHAEL MCLAUGHLIN

WINTER

■ ■ ■

NEW YEAR'S DAY OPEN HOUSE

January 1 offers a unique opportunity: You can host the first party of the new year. If your guest list is long, consider planning an open house from, say, two to six in the afternoon. This strategy offers great flexibility to guests and host alike. Those who had a late New Year's Eve needn't arise or arrive before their heads are cleared. People with other plans can stop by when convenient. Food can be prepared in quantity but put out in reasonable portions and replenished as needed. ~ Your refreshment menu will include Cognac eggnog, raspberry-infused Champagne punch and also hot spiced cider that contains no alcohol whatsoever. Finger foods – skewered sausage and peppers, *crostini* with pea puree and shallots in red wine – can be placed about the room or included on the buffet table. The main dishes include the traditional foods said to bring good luck in the coming year–fresh fish, pork and sauerkraut. There are black-eyed peas to bring wealth and braised mustard greens to benefit your health. And since some of your friends will be resolute about resolutions, dessert is simple – a fresh winter fruit salad and wedges of pungent but buttery ginger shortbread.

■ ■ ■

Crostini
with Pea Puree

Marinated Pork
and Red Cabbage

Shallots
in Red Wine

Skewered Sausages
and Peppers

Seppi Renggli's
Roasted
Whole Salmon

Orzo Salad
with Carrots
and Parsley

144

NEW YEAR'S DAY OPEN HOUSE

Serves 50 to 60

COGNAC EGGNOG

CHAMPAGNE PUNCH

HOT SPICED CIDER

Skewered Sausages and Peppers

Crostini with Pea Puree

*Seppi Renggli's Roasted Whole Salmon
with Fresh Herb Dressing*

Marinated Pork and Red Cabbage

Holiday Choucroute

Pennies and Dollars

Braised Mustard Greens

Orzo Salad with Carrots and Parsley

Shallots in Red Wine

Wintry Fruit Salad

Ginger Shortbread

COGNAC EGGNOG

This heady potion will ensure good spirits and holiday cheer. Serve it chilled in a punch bowl or glass pitcher and let your guests indulge themselves. Eggnog will keep in the refrigerator for up to one week.

8 EGGS
¾ CUP SUGAR
3 CUPS MILK
2 CUPS HEAVY CREAM
1¼ CUPS COGNAC
1 TEASPOON VANILLA EXTRACT
¾ TEASPOON FRESHLY GRATED NUTMEG

1~ In a large bowl, whisk the eggs with ¼ cup of the sugar until the mixture falls in a ribbon when the whisk is lifted, about 2 minutes.
2~ In a heavy medium saucepan, combine the milk and cream with the remaining ½ cup sugar. Bring to a boil, stirring to dissolve the sugar. Whisk all of the hot liquid into the egg/sugar mixture.
3~ Let the eggnog cool for 5 minutes. Stir in the Cognac, vanilla and nutmeg. Pour the eggnog into two 1-quart bottles, cover and let cool; then refrigerate.

MAKES ABOUT 2 QUARTS
RECIPE BY DIANA STURGIS

CHAMPAGNE PUNCH

You might want to make several batches of this punch and place them in different areas of the room to help avoid congestion at the bar.

2 PACKAGES (10 OUNCES EACH) FROZEN
    RASPBERRIES, THAWED
2 CUPS BRANDY
2 CUPS RASPBERRY BRANDY
½ CUP ORANGE-FLAVORED LIQUEUR, SUCH
    AS COINTREAU, TRIPLE SEC OR CURAÇAO
1 QUART CLUB SODA, CHILLED
2 BOTTLES (750 ML EACH) CHAMPAGNE OR
    SPARKLING WINE, CHILLED

1~ About 1 hour before serving, combine the raspberries, brandy, raspberry brandy and orange-flavored liqueur in a large punch bowl.
2~ Just before serving, place a block of ice in the punch bowl (or fill the bowl one-third full with ice cubes). Pour in the club soda and Champagne and stir gently. Serve the punch in cups or tall Champagne glasses.

SERVES 20
RECIPE BY W. PETER PRESTCOTT

HOT SPICED CIDER

Your New Year's Day menu might include a non-alcoholic drink. This formula for making hot apple cider steeped with spices can be multiplied at will to satisfy a crowd. Serve it in pitchers or thermal carafes situated at strategic locations around the room. It will make your house smell deliciously welcoming.

6 CUPS UNFILTERED APPLE CIDER
¼ CUP MAPLE SYRUP, OR TO TASTE
1 CINNAMON STICK, BROKEN UP
½ TEASPOON ALLSPICE BERRIES
¼ TEASPOON WHOLE CLOVES

1~ In a large saucepan, combine all of the ingredients. Cover and simmer for 5 minutes, or until heated through.
2~ Strain the cider into a pitcher or carafe and serve hot, in cups.

MAKES 6 CUPS
RECIPE BY ELIZABETH SCHNEIDER

SKEWERED SAUSAGES AND PEPPERS

You might want to use a combination of sweet *and* hot Italian sausages to make these skewered hors d'oeuvre. Don't forget—you'll need 40 short wooden skewers that have been soaked in cold water for one hour to prevent them from scorching under the broiler.

3 OR 4 RED BELL PEPPERS (1½ POUNDS),
   CUT INTO 1-INCH SQUARES
2 OR 3 GREEN BELL PEPPERS (1 POUND),
   CUT INTO 1-INCH SQUARES
3 TABLESPOONS OLIVE OIL
3 GARLIC CLOVES, SMASHED AND PEELED
¼ CUP CHOPPED FRESH PARSLEY
½ CUP WELL-DRAINED, CANNED ITALIAN
   PEELED TOMATOES
½ TEASPOON SALT
2 POUNDS SWEET OR HOT ITALIAN SAUSAGE

1~ Set aside 40 pieces each of the red and green peppers. Heat the oil in a medium nonreactive saucepan or stovetop casserole. Add the garlic and parsley and cook over moderately low heat until the garlic is fragrant and softened but not browned, 2 to 3 minutes. Add the remaining red and green peppers, cover the pan and cook until the peppers are slightly limp, about 8 minutes. Add the tomatoes and salt. Partially cover and cook until the peppers are soft, about 30 minutes.
2~ In a blender or food processor, puree the pepper-tomato mixture until smooth. Strain through a sieve into a small nonreactive saucepan. Cook over low heat, stirring occasionally, until the sauce is reduced enough to coat a spoon, about 5 minutes. *(The sauce can be made up to a day ahead. Let cool, then cover and refrigerate.)*
3~ Prick each sausage in 4 or 5 places. Place in a medium saucepan and add cold water to cover. Bring to a boil over high heat, reduce the heat to moderate and simmer for 8 minutes. Drain the sausages. When they are cool enough to handle, cut into ¾-inch-long pieces. *(The sausages can be prepared up to a day ahead. Wrap well and refrigerate.)*
4~ Assemble each portion by spearing 1 piece of red pepper, a piece of sausage and then 1 piece of green pepper on the end of a soaked wooden skewer. *(This stuzzichino can be assembled up to 2 hours ahead. Wrap in plastic and set aside at room temperature.)*
5~ Preheat the broiler. Place the skewers on a rack over a broiler pan. Broil for 4 minutes, until the sausages are lightly browned. Turn and broil for 4 minutes longer, or until lightly browned all over. Reheat the pepper-tomato sauce if necessary. Arrange the skewers on a tray and serve them along with the warm sauce for dipping.

MAKES 40 SKEWERS
RECIPE BY NANCY VERDE BARR

145

CROSTINI WITH PEA PUREE

146

If you choose to serve this as an hors d'oeuvre, cut each slice of bread in half. The pancetta, garlic and pea combination is delicious.

5 OUNCES PANCETTA, THINLY SLICED
4 GARLIC CLOVES
¼ CUP PLUS 2 TABLESPOONS OLIVE OIL
¾ POUND FRESH PEAS, OR 1 PACKAGE
(10 OUNCES) FROZEN PEAS
¼ CUP CHOPPED FRESH PARSLEY
¼ TEASPOON SALT
¼ TEASPOON FRESHLY GROUND PEPPER
18 SLICES OF ITALIAN BREAD, CUT ⅜ INCH
THICK

1~ Finely chop enough of the pancetta to yield ½ cup. In a large skillet, cook the chopped pancetta over moderate heat until crisp, about 5 minutes. Drain on paper towels; set aside.
2~ In a food processor, puree the remaining pancetta with 3 of the garlic cloves. Scrape the puree into a large skillet, add 2 tablespoons of the olive oil and cook over moderately low heat until the garlic is just golden, about 4 minutes. Add the fresh peas, 2 tablespoons of the parsley, the salt, pepper and ¼ cup of water. Cook until the peas are completely tender, 15 to 20 minutes. If using frozen peas, omit the water and cook for only 10 minutes.

3~ In a food processor, puree the cooked peas until smooth. Strain to remove the skins. Add 1 tablespoon of the olive oil and the remaining 2 tablespoons parsley and mix to blend well.
4~ Preheat the oven to 400°. Bake the bread slices directly on the oven rack until lightly toasted, about 4 minutes. Cut the remaining garlic clove in half and rub over one side of the toast slices. Brush the garlic-rubbed sides with the remaining 3 tablespoons olive oil. Spread 1 scant tablespoon of the pea puree over each toast slice and sprinkle with the reserved crisp pancetta.

SERVES 6 AS AN APPETIZER OR MAKES 36 HORS D'OEUVRE
RECIPE BY NANCY VERDE BARR

SEPPI RENGGLI'S ROASTED WHOLE SALMON

This fabulous fish, served by Seppi Renggli, chef at The Four Seasons in New York City, makes a grand presentation for an important party. Roasting brings out the finest flavor of the fish and doesn't perfume your kitchen with the smells of the sea the way poaching does. Order your fish well in advance so it is as fresh as possible for your party. Begin preparations three to four hours before you plan to serve the fish.

8-POUND WHOLE SALMON, AS FRESH AS
POSSIBLE
2 TABLESPOONS SALT
1 TABLESPOON FRESHLY GROUND PEPPER
2½ LEMONS
LARGE BOUQUET OF MIXED FRESH HERBS
SUCH AS TARRAGON, OREGANO,
ROSEMARY, BASIL, DILL, SAGE
GREEN TOPS FROM 1 OR 2 LEEKS
4 OR 5 DRIED FENNEL BRANCHES
(OPTIONAL)
PARSLEY OR JAPANESE RADISH SPROUTS
AND LEMON SLICES, FOR GARNISH
FRESH HERB DRESSING (AT RIGHT)
LEMON WEDGES

1~ Rinse the fish and dry well. With a very sharp knife, score the fish in a chevron pattern at ¼-inch intervals, cutting ½-inch deep from the backbone halfway down the side of the fish on a diagonal away from the head and then scoring the bottom half in the same way, slanting in the opposite direction.

FRESH HERB DRESSING

2~ Combine the salt and pepper. (Chef Renggli grinds 2 parts coarse salt to 1 part black peppercorns in a spice mill.) Liberally season one side of the fish with 2 to 3 teaspoons of this mixture. Squeeze on the juice of 1 lemon and rub the seasonings into the fish. Turn the salmon over and season the second side in the same way. Season the cavity of the fish with about ½ tablespoon of the salt and pepper mixture and the juice of half a lemon. Stuff the cavity with the herbs, leek greens and dried fennel if you have it; there should be plenty of greenery sticking out of the fish. Place on a rack or a tray lined with paper towels and refrigerate uncovered for 2 to 3 hours.

3~ Preheat the oven to 400°. Turn a large jelly-roll pan upside-down and oil the bottom.

4~ Remove the salmon from the refrigerator and pat dry with paper towels. Place on the inverted pan, diagonally if necessary to fit. Place the pan in a larger pan or on a very large piece of aluminum foil folded to make a lip to catch any drippings.

5~ Roast uncovered in the middle of the oven without turning for 40 minutes, or until the center of the fish registers 125° on an instant-reading thermometer.

6~ If the skin is not crisp at this point, broil about 4 inches from the heat for 2 to 3 minutes. If the salmon won't fit in your broiler, don't worry, it will taste delicious anyway.

7~ Slide the fish from the pan onto a large platter or attractive cutting board. Garnish simply with parsley or Japanese radish sprouts and lemon slices. Let sit for 10 minutes.

8~ To serve, slice the crisp skin down the length of the backbone. Then cut through the skin crosswise at 3-inch intervals. Remove the skin (it will lift or peel right off the fish) and carve separately into 18 to 24 pieces, depending on how many people you are serving. Then carve the salmon down to the backbone into roughly 3-by-1- to 1½-inch pieces, transferring each piece to a plate as you carve. Spoon 1 to 2 teaspoons of Fresh Herb Dressing over each piece of fish and add a piece of the crackly skin to each plate. Encourage guests to help themselves to lemon wedges, set out in 3 or 4 bowls.

SERVES 18 TO 24
RECIPE BY SEPPI RENGGLI
THE FOUR SEASONS, NEW YORK CITY

Use any or all of the herbs called for. If you do not have fresh tarragon or chervil, increase the parsley and chives.

¼ CUP MINCED FRESH PARSLEY
¼ CUP MINCED FRESH CHIVES
2 TABLESPOONS MINCED FRESH TARRAGON
2 TABLESPOONS MINCED FRESH CHERVIL
2 TABLESPOONS MINCED JAPANESE RADISH SPROUTS (OPTIONAL)
3 TABLESPOONS FRESH LEMON JUICE
½ TEASPOON FRESHLY GROUND PEPPER
½ TEASPOON MINCED FRESH JALAPEÑO OR SEVERAL DASHES OF CAYENNE
½ CUP EXTRA-VIRGIN OLIVE OIL

1~ Shortly before serving the fish, blend together all of the ingredients in a bowl.

2~ Transfer to a serving bowl and spoon over each portion of fish.

MAKES ABOUT 1 CUP
RECIPE BY SEPPI RENGGLI
THE FOUR SEASONS, NEW YORK CITY

MARINATED PORK AND RED CABBAGE

148

Since this dish is served at room temperature, it can be made a day ahead of time—handy for any host or hostess who's expecting 50 guests the day after New Year's Eve.

3 POUNDS BONELESS LOIN OF PORK, TRIMMED
1 TABLESPOON CRUMBLED DRIED SAGE
1 TABLESPOON GROUND GINGER
2 CUPS SWEET MARSALA
2 CUPS APPLE JUICE OR CIDER
⅔ CUP SAFFLOWER OIL
⅓ CUP OLIVE OIL
¼ CUP RICE WINE VINEGAR
6 SCALLIONS WITH 1 INCH OF GREEN, MINCED
2 GARLIC CLOVES, SMASHED
2 TABLESPOONS SOY SAUCE
2 TEASPOONS SUGAR
3 TABLESPOONS DIJON-STYLE MUSTARD
1 TABLESPOON FRESH LEMON JUICE
1 TEASPOON SALT
1 SMALL HEAD OF RED CABBAGE, VERY THINLY SLICED (6 TO 7 CUPS)
1 LARGE GRANNY SMITH APPLE—PEELED, CORED AND COARSELY CHOPPED
½ CUP PLAIN YOGURT

1~ Preheat the oven to 325°.
2~ Rub the pork all over with the sage, then the ginger. Place in a nonreactive roasting pan. Roast the pork for 1 hour and 15 minutes, or until the internal temperature reaches 145°.
3~ In a medium nonreactive saucepan, combine the Marsala, apple juice, safflower oil, olive oil, rice vinegar, scallions, garlic, soy sauce and sugar. Bring to a simmer over moderate heat.
4~ Pour the hot marinade over the meat and let cool to room temperature, turning once or twice. Cover with plastic wrap and refrigerate overnight.
5~ Meanwhile, in a large bowl, stir together the mustard, lemon juice and salt. Add the cabbage, toss, cover with plastic wrap and refrigerate overnight.
6~ About 1 hour before serving, remove the meat from the marinade and thinly slice on the diagonal. Reserve the marinade. Arrange the pork on a large platter. Pour the marinade into a measuring cup and use a ladle to skim off and discard the oil on top. Brush the pork with ¼ cup of the marinade.
7~ Add the apple and yogurt to the cabbage and toss well. Add ½ cup of the marinade; toss again. Arrange the cabbage alongside the meat.

SERVES 8 TO 10
RECIPE BY W. PETER PRESTCOTT

HOLIDAY CHOUCROUTE

This is a robust and spectacular wintertime dish. And, all by itself, it fulfills the New Year's Day good-luck "requirements" for pork and sauerkraut.

¼ CUP PLUS 2 TABLESPOONS FRESH RENDERED PORK OR GOOSE FAT
2 LARGE SPANISH ONIONS (2½ POUNDS), THINLY SLICED
6 CUPS PORK STOCK
6 POUNDS FRESH SAUERKRAUT, RINSED AND SQUEEZED DRY
1 POUND DOUBLE-SMOKED SLAB BACON, CUT CROSSWISE INTO 3 PIECES
2 CUPS DRY WHITE WINE
6 IMPORTED BAY LEAVES
1 TEASPOON THYME
10 JUNIPER BERRIES
5 GARLIC CLOVES, PEELED
8 OUNCES DRIED PEARS, CUT INTO THIN STRIPS*
36 SMALL RED POTATOES (ABOUT 4 POUNDS)
1 POUND BRATWURST
½ POUND POLISH SAUSAGE
1 POUND KNOCKWURST
1 POUND WEISSWURST
½ POUND COCKTAIL FRANKS
KALE, FOR GARNISH
*AVAILABLE AT NATURAL FOOD STORES

1~ In a large stovetop casserole, melt 2 tablespoons of the pork fat over moderate heat. Add the onions and cook, stirring frequently, until caramelized to a deep golden brown, about 1 hour.

PENNIES AND DOLLARS

2~ Add the pork stock, sauerkraut, bacon, wine, bay leaves, thyme, juniper berries, garlic and pears. Place over moderately low heat and simmer, partially covered, for 3 hours, stirring occasionally. (Add water ½ cup at a time if the sauerkraut begins to stick.)

3~ Let cool to room temperature. Cover and refrigerate at least overnight or for up to 1 week to let the flavors mellow.

4~ Preheat the oven to 375°.

5~ Melt the remaining ¼ cup of pork fat in a baking pan large enough to hold the potatoes in a single layer. Add the potatoes and toss to coat with the fat. Roast the potatoes for about 30 minutes, or until fork tender. (When the potatoes are done, reduce the oven temperature to 150°.)

6~ Meanwhile, warm the sauerkraut slowly over moderate heat until simmering. Add the bratwurst and Polish sausage, burying them in the sauerkraut. Simmer until the bratwurst is no longer pink inside, 30 to 35 minutes. Wrap the meats in foil and keep warm in the oven.

7~ Bury the weisswurst and knockwurst in the sauerkraut and simmer until plumped, about 20 minutes. During the last 10 minutes of cooking, add the cocktail franks to the sauerkraut. Wrap the weisswurst, knockwurst and cocktail franks in foil and keep warm in the oven until ready to serve.

8~ To serve, garnish the rim of a very large platter with kale. Mound the sauerkraut on the platter. Slice the sausages and arrange on top.

SERVES 10 TO 12
RECIPE BY ANNE DISRUDE

According to Edna Lewis, professional chef and chronicler of American cooking, a fresh hog's head or hog jowl is the essential ingredient for an authentic Virginia New Year's dish of black-eyed peas. A more widely available and less cumbersome substitute is fresh pork belly. Almost any kind of pork, however, is endowed with money-making symbolism and has evolved into the representative piggy bank. Start this dish the night before to give the black-eyed peas a chance to soak.

1 POUND DRIED BLACK-EYED PEAS,
   PICKED OVER
1½ POUNDS FRESH PORK BELLY, CUT INTO
   1½-INCH CUBES
1 CUP CHOPPED ONION
2 TEASPOONS SALT
FRESHLY GROUND BLACK PEPPER
3 TABLESPOONS BACON FAT
2 BUNCHES OF WATERCRESS, WASHED AND
   THOROUGHLY DRIED

1~ Soak the peas for at least 12 hours in water to cover.

2~ Place a large stovetop casserole over moderately high heat and add the pork. Sear the pork pieces on all sides until golden brown. Add the onion and cook for 1 to 2 minutes over moderately low heat, until wilted and just beginning to brown. Remove the casserole from the heat.

3~ Drain the black-eyed peas, rinse, and drain again. Add the peas to the casserole with 2 cups cold water and the salt. Bring to a simmer. (Once the contents of the casserole begin to simmer, the water should just barely cover the black-eyed peas.) Cover the casserole and cook over low heat until the black-eyed peas are tender, about 1 hour, 15 minutes. Do not overcook. (*The dish may be prepared in advance up to this point—set aside, covered, at room temperature until ready to serve; then reheat and proceed with the recipe.*)

4~ Transfer ½ cup of peas from the casserole to a bowl. Mash them with a fork. Gently swirl them back into the casserole to thicken the liquid slightly. Season with pepper to taste.

5~ Just before serving, heat the bacon fat in a very large skillet or a wok. Add the watercress and cook, stirring, until wilted and bright green, 1 to 2 minutes. Sprinkle with a pinch of salt, stir gently and remove from the pan.

6~ To serve, heap the black-eyed peas in a deep serving platter and arrange the watercress around them.

SERVES 8
RECIPE BY EDNA LEWIS

149

BRAISED MUSTARD GREENS

150

Feel free to make several batches of these greens. As legend has it, the more you eat, the better your luck in the new year will be.

2 TABLESPOONS EXTRA-VIRGIN OLIVE OIL
1 MEDIUM ONION, COARSELY CHOPPED
2 SMALL SHALLOTS, MINCED
2 SMALL GARLIC CLOVES, FINELY MINCED
2 TABLESPOONS CHICKEN STOCK OR
    CANNED BROTH
2 POUNDS FRESH MUSTARD GREENS,
    RINSED, WITH LARGE STEMS REMOVED
2 TEASPOONS FRESH LIME JUICE
½ TEASPOON SALT
¼ TEASPOON FRESHLY GROUND PEPPER

1~ In a large stovetop casserole, heat the oil over moderate heat. Add the onion, shallots and garlic and cook until golden, 8 to 10 minutes.
2~ Add the chicken stock to the casserole. Arrange the mustard greens on top of the onion. Cover and cook, turning the greens several times, until tender, about 20 minutes. (The mustard greens will reduce in volume.) Season with the lime juice, salt and pepper. Toss and serve.

SERVES 6
RECIPE BY LEE BAILEY

ORZO SALAD WITH CARROTS AND PARSLEY

Cooked orzo bears a striking resemblance to rice. In this recipe, the pearly grains of pasta are turned bright yellow by the saffron.

2½ TEASPOONS SALT
½ TEASPOON SAFFRON THREADS
1 BOX (16 OUNCES) ORZO
1 POUND CARROTS—PEELED, CUT INTO
    2- TO 3-INCH LENGTHS AND THEN
    INTO FINE JULIENNE
3 TABLESPOONS DIJON-STYLE MUSTARD
2 TABLESPOONS WHITE WINE VINEGAR
1 TEASPOON FRESHLY GROUND PEPPER
½ TEASPOON DRIED THYME
½ CUP EXTRA-VIRGIN OLIVE OIL
2 BUNCHES OF PARSLEY, FINELY CHOPPED

1~ In a large saucepan or stovetop casserole, bring 3 quarts of water to a boil. Add 2 teaspoons of the salt and the saffron. Remove from the heat, cover and set aside for 10 minutes.
2~ Return the saffron water to a simmer. Add the orzo and cook for 7 minutes, stirring frequently. Add the carrots and continue to cook until the orzo and carrots are tender but firm to the bite, about 2 minutes longer. Drain and rinse under cold running water. Drain well.
3~ In a large bowl, whisk together the mustard, vinegar, pepper, thyme and the remaining ½ teaspoon salt. Whisk in the olive oil. Add the drained orzo and carrots and toss well. *(The salad can be prepared to this point up to 3 days ahead and refrigerated, covered. Let return to room temperature.)* Stir in the parsley shortly before serving.

SERVES 12
RECIPE BY BOB CHAMBERS

SHALLOTS IN RED WINE

When peeling the shallots, barely trim the root end to keep the shallots intact during cooking. You might want to leave the other end long, just for the look of it.

1 POUND LARGE SHALLOTS, PEELED
2 TABLESPOONS SUGAR
1 SMALL SPRIG OF FRESH ROSEMARY OR
    ¼ TEASPOON DRIED
¼ CUP EXTRA-VIRGIN OLIVE OIL
⅛ TEASPOON COARSELY GROUND PEPPER
1 BOTTLE (750 ML) DRY RED WINE

1~ In a medium bowl, toss the shallots with the sugar and rosemary. In a medium nonreactive skillet, heat the olive oil. Add the shallots and cook over moderate heat, tossing frequently, until browned, 5 to 7 minutes. Add the pepper and wine and simmer until the shallots can be easily pierced with a fork, 20 to 25 minutes.
2~ Using a slotted spoon, transfer the shallots and rosemary to a 1-quart jar. Boil the liquid in the skillet over high heat until reduced to 1¼ cups, 10 to 15 minutes.
3~ Pour the reduced liquid over the shallots. Let cool completely, then cover and refrigerate. These shallots will keep in the refrigerator for several months.

MAKES ABOUT 30 SHALLOTS
RECIPE BY ANNE DISRUDE

WINTRY FRUIT SALAD

By the time guests find their way to the dessert table, they'll be stuffed. Most will be more than happy with a small cup of fruit. Be sure to double or triple the recipe, as necessary, to serve your crowd.

3 KIWIS—PEELED, QUARTERED AND SLICED
¼ INCH THICK
2 APPLES—PEELED, QUARTERED, CORED
AND SLICED ¼ INCH THICK
1 FIRM, RIPE PEAR—PEELED, QUARTERED,
CORED AND SLICED ¼ INCH THICK
1 CANTALOUPE—HALVED, SEEDED AND
SCOOPED INTO LITTLE BALLS WITH
A MELON BALLER
1 HONEYDEW MELON—HALVED, SEEDED
AND SCOOPED INTO LITTLE BALLS WITH
A MELON BALLER
1 PAPAYA—PEELED, HALVED, SEEDED AND
CUT INTO 2-BY-¼-INCH STRIPS
1 PINT FRESH RASPBERRIES OR
STRAWBERRIES
¼ CUP SUGAR
3 TABLESPOONS FRESH LEMON JUICE

1~ In a large glass bowl, combine all of the fruit. Sprinkle on the sugar and lemon juice and toss gently.
2~ Cover with plastic wrap and refrigerate for 2 hours, or overnight, before serving.

SERVES 16
RECIPE BY MIMI RUTH BRODEUR

GINGER SHORTBREAD

It's a lucky thing that shortbread wedges store so well in a sealed tin. When friends compliment you on New Year's Day, you can actually say, "Oh, they're nothing—I made them last year." These, however, are definitely something.

¾ CUP SIFTED CORNSTARCH
⅔ CUP SIFTED ALL-PURPOSE FLOUR
½ CUP SIFTED CONFECTIONERS' SUGAR
¼ POUND (1 STICK) PLUS 2⅔ TABLESPOONS
UNSALTED BUTTER, SOFTENED
⅓ CUP VERY THINLY SLICED CANDIED
GINGER, NOT LONGER THAN ¾ INCH

1~ Preheat the oven to 325°. Butter a 9-inch round springform or cake pan.
2~ In a small bowl, stir together the cornstarch, flour and confectioners' sugar.
3~ In a medium mixer bowl, beat the butter until light and creamy, about 3 minutes. Gradually beat in the dry ingredients until well blended. Stir in the ginger.
4~ Press the dough evenly into the prepared pan. Using a sharp knife, score the dough into 12 pie-shaped wedges. With the tines of a fork, pierce the dough along the score lines, then use the fork to crimp the outer edges as you would a pie.
5~ Bake the shortbread for 40 to 45 minutes, turning the pan midway through to insure even baking, until light golden. While the shortbread is still warm, again pierce the score lines with the fork. Run a sharp knife around the edge. Set the pan on a rack and let cool completely.
6~ Using a sharp knife, cut along the score lines and remove the wedges of shortbread from the pan. If using a springform pan, remove the sides first. (These shortbread cookies will keep for up to 2 weeks at room temperature in an airtight container.)

MAKES 12 WEDGES
RECIPE BY MARGARET FOX

151

■ ■ ■

NATIONAL PIE DAY
CELEBRATION

When you're entertaining more than just a few people, it's wise to keep the menu as simple as possible. Here's one that will feed 15 people and comes with a built-in reason to celebrate: National Pie Day, January 23. It gives you the excuse and the menu for a relaxed mid-winter gathering. ∼ So invite a bunch of friends and serve up entrée pies such as a rich chicken pot pie in phyllo, a glorious seafood gumbo pie, a celestial beef pie topped with mashed potatoes and a vegetarian ratatouille pie in basil pastry. Slip in a salad if you want to; it might be welcome. ∼ Dessert is – you guessed it – more pies, this time a range of fruit and cream types. You'll rekindle sated appetites with a selection that includes cherry pie, apple-quince pie, coconut meringue pie and a truly superb lime cream pie. Have some vanilla ice cream on hand for those who must have their pie à la mode. And if there are Anglophiles in the group, you can melt a slab of well-aged Cheddar atop the apple-quince pie.

■ ■ ■

*New-Fashioned
Chicken
Pot Pie with
Phyllo Crust*

*Heavenly Beef Pie
with Rich
Mashed Potato
Topping*

*Ratatouille Pie
with Basil Crust*

*Biscuit-Cloaked
Seafood
Gumbo Pie*

GREEN SALAD WITH LEMON AND FENNEL

NATIONAL PIE DAY CELEBRATION

Serves 15

SAUVIGNON BLANC
OR SPARKLING CIDER

New-Fashioned Chicken Pot Pie with Phyllo Crust

Biscuit-Cloaked Seafood Gumbo Pie

Heavenly Beef Pie with Rich Mashed Potato Topping

Ratatouille Pie with Basil Crust

Green Salad with Lemon and Fennel

COFFEE AND TEA

Apple-Quince Pie

All-Season Cherry Pie

Coconut Meringue Pie

Fluffy Lime Cream Pie

vanilla ice cream

To get most of the work for this salad out of the way ahead of time, rinse, dry and trim the greens up to 6 hours before serving. Wrap in a dampened kitchen towel and refrigerate. They will be nicely crisped by the time the salad is assembled. You'll want to double the recipe for a National Pie Day celebration.

1 LEMON
3 FENNEL BULBS
¼ CUP SAFFLOWER OIL
¼ CUP LIGHT OLIVE OIL
1 TEASPOON CRUSHED FENNEL SEEDS
½ TEASPOON SALT
¼ TEASPOON COARSELY CRACKED BLACK PEPPER
1 BUNCH OF WATERCRESS, LARGE STEMS REMOVED
3 HEADS OF BIBB LETTUCE, SEPARATED INTO LEAVES
1 HEAD OF BOSTON LETTUCE, TORN INTO PIECES

1~ Remove the lemon zest in long strips with a vegetable peeler. Cut lengthwise into very fine julienne. Wrap in plastic wrap to keep moist.
2~ Remove and discard the green tops of the fennel. Cut out the cores and remove any tough outer sections. Cut the bulbs lengthwise into thin strips. In a medium bowl, toss the fennel strips with the juice of ½ lemon. Cover with ice water and let stand until crisp, about 30 minutes. Drain and spin or pat dry.

3~ In a small bowl, whisk together the safflower and olive oils, fennel seeds, salt, pepper and the strained juice of the remaining ½ lemon.
4~ To assemble the salad, toss the fennel with 2 tablespoons of the dressing. In a separate bowl, combine the watercress and Bibb and Boston lettuce. Toss the greens with the remaining dressing.
5~ Mound the fennel in the center of the greens. Top the fennel with the lemon julienne and additional cracked black pepper.

SERVES 8
RECIPE BY FOOD & WINE

NEW-FASHIONED CHICKEN POT PIE WITH PHYLLO CRUST

Chicken pot pie with a secret ingredient? Yes, jicama, that sweet, super-crisp tuber frequently found in Mexican cuisine. Jicama's crunch holds up remarkably well even after long cooking.

1 CHICKEN (ABOUT 3½ POUNDS)
1 LARGE ONION, UNPEELED
2 CARROTS—1 CHOPPED, 1 CUT INTO
   ¼-INCH DICE
1 CELERY RIB, CHOPPED
1 TURNIP, PEELED AND CHOPPED
1 PARSNIP, PEELED AND CHOPPED
4 SPRIGS OF PARSLEY
4 CUPS CHICKEN STOCK OR CANNED BROTH
1 TEASPOON CIDER VINEGAR
1 LARGE LEEK (WHITE AND TENDER
   GREEN), CHOPPED
1 SMALL JICAMA (½ POUND), PEELED AND
   CUT INTO ¼-INCH DICE
5 TABLESPOONS UNSALTED BUTTER
1½ TABLESPOONS ALL-PURPOSE FLOUR
1 CUP HEAVY CREAM
PINCH OF GROUND ALLSPICE
PINCH OF FRESHLY GRATED NUTMEG
½ TEASPOON SALT
¼ TEASPOON FRESHLY GROUND PEPPER
8 SHEETS OF PHYLLO DOUGH
1 TABLESPOON FINE BREAD CRUMBS

1~ In a large saucepan, combine the chicken, onion, chopped carrot, celery, turnip, parsnip, parsley, chicken stock and vinegar. Add enough water to cover the chicken and bring to a boil. Reduce the heat and simmer, partially covered, until the chicken is tender and white throughout, about 50 minutes. Remove from the heat and let cool for 30 minutes.

2~ When the chicken is cool enough to handle, discard the skin and bones; cut the meat into bite-size pieces. Strain the cooking liquid and reserve.

3~ In a medium saucepan, cover the leek with 1½ cups of the reserved cooking liquid and bring to a boil. Add the diced carrot and cook over moderately low heat until softened, about 10 minutes. Stir in the jicama and cook until softened slightly, about 5 minutes longer. Using a slotted spoon, remove the vegetables to a bowl and reserve. If necessary, add enough of the reserved cooking liquid to the pan to make 1 cup; set aside.

4~ In another medium saucepan, melt 2 tablespoons of the butter over moderately low heat. Whisk in the flour and cook, stirring constantly, for about 2 minutes without coloring. Whisk in the reserved 1 cup of cooking liquid and bring to a boil. Boil, stirring frequently, for 3 minutes. Whisk in the cream, allspice and nutmeg and return to a boil. Cook, stirring frequently, until thick, about 8 minutes. Remove from the heat and let cool, stirring occasionally. Stir in the chicken, cooked vegetables and the salt and pepper. Transfer the stew to a shallow 10-inch round baking dish.

5~ Preheat the oven to 425°.

6~ Melt the remaining 3 tablespoons butter. On a work surface, lightly brush 2 sheets of the phyllo dough with melted butter and sprinkle with 1 teaspoon of the bread crumbs. Repeat twice more with the remaining phyllo, melted butter and bread crumbs, reserving a little of the butter. Place the last 2 sheets of phyllo on top and brush with butter. Invert the phyllo dough onto the baking dish and trim the sides to ½ inch beyond the edge. Brush the top and sides lightly with the remaining butter. Tuck under the sides.

7~ Cut a hole in the center of the pie and bake for 30 minutes, or until the top is golden and crisp.

SERVES 6
RECIPE BY PHILLIP STEPHEN SCHULZ

155

BISCUIT-CLOAKED SEAFOOD GUMBO PIE

156

From a recipe born in the heart of Cajun country in New Iberia, Louisiana, this rich, dark and flavorful gumbo is an absolutely authentic bayou dish.

GUMBO:

3 TABLESPOONS PLUS 1 TEASPOON
    VEGETABLE OIL
3 TABLESPOONS ALL-PURPOSE FLOUR
3 TABLESPOONS UNSALTED BUTTER
¾ POUND SMOKED SAUSAGE, SLICED
¾ POUND COOKED BONELESS HAM STEAK,
    CUT INTO 2-BY-¼-INCH STRIPS
1 LARGE ONION, CHOPPED
2 GARLIC CLOVES, MINCED
½ GREEN BELL PEPPER, CHOPPED
½ RED BELL PEPPER, CHOPPED
1 SMALL CELERY RIB, MINCED
3 TABLESPOONS LONG-GRAIN WHITE RICE
2 CUPS CHICKEN STOCK OR CANNED BROTH
2 TEASPOONS FRESH LEMON JUICE
½ TEASPOON CAYENNE
¾ POUND UNCOOKED SHRIMP, SHELLED
    AND DEVEINED
½ POUND OKRA, SLICED
SALT AND FRESHLY GROUND BLACK PEPPER

BISCUIT TOPPING:

2 CUPS ALL-PURPOSE FLOUR
1 TABLESPOON BAKING POWDER
2 TEASPOONS SUGAR
½ TEASPOON BAKING SODA
½ TEASPOON SALT
6½ TABLESPOONS COLD UNSALTED BUTTER
¾ CUP BUTTERMILK

1~ *Make the Gumbo:* In a heavy medium skillet, combine 3 tablespoons of the oil with the flour and cook over moderately low heat, stirring occasionally, until the roux is dark mahogany in color, about 1 hour. Do not let burn. Immediately remove from the heat. *(The roux can be prepared ahead and will keep indefinitely. Let cool, then cover and refrigerate.)*

2~ In a medium stovetop casserole, melt 2 tablespoons of the butter with the remaining 1 teaspoon oil. Add the sliced sausage and cook over moderate heat until well browned, about 5 minutes. Transfer to a plate with a slotted spoon. Add the ham strips to the casserole and cook until lightly browned, about 7 minutes; add to the plate with the sausage slices.

3~ Add the remaining 1 tablespoon butter and the onion to the casserole. Cook over moderate heat, stirring constantly, until softened and translucent, about 2 minutes. Reduce the heat to moderately low and add the garlic, green and red bell peppers, celery and rice. Cook, stirring, for 5 minutes longer.

4~ Reheat the brown roux if necessary. Scrape it into the casserole with the vegetables and rice. Stir in the chicken stock and lemon juice.

Bring to a boil over high heat. Add the sausage and ham, reduce the heat to moderately low and cook, covered, for 20 to 25 minutes.

5~ Stir in the cayenne, shrimp and okra and season with salt and black pepper to taste. Cook, stirring once or twice, for 2 minutes. Remove from the heat. *(The recipe can be prepared to this point up to 2 days ahead. Let cool, then cover and refrigerate. Reheat before proceeding.)*

6~ *Make the Biscuits:* Preheat the oven to 450°.

7~ In a medium bowl, combine the flour, baking powder, sugar, baking soda and salt. Cut in 5½ tablespoons of the butter until the mixture resembles coarse crumbs. Stir in the buttermilk until a soft dough forms.

8~ On a lightly floured surface, roll out the dough ½ inch thick. Using a 2½-inch round cutter, stamp out 12 biscuits.

9~ Melt the remaining 1 tablespoon butter. Pour the hot gumbo into a shallow 9-inch round baking dish. Arrange the biscuits on top and brush with the melted butter.

10~ Bake until the biscuits are puffed and golden brown, about 20 minutes. Serve hot.

SERVES 6
RECIPE BY PHILLIP STEPHEN SCHULZ

HEAVENLY BEEF PIE WITH RICH MASHED POTATO TOPPING

This dish is of mixed heritage—not really a shepherd's pie, but a combination of two freely adapted Alice B. Toklas recipes that make an entirely new French connection.

BEEF FILLING:

2 POUNDS TRIMMED BONELESS SIRLOIN STEAK (½ INCH THICK), CUT INTO 1-INCH PIECES

½ CUP COGNAC

¼ POUND SALT PORK, CUT INTO ¼-INCH DICE

5 TABLESPOONS UNSALTED BUTTER

1 TABLESPOON VEGETABLE OIL

12 SMALL WHITE ONIONS, PEELED

1 TABLESPOON ALL-PURPOSE FLOUR

2 CUPS DRY RED WINE

BOUQUET GARNI: 3 SPRIGS OF ITALIAN FLAT-LEAF PARSLEY, 1 SPRIG OF THYME, 1 BAY LEAF, 5 WHOLE PEPPERCORNS AND 1 CRUSHED GARLIC CLOVE TIED IN CHEESECLOTH

1½ CUPS SMALL MUSHROOM CAPS

MASHED POTATO TOPPING:

2½ POUNDS BAKING POTATOES

½ TEASPOON SALT

⅛ TEASPOON FRESHLY GROUND WHITE PEPPER

⅛ TEASPOON FRESHLY GRATED NUTMEG

4½ TABLESPOONS UNSALTED BUTTER, MELTED

2 EGG YOLKS

3 TABLESPOONS HEAVY CREAM

1~ *Prepare the Beef Filling:* Put the steak in a shallow glass or ceramic dish and pour ⅓ cup of the Cognac over it. Cover and let stand at room temperature for 3 hours, or refrigerate for 6 hours.

2~ In a small saucepan, cover the salt pork with water and bring to a boil; boil for 4 minutes. Drain well.

3~ In a heavy nonreactive saucepan or stovetop casserole, melt 3 tablespoons of the butter in the oil over moderately high heat. Remove the steak from the dish and pat dry with paper towels. Add the meat to the pan in batches and cook, turning, until well browned, about 5 minutes. Transfer to a plate.

4~ In the same pan, cook the salt pork over moderately high heat until golden brown, 3 to 5 minutes. Remove and add to the beef.

5~ Cut a cross in the root end of each onion. Add to the pan and cook, tossing, until golden brown, 3 to 5 minutes. Using a slotted spoon, transfer to a bowl.

6~ Drain off all but 1 tablespoon of the drippings from the pan. Whisk in the flour and cook over low heat, stirring constantly, for about 2 minutes without coloring. Whisk in the wine and ½ cup of water. Bring to a boil, scraping the sides and bottom of the pan with a wooden spoon.

7~ Return the meat to the pan and add the bouquet garni. Pour the remaining Cognac into a small saucepan and carefully ignite. When the flames subside, pour over the meat. Cover and cook over moderately low heat for 1 hour.

8~ Add the onions and cook, partially covered, until the meat and onions are just tender and the sauce is thickened, about 30 minutes.

9~ Meanwhile, in a large skillet, melt the remaining 2 tablespoons butter over moderately high heat. Add the mushroom caps and sauté, turning, until browned on both sides, about 5 minutes. Remove and set aside. When the meat and onions are tender, stir in the mushrooms and remove from the heat.

10~ *Make the Mashed Potato Topping:* Preheat the oven to 400°.

11~ Bake the potatoes until tender, about 1 hour; leave the oven on. When cool enough to handle, cut the potatoes in half and scoop out the insides; discard the skins. Rice the potatoes into a bowl and beat in the salt, white pepper, nutmeg and 4 tablespoons of the melted butter. Beat in the egg yolks and cream.

12~ Spoon the beef stew into a 1½-quart shallow baking dish about 2 inches deep; discard the bouquet garni. Spread the mashed potatoes over the top. Drizzle on the remaining 1½ teaspoons melted butter. Bake in the upper third of the oven for 15 minutes. If the top is not browned, run the pie under the broiler for 1 or 2 minutes.

SERVES 6
RECIPE BY PHILLIP STEPHEN SCHULZ

RATATOUILLE PIE WITH BASIL CRUST

158

This is one for the vegetarian crowd to be sure, but it's not to be passed up even if you aren't a card-carrying member of the no-meat contingent.

BASIL CRUST:

1½ CUPS PLUS 1 TEASPOON ALL-PURPOSE FLOUR
1 TEASPOON SUGAR
½ TEASPOON SALT
6 TABLESPOONS VEGETABLE SHORTENING
1 EGG YOLK
1 TEASPOON RED WINE VINEGAR
2 TO 3 TABLESPOONS COLD WATER
2 TABLESPOONS CHOPPED FRESH BASIL

RATATOUILLE:

1 LARGE EGGPLANT (ABOUT 1½ POUNDS)
¾ TEASPOON SALT
½ CUP EXTRA-VIRGIN OLIVE OIL
2 SMALL ZUCCHINI (ABOUT 1 POUND), SLICED
1 TABLESPOON UNSALTED BUTTER
1 LARGE ONION, THINLY SLICED
2 LARGE GARLIC CLOVES, MINCED
1 MEDIUM GREEN BELL PEPPER, THINLY SLICED
1 MEDIUM RED BELL PEPPER, THINLY SLICED
2 MEDIUM TOMATOES, PEELED AND CUT INTO ½-INCH WEDGES
¼ TEASPOON FRESHLY GROUND BLACK PEPPER

½ TEASPOON HOT HUNGARIAN PAPRIKA
¼ CUP CHOPPED FRESH PARSLEY
2 TABLESPOONS CHOPPED FRESH BASIL
2 CUPS GRATED ITALIAN FONTINA CHEESE (ABOUT 6 OUNCES)
½ CUP FRESHLY GRATED PARMESAN CHEESE
1 EGG WHITE, LIGHTLY BEATEN

1~ *Make the Basil Crust:* In a medium bowl, combine 1½ cups of the flour with the sugar and salt. Cut in the shortening until the mixture resembles coarse crumbs. Lightly beat the egg yolk with the vinegar, water and basil. Mix the liquid into the flour mixture just until a soft dough forms. Sprinkle with the remaining 1 teaspoon flour, cover with plastic wrap and refrigerate for 1 hour.

2~ *Prepare the Ratatouille:* Halve the eggplant lengthwise and cut crosswise into ¼-inch-thick slices. Put the eggplant in a colander, sprinkle with ½ teaspoon of the salt and let stand for 30 minutes. Pat the eggplant with damp paper towels until dry to remove the salt.

3~ In a large heavy skillet, heat 2 tablespoons of the oil over moderately high heat. Add the eggplant slices in batches and sauté, tossing, until golden, about 2½ minutes per side. Repeat with the remaining eggplant, adding up to 5 tablespoons more oil as needed. Drain the eggplant on paper towels, then transfer to a bowl.

4~ Add the remaining 1 tablespoon of oil to the same skillet, add the zucchini and cook over high heat, tossing constantly, until golden, 2 to 3 minutes. Reduce the heat to moderate

and cook until soft, about 3 minutes longer. Drain and add to the eggplant in the bowl.

5~ Wipe the skillet clean. Add the butter and melt over moderate heat. Add the onion and cook for 2 minutes. Stir in the garlic and green and red bell peppers, cover and cook until the peppers are soft, about 5 minutes. Stir in the tomatoes, remaining ¼ teaspoon salt, black pepper and paprika. Increase the heat to high and cook until all the liquid has evaporated, 2 to 3 minutes. Remove from the heat and add the eggplant, zucchini, parsley and basil; mix well.

6~ Preheat the oven to 425°.

7~ Spoon one-third of the ratatouille into a buttered 10-inch glass or ceramic quiche dish. Sprinkle with one-third each of the Fontina and Parmesan cheeses. Continue layering until all of the ingredients are used, ending with the Parmesan cheese.

8~ Roll out the pastry on a lightly floured board and lay it over the dish. Trim and flute the edges. Cut a slash in the center of the pie. Brush the pastry with the beaten egg white.

9~ Bake for 25 minutes, or until golden brown. Let stand for 5 minutes before serving.

SERVES 6
RECIPE BY PHILLIP STEPHEN SCHULZ

APPLE-QUINCE PIE

What a combination. If you're not familiar with quinces, it's time to get to know this excellent ingredient.

FLAKY PIE DOUGH:
2¼ CUPS ALL-PURPOSE FLOUR
¾ TEASPOON SALT
¾ CUP COLD VEGETABLE SHORTENING
5 TO 6 TABLESPOONS ICE WATER

FILLING:
4 TART GREEN APPLES—PEELED, CORED AND CUT INTO ½-INCH SLICES
2 RIPE QUINCES—PEELED, CORED AND CUT INTO ⅛-INCH SLICES
GRATED ZEST AND JUICE OF 1 MEDIUM LEMON
¾ CUP SUGAR
1 TABLESPOON ALL-PURPOSE FLOUR
3 TABLESPOONS UNSALTED BUTTER, CUT INTO ½-INCH DICE

1~ *Make the Dough:* In a large bowl, combine the flour and salt. Cut in the shortening until the mixture resembles very coarse meal with some pieces of shortening the size of corn kernels still visible.

2~ Sprinkle 5 tablespoons of the ice water over the mixture, tossing to moisten evenly. Gather the dough into a ball, adding up to 1 tablespoon more ice water if the dough is too dry.

3~ Divide the dough in half and pat each piece into a 6-inch disk. Wrap separately in plastic wrap and refrigerate for at least 30 minutes. *(The pie dough can be made several days ahead of time.)*

4~ Preheat the oven to 400°.

5~ *Prepare the Filling:* In a large bowl, toss together the apples, quinces, lemon zest, lemon juice, sugar and flour.

6~ On a lightly floured surface, roll out one disk of pastry to a 12-inch circle, about ⅛ inch thick. Fit the pastry into a 9-inch ovenproof glass pie plate. Roll out the top crust in the same manner.

7~ Mound the fruit mixture in the lined pie plate and dot with the butter. Moisten the rim of the pie shell with water and lay the top crust over the fruit.

8~ Using scissors, trim the edges of the dough so that they extend no more than ¾ inch beyond the rim of the plate. Roll the dough under and crimp to make an attractive border. Cut at least 5 steam vents in the top crust.

9~ Bake the pie in the lower third of the oven for 25 minutes. Reduce the oven temperature to 350° and bake for 35 to 40 minutes longer, or until the crust is golden brown and the fruit is tender. Let cool for at least 2 hours before serving.

SERVES 8 TO 10
RECIPE BY MICHAEL JAMES

ALL-SEASON CHERRY PIE

159

Since the season for fresh sour cherries is so short, you can use canned cherries for this pie. Don't worry—Rose Levy Beranbaum perks them up in a special way.

2 CANS (16 OUNCES EACH) TART, RED PITTED CHERRIES, PACKED IN WATER
¾ CUP CHERRY KIJAFA
¾ CUP SUGAR
2 TABLESPOONS CORNSTARCH
PINCH OF SALT
¼ TEASPOON ALMOND EXTRACT
PÂTE BRISÉE PIE SHELL (PAGE 39)

1~ Pour the cherries into a colander set over a bowl and let them drain for 30 minutes. Press lightly to extract as much liquid as possible without crushing the cherries. Reserve ¼ cup of cherry juice; discard the remainder.

2~ In a medium nonreactive saucepan, combine the reserved cherry juice, the Cherry Kijafa and the sugar. Stir to dissolve the sugar. Add the cherries and bring just to a boil over moderately high heat. Cover and remove from the heat. Let cool to room temperature, then transfer the cherries and liquid to a jar, cover and macerate at room temperature for at least 12 hours, or overnight.

3~ Pour the cherries back into a colander set over a bowl and let drain for 30 minutes. Reserve all of the liquid.

4~ In a medium nonreactive saucepan, boil the reserved liquid over high heat until it is reduced to 1 cup, 5 to 8 minutes. Cover and let cool to room temperature.

RECIPE CONTINUES ON THE NEXT PAGE

ALL-SEASON CHERRY PIE CONTINUED

5~ Stir the cornstarch and salt into the cooled liquid until the cornstarch dissolves. Add the cherries and bring to a boil over moderately high heat, stirring constantly, until the liquid is smooth and thick. Reduce the heat to moderately low and simmer, stirring, for 1 minute; remove from the heat. Stir in the almond extract.

6~ Pour the cherries into the baked pie shell. Let cool to room temperature before unmolding from the pan.

SERVES 6 TO 8
RECIPE BY ROSE LEVY BERANBAUM

COCONUT MERINGUE PIE

No pie party could be without one of the all-time favorites—coconut meringue pie.

2 CUPS MILK
1¼ CUPS SUGAR
5 EGGS, SEPARATED
½ CUP ALL-PURPOSE FLOUR
¼ CUP HEAVY CREAM
1 TEASPOON VANILLA EXTRACT
2 TABLESPOONS UNSALTED BUTTER
¾ CUP PLUS 2 TABLESPOONS
  UNSWEETENED SHREDDED
  COCONUT (ABOUT 2½ OUNCES)*
PREBAKED PIE SHELL (AT RIGHT)
½ TEASPOON CREAM OF TARTAR
¼ TEASPOON SALT
*AVAILABLE AT HEALTH FOOD STORES

1~ In a large heavy saucepan, bring the milk to a simmer over moderately low heat.

2~ Meanwhile, in a medium bowl, gradually beat ½ cup of the sugar into the egg yolks. Beat until the mixture thickens slightly and lightens in color, about 5 minutes. Beat in the flour.

3~ Gradually whisk the hot milk into the egg mixture in a thin stream. Beat in the heavy cream and vanilla.

4~ Pour the custard back into the saucepan and cook over moderately high heat, whisking constantly, until it boils and thickens. Continue to beat over heat until the custard is smooth and has no raw flour taste, 1 to 2 minutes. Remove from the heat and beat in the butter. Stir in ¾ cup of the coconut.

5~ Pour the coconut custard into the baked pie shell, press a piece of plastic wrap directly onto the surface to prevent a skin from forming and refrigerate until chilled and set, about 2 hours.

6~ Preheat the oven to 400°.

7~ In a large bowl, combine the egg whites, cream of tartar and salt. Set the bowl over a pan of simmering water. Whisk slowly until the egg whites are slightly warmed.

8~ Remove the bowl from the heat and beat the egg whites with an electric mixer at medium speed until soft peaks form. At high speed, gradually beat in the remaining ¾ cup sugar, 1 tablespoon at a time, until stiff shiny peaks form.

9~ Using a metal spatula, spread the meringue over the coconut custard, swirling it decoratively into standing peaks. Set the pie in the oven and bake for 5 minutes, or until the meringue peaks begin to brown. Garnish the pie with the remaining 2 tablespoons coconut. Let cool, then cover and refrigerate. Serve the pie well chilled.

SERVES 8 TO 10
RECIPE BY MICHAEL JAMES

PREBAKED PIE SHELL

1½ CUPS ALL-PURPOSE FLOUR
¼ TEASPOON SALT
½ CUP COLD VEGETABLE SHORTENING
3 TO 4 TABLESPOONS ICE WATER

1~ In a large bowl, combine the flour and salt. Cut in the shortening until the mixture resembles very coarse meal with some pieces of shortening the size of corn kernels still visible; do not overmix. Sprinkle on 3 tablespoons of the ice water, tossing to moisten evenly. Gather the dough into a ball, adding up to 1 tablespoon more ice water if necessary. Flatten into a 6-inch disk, wrap and refrigerate for at least 30 minutes.

2~ On a lightly floured surface, roll out the dough to a 12-inch circle, about ⅛ inch thick. Fit the pastry into a 9-inch ovenproof glass pie plate. Trim the dough to ¾ inch beyond the rim of the dish. Fold the excess dough under the pastry and crimp the edge. With a fork, prick the dough all over. Freeze the pastry shell for 30 minutes.

3~ Meanwhile, preheat the oven to 450°.

4~ Line the pie shell with a sheet of aluminum foil and fill with pie weights or dried beans. Bake for 10 minutes, or until dry. Remove the foil and weights. Reduce the oven temperature to 400° and bake the pie shell for 15 minutes longer, or until lightly browned.

MAKES ONE 9-INCH CRUST
RECIPE BY MICHAEL JAMES

FLUFFY LIME CREAM PIE

This pie is really quite different. Stiffly beaten egg whites are folded into the lime filling and the pie is baked just briefly. When the chilled pie is piled with whipped cream, it becomes even fluffier. Be sure to leave time in your schedule; this pie needs to chill for 6 hours.

CRUMB SHELL:
1½ CUPS FINE GRAHAM CRACKER CRUMBS
¼ CUP SUGAR
⅓ CUP MELTED UNSALTED BUTTER

FILLING:
3 EGGS, SEPARATED AND AT ROOM
    TEMPERATURE
½ CUP FRESH LIME JUICE (FROM ABOUT
    4 LIMES)
1 CAN (14 OUNCES) SWEETENED
    CONDENSED MILK
¼ TEASPOON SALT
1 TABLESPOON SUGAR

TOPPING:
1 CUP HEAVY CREAM
3 TABLESPOONS SUGAR, PREFERABLY
    SUPERFINE
4 THIN LIME SLICES, HALVED

1~ *Prepare the Crumb Shell:* Preheat the oven to 375°.

2~ In a medium bowl, combine the crumbs, sugar and melted butter and toss until the crumbs are coated with butter. Place in a 9-inch pie pan and lightly press over the bottom and up the sides to make a shell of even thickness.

3~ Bake for 8 minutes, until set and lightly browned. Let cool on a rack. Reduce the oven temperature to 300°.

4~ *Prepare the Filling:* In a large mixing bowl, beat the egg yolks until light in color. Gradually beat in the lime juice and then the condensed milk.

5~ Using clean beaters and bowl, beat the egg whites with the salt until soft peaks form. Gradually add the sugar and continue beating until stiff peaks form. Using a rubber spatula, quickly but gently fold one-third of the beaten egg whites into the yolk mixture. Fold in the remaining egg whites. Pile into the pie shell.

6~ Bake the pie for 15 minutes. Let cool to room temperature on a rack. Refrigerate for at least 6 hours or overnight.

7~ *Prepare the Topping:* Beat the heavy cream at high speed until soft peaks form. Gradually add the 3 tablespoons sugar and continue beating until just stiff. Spread half of the whipped cream over the pie. Using a spoon or a pastry bag with a decorative tip, make 7 rosettes or mounds of whipped cream around the edge of the pie and one in the center. Top each mound with half of a lime slice. Serve chilled. If not serving immediately, refrigerate for up to 1 hour.

SERVES 8
RECIPE BY JIM FOBEL

■ ■ ■

SUPER BOWL SUNDAY
LAP FOOD

If you're planning a party that centers around a television event, it's wise to keep the group small. Too many people leads to too much talking, too much walking in front of the screen, less than perfect sight lines, and ultimately you miss out on the action of the show. If you're entertaining for the Super Bowl, your safest strategy is to plan for people to eat off lap trays from their seats in front of the set. Don't tackle more than you can handle; the goal here is to provide plenty of tasty sustenance during the action of the game. ∼ Kick off with an open bar of good beer, sturdy wine and the basic liquors and mixers. You might keep some pretzels, nuts and chips available on the sidelines, or pass them around during time-outs. At halftime, set up a buffet that offers overstuffed sandwiches – barbecued pork with slaw, flank steak with Roquefort and a chicken and avocado club. Spoon some of the Tuscan-style white bean salad on each plate. As a defensive ploy that will thwart any possible complaints or penalties, end the meal with Simply Super Chocolate-Chunk Cookies, made especially to close the best TV dinner we've ever tasted.

■ ■ ■

*BBQ Pork
Sandwiches with
Five-Vegetable Slaw*

*Flank Steak
Sandwiches with
Roquefort Cheese*

164

SUPER BOWL SUNDAY LAP FOOD

Serves 6 to 8

PREMIUM BEER
BOURBON, SCOTCH, GIN AND VODKA
RED WINE

pretzels, potato chips and nuts

*BBQ Pork Sandwiches with
Five-Vegetable Slaw*

*Flank Steak Sandwiches with
Roquefort Cheese*

Chicken and Avocado Club Sandwiches

Tuscan-Style White Bean Salad

pickles and relishes

COFFEE

Simply Super Chocolate-Chunk Cookies

BBQ PORK SANDWICHES WITH FIVE-VEGETABLE SLAW

Spicy roast pork and crisp coleslaw add up to a down-home sandwich with uptown taste.

¼ CUP PLUS 2 TABLESPOONS
    DARK MOLASSES
⅓ CUP CIDER VINEGAR
¼ CUP TOMATO PASTE
4 LARGE GARLIC CLOVES, MINCED
1 TEASPOON GROUND CUMIN
¼ TEASPOON CAYENNE PEPPER
½ TEASPOON PAPRIKA
½ TEASPOON GROUND CORIANDER
½ TEASPOON SALT
¼ TEASPOON FRESHLY GROUND
    BLACK PEPPER
1½ POUNDS BONELESS PORK SHOULDER,
    CUT INTO 2-INCH CUBES
2 IMPORTED BAY LEAVES
4 LARGE, SOFT SESAME-TOPPED BUNS
FIVE-VEGETABLE SLAW (AT RIGHT)

1~ Preheat the oven to 325°.
2~ In a medium bowl, whisk together the molasses, vinegar, tomato paste, garlic, cumin, cayenne, paprika, coriander, salt and black pepper. Place the pork cubes and bay leaves in a large shallow nonreactive baking dish. Add the molasses mixture and stir well to coat.

3~ Cover with foil and bake until the pork is very tender, about 1½ hours.
4~ Remove the meat from the sauce and shred with a knife; remove the bay leaves. Return the shredded meat to the baking dish and mix with the sauce.
5~ Slice the buns in half. Spoon the pork onto the bottom halves of the buns and mound ½ cup or more of the Vegetable Slaw on top. Cover with the bun tops and serve the remaining slaw on the side.

SERVES 4
RECIPE BY MARCIA KIESEL

FIVE-VEGETABLE SLAW

This makes a light, colorful side dish as well as a sandwich topping. It tastes even better the day after it is made.

4 CUPS FINELY SHREDDED GREEN CABBAGE
½ CUP THINLY SLICED RED BELL PEPPER
½ CUP THINLY SLICED GREEN BELL PEPPER
½ MEDIUM CUCUMBER—PEELED, HALVED LENGTHWISE, SEEDED AND THINLY SLICED
3 SCALLIONS, THINLY SLICED ON THE DIAGONAL
⅓ CUP MAYONNAISE, PREFERABLY HOMEMADE
1 TABLESPOON CIDER VINEGAR
¼ TEASPOON SALT
¼ TEASPOON FRESHLY GROUND BLACK PEPPER

1~ In a large bowl, toss together the cabbage, red and green bell peppers, cucumber and scallions. Mix in the mayonnaise, vinegar, salt and black pepper.
2~ Cover and refrigerate for up to 2 days before serving.

MAKES ABOUT 4½ CUPS
RECIPE BY MARCIA KIESEL

FLANK STEAK SANDWICHES WITH ROQUEFORT CHEESE

Snow peas add color and crunch to this beefy sandwich, and the Roquefort spread provides a tangy kick.

2 TEASPOONS BALSAMIC VINEGAR
1 TEASPOON DIJON-STYLE MUSTARD
½ TEASPOON CHOPPED FRESH TARRAGON OR ½ TEASPOON DRIED
¼ TEASPOON THYME
¼ TEASPOON SALT
⅛ TEASPOON FRESHLY GROUND PEPPER
⅓ CUP PLUS 2 TABLESPOONS OLIVE OIL
¾ POUND FLANK STEAK, IN ONE PIECE
3 OUNCES ROQUEFORT CHEESE, AT ROOM TEMPERATURE
2 OUNCES CREAM CHEESE, AT ROOM TEMPERATURE
2 TEASPOONS FRESH LEMON JUICE
¼ CUP CHOPPED TOASTED WALNUTS
6 OUNCES SNOW PEAS, TRIMMED
2 KAISER (HARD) ROLLS, SPLIT

1~ In a small bowl, whisk together the vinegar, mustard, tarragon, thyme, salt and pepper. Gradually whisk in ⅓ cup of the oil until well blended. Place the flank steak in a bowl and pour all but 2 tablespoons of the vinaigrette over the meat. Cover and let marinate, turning occasionally, for 1 hour at room temperature or overnight in the refrigerator.
2~ In a food processor or blender, puree the Roquefort, cream cheese and lemon juice until smooth. Season with pepper to taste. Scrape into a small bowl and stir in the walnuts.

3~ In a large skillet, heat 1 tablespoon of the olive oil over high heat. Add the snow peas and sauté until bright green but still crisp, about 1 minute. Remove and set aside. Add the remaining 1 tablespoon olive oil to the skillet and reduce the heat to moderately high. Add the flank steak and sauté, turning once, until medium-rare, 4 to 6 minutes per side. Slice the steak diagonally into thin strips.
4~ In a medium bowl, toss the sliced steak and pea pods with the remaining 2 tablespoons vinaigrette. Spread the Roquefort mixture evenly over both sides of each roll and fill with the steak and snow peas.

SERVES 2
RECIPE BY MIMI RUTH BRODEUR

165

CHICKEN AND AVOCADO CLUB SANDWICHES

166

In this new twist on an old favorite, an avocado puree embellishes the mayonnaise, and wheat pita rounds stand in for the traditional white toast. Offer plenty of napkins with this one.

3 TABLESPOONS CHAMPAGNE VINEGAR OR WHITE WINE VINEGAR
1 TABLESPOON FRESH LEMON JUICE
⅛ TO ¼ TEASPOON HOT PEPPER SAUCE
3 GARLIC CLOVES, MINCED
1 TEASPOON FRESH THYME OR ½ TEASPOON DRIED
¾ TEASPOON SALT
⅛ TEASPOON FRESHLY GROUND PEPPER
½ CUP PLUS 2 TABLESPOONS OLIVE OIL
2 SKINLESS, BONELESS CHICKEN BREAST HALVES (6 OUNCES EACH), POUNDED ⅛ INCH THICK
1 SMALL AVOCADO, PEELED AND PITTED
2 TABLESPOONS MAYONNAISE
8 SLICES OF BACON
3 WHOLE WHEAT PITA POCKETS (ABOUT 6 INCHES IN DIAMETER), SPLIT INTO ROUNDS
4 LETTUCE LEAVES
1 LARGE RIPE TOMATO, THINLY SLICED
1 SMALL RED ONION, THINLY SLICED

1~ In a small bowl, whisk together the vinegar, lemon juice, hot sauce, garlic, thyme, salt and pepper. Gradually whisk in the olive oil until well blended. Pour half of the vinaigrette over the chicken breasts; cover and let them marinate for 1 hour at room temperature or overnight in the refrigerator. Reserve the remaining vinaigrette.

2~ In a food processor or blender, puree the avocado with the mayonnaise and the remaining vinaigrette until smooth.

3~ In a large skillet, fry the bacon over moderately high heat until crisp, about 5 minutes. Remove and drain on paper towels. Pour off all but 2 tablespoons of the fat and return the skillet to the heat. Add the chicken breasts and sauté, turning once, until white throughout but still juicy, about 2 minutes. Remove and let cool to room temperature.

4~ Spread half of the avocado puree evenly over 2 of the pita rounds. Layer the puree with half of the lettuce, tomato, bacon and onion and top with a chicken breast. Place another pita round on top of the chicken and cover with the remaining avocado puree, lettuce, tomato, bacon and onion. Cover the sandwiches with the remaining pita rounds. Cut into quarters before serving.

SERVES 2
RECIPE BY MIMI RUTH BRODEUR

TUSCAN-STYLE WHITE BEAN SALAD

You'll want to make this salad throughout the year, and you can—among the ingredients, only the tomatoes are seasonal and these days, you can find decent ones even in the middle of winter.

2 CUPS DRIED CANNELLINI (ABOUT 12 OUNCES), GREAT NORTHERN WHITE OR CRANBERRY BEANS (SEE NOTE)
1 SMALL YELLOW ONION
2 GARLIC CLOVES
4 SPRIGS OF FRESH SAGE OR THYME, OR ¼ TEASPOON DRIED THYME
4 FRESH PLUM TOMATOES
2½ TEASPOONS SALT
1 TEASPOON FRESHLY GROUND PEPPER
1 SMALL RED ONION, CHOPPED
1 SMALL CELERY RIB WITH LEAVES, CUT INTO ¼-INCH DICE
¼ CUP THINLY SLICED SCALLION GREENS
2 TABLESPOONS SHREDDED FRESH BASIL
1 TABLESPOON CHOPPED PARSLEY
⅓ CUP EXTRA-VIRGIN OLIVE OIL
3 TABLESPOONS LEMON JUICE

1~ Either soak the dried beans overnight in cold water to cover by 4 inches or place in a large saucepan with several inches of water to cover and bring to a boil. Boil, covered, for 2 minutes, then remove from the heat and let stand for 1 hour. Drain the beans.

2~ Place in a large saucepan and cover with 4 inches of fresh cold water. Cover and bring to a boil over high heat. Tuck the yellow onion, garlic and 2 sprigs of the sage in with the beans. Simmer over low heat until the beans are tender but not mushy, about 1½ hours. Drain the beans; discard the onion, garlic and sage.

3~ Core and seed one of the tomatoes and cut it into ¾-inch dice. Cut the remaining 3 tomatoes lengthwise into 6 wedges each and set aside. Finely chop the remaining 2 sprigs of sage.

4~ Place the beans in a large mixing bowl and season with the salt and pepper. Add the chopped tomato and sage, the red onion, celery, scallion greens, basil, parsley, olive oil and lemon juice. Toss gently with 2 rubber spatulas to combine the ingredients without crushing the beans. Cover and set aside for at least 1 hour at room temperature to blend the flavors. *(The recipe can be prepared a day in advance up to this point and refrigerated, covered.)*

5~ Transfer the salad to a serving bowl or platter and surround with the tomato wedges. Serve at room temperature.

Note: If fresh cranberry beans are available, use 3 pounds (weighed in the pod), shelled. Begin at Step 2, but cook the beans for only about 20 minutes, until tender. If you prefer to use canned beans, use 2 cans (19 ounces each) of cannellini. Simply rinse and drain, then proceed to Step 3.

SERVES 6 TO 8
RECIPE BY RICHARD SAX

SIMPLY SUPER CHOCOLATE-CHUNK COOKIES

Serve these super-size, super-chunk cookies to all of your superlative friends.

2⅓ CUPS ALL-PURPOSE FLOUR
1 TEASPOON BAKING SODA
½ TEASPOON SALT
½ POUND (2 STICKS) UNSALTED BUTTER, AT ROOM TEMPERATURE
1 CUP PACKED DARK BROWN SUGAR
½ CUP GRANULATED SUGAR
2 EGGS, AT ROOM TEMPERATURE
9 OUNCES BITTERSWEET CHOCOLATE, CUT INTO ½-INCH PIECES
1½ CUPS COARSELY CHOPPED PECANS (ABOUT 6 OUNCES)

1~ Preheat the oven to 375°.

2~ In a medium bowl, toss together the flour, baking soda and salt.

3~ In a large bowl, beat the butter with an electric mixer, until soft and creamy, about 3 minutes. Gradually beat in the brown sugar and granulated sugar. Add the eggs one at a time. On low speed, gradually add the flour mixture, ½ cup at a time. Stir in the chocolate and the nuts.

4~ Fill a ¼-cup measuring cup with cookie dough. Drop the entire ¼ cup of dough onto an ungreased baking sheet for each cookie, allowing 3 inches in between for spreading. Flatten each cookie slightly with a fork. Bake for 15 to 17 minutes, or until lightly golden. Cool the cookies on a rack. Store airtight.

MAKES ABOUT 20
RECIPE BY DIANA STURGIS

■   ■ ■   ■   **1 6 7**

For the Record: Teams and Scores from Super Bowl I to XXIII

Green Bay Packers 35, Kansas City Chiefs 10
Green Bay Packers 33, Oakland Raiders 14
New York Jets 16, Baltimore Colts 7
Kansas City Chiefs 23, Minnesota Vikings 7
Baltimore Colts 16, Dallas Cowboys 13
Dallas Cowboys 24, Miami Dolphins 3
Miami Dolphins 14, Washington Redskins 7
Miami Dolphins 24, Minnesota Vikings 7
Pittsburgh Steelers 16, Minnesota Vikings 6
Pittsburgh Steelers 21, Dallas Cowboys 17
Oakland Raiders 32, Minnesota Vikings 14
Dallas Cowboys 27, Denver Broncos 10
Pittsburgh Steelers 35, Dallas Cowboys 31
Pittsburgh Steelers 31, L.A. Rams 19
Oakland Raiders 27, Philadelphia Eagles 10
San Francisco 49ers 26, Cincinnati Bengals 21
Washington Redskins 27, Miami Dolphins 17
L.A. Raiders 38, Washington Redskins 9
San Francisco 49ers 38, Miami Dolphins 16
Chicago Bears 46, New England Patriots 10
New York Giants 39, Denver Broncos 20
Washington Redskins 42, Denver Broncos 10
San Francisco 49ers 16, Cincinnati Bengals 13

■   ■ ■   ■

■ ■ ■

A
MOST EXTRAVAGANT
DINNER

This is the most playful menu in this book. Chances are you'll never serve all of these extravagant dishes in a single meal. But anytime you want to insert one delicious and improvident course into a menu of dishes, look here for recipes that require some of the most highly prized ingredients on earth. ∼ If you have some truly outstanding occasion to celebrate, of course, you can make the whole menu. This is a dinner to celebrate getting a multimillion-dollar client, making partner or just to rejoice in a big end-of-year bonus. ∼ We give you hors d'oeuvre that put the finest smoked salmon and caviar to excellent use. Whichever first course you choose – the duck or goose *foie gras* on slices of toasted brioche or the ragout of snails and wild mushrooms with tarragon – you cannot go wrong. The main course – rare leg of lamb served with *rösti* topped with a dollop of scrambled eggs with black truffles – pushes this dinner into the realm of the sublime. For dessert, choose between the Pears Poached in Sauternes and the Frozen Chocolate Mascarpone Cream with Toasted Hazelnuts. Or if both are on the agenda, sip a tot of Poire William in between.

Butterflied Leg
of Lamb

Rösti
topped with
Scrambled Eggs with
Black Truffles

■ ■ ■

170

A
MOST EXTRAVAGANT
DINNER

Serves 6

TOP-QUALITY CHAMPAGNE

*Smoked Salmon Cornets with
Horseradish Cream*

Polenta and Mushroom Canapés

Caviar Roulade

foie gras on toasted brioche with

CHÂTEAU D'YQUEM 1971

or

*Ragout of Snails and
Wild Mushrooms with Tarragon with*

CHÂTEAU TALBOT 1976

CHÂTEAU HAUT-BRION 1966

Butterflied Leg of Lamb

*Rösti
topped with
Scrambled Eggs with Black Truffles*

Salade Blanche

Frozen Chocolate Mascarpone Cream

or

Pears Poached in Sauternes with

CHÂTEAU D'YQUEM 1971

COGNACS, EAUX-DE-VIE AND ESPRESSO

SMOKED SALMON
CORNETS WITH
HORSERADISH CREAM

Tiny jewel-like bites of smoked salmon make
just the right start to an evening of celebration
and revelry.

10 OUNCES THINLY SLICED SCOTCH OR
OTHER GOOD-QUALITY SMOKED
SALMON
6 THIN SLICES OF SQUARE PUMPERNICKEL
BREAD
½ CUP HEAVY CREAM
2 TABLESPOONS WELL-DRAINED PREPARED
WHITE HORSERADISH

1~ Cut the salmon slices into 2-inch squares and
refrigerate between sheets of waxed paper.
Reserve the scraps for another use.
2~ Trim off the bread crusts and cut each slice of
bread into 6 small triangles. Wrap in plastic
wrap to prevent drying out.
3~ Beat the cream until stiff peaks form. Fold in
the horseradish.
4~ To assemble, roll the squares of salmon into
small cornets. Place one on each bread trian-
gle. Using a small pastry bag with a star tip,
pipe the horseradish cream into the cornets.
Refrigerate, covered, for up to 3 hours before
serving.

MAKES 36 HORS D'OEUVRE
RECIPE FROM THE FOUR SEASONS
NEW YORK CITY

POLENTA AND
MUSHROOM CANAPÉS

Pretty to look at and easy to eat, these pre-
cious-looking canapés do not require a lot of
last-minute hands-on fuss.

¾ TEASPOON SALT
½ CUP INSTANT POLENTA
FRESHLY GROUND PEPPER
2 OUNCES DRIED PORCINI MUSHROOMS
25 MUSHROOMS WITH 1-INCH CAPS
JUICE OF 1 LEMON
3 TABLESPOONS UNSALTED BUTTER
3 TABLESPOONS OLIVE OIL
1 TABLESPOON MINCED SHALLOT
1 TEASPOON MINCED GARLIC
1 TABLESPOON TOMATO PASTE
1 ROASTED RED BELL PEPPER,
CUT INTO ¼-INCH STRIPS
25 FRESH BASIL LEAVES

1~ In a medium saucepan, bring 1½ cups of water
and the salt to a boil over high heat. Add the
polenta in a thin stream, reduce the heat to
moderate and cook, stirring constantly, until
the polenta masses together and pulls away
from the side of the pan, about 5 minutes.
Season with pepper.
2~ Turn the polenta into an oiled 8-inch square
pan. Quickly spread into an even layer. Cover
and refrigerate overnight. *(The polenta can be
made up to 2 days ahead; let return to room
temperature before proceeding.)*
3~ Soak the porcini in hot water to cover until
soft, about 30 minutes. Rinse the porcini and
squeeze dry. Mince the porcini and set aside.

CAVIAR ROULADE

4~ Separate the mushroom caps and stems. Mince the stems and set aside. Using a small sharp knife, flute the mushrooms by holding the blade at an angle to the top of the cap and swiveling the mushroom. In a large bowl, combine 3 cups of water with the lemon juice. As the mushroom caps are fluted, drop them into the acidulated water.

5~ In a large skillet, melt 2 tablespoons of the butter in the oil over moderately high heat. Add the shallot and garlic and cook until fragrant, about 1 minute. Add the porcini and sauté for 2 minutes. Add the mushroom stems and sauté for 2 minutes longer. Add the tomato paste and cook, stirring occasionally, until most of the liquid evaporates but the mixture is still moist enough to mass together, 5 to 10 minutes. Season with salt and pepper to taste. *(The filling can be made up to 2 days ahead. Refrigerate, covered; let return to room temperature before proceeding.)*

6~ Melt the remaining 1 tablespoon butter over low heat; set aside. Preheat the oven to 500°.

7~ Cut the polenta into 1½-inch squares; arrange the squares on a baking sheet. Arrange a strip of red pepper diagonally across each square. Pat the mushroom caps dry. Stuff each cap with filling and place, filled-side down, on top of a polenta square. Brush lightly with the melted butter. Bake until just warmed through, about 3 minutes. Garnish each canapé with a basil leaf.

MAKES ABOUT 2 DOZEN
RECIPE BY NEW YORK PARTIES

Caviar is festive under any circumstances. Here, it is served on a slice of soufflélike sponge.

4 TABLESPOONS UNSALTED BUTTER
½ CUP SIFTED ALL-PURPOSE FLOUR
2 CUPS HOT MILK
4 EGGS, SEPARATED
PINCH OF SALT
3 OUNCES CREAM CHEESE, SOFTENED
1 CUP SOUR CREAM
4 OUNCES CAVIAR

1~ Preheat the oven to 425°. Lightly butter a 10-by-15-inch jelly-roll pan. Line the pan with parchment or waxed paper. Lightly butter the paper; dust with flour and tap out any excess.

2~ In a medium saucepan, melt the butter over low heat. Stir in the flour, increase the heat to moderately high and cook for 1 minute. Pour in the hot milk and cook, whisking constantly, until the mixture is thick and smooth, about 1 minute.

3~ Remove from the heat and beat in the egg yolks, 1 at a time, beating well after each addition.

4~ In a large bowl, beat the egg whites with the salt until stiff but not dry. Gently fold the beaten whites into the base until no streaks remain.

5~ Pour the batter into the pan and spread evenly. Bake for about 15 minutes, or until the cake springs back to the touch and is golden brown on top. Let cool for 10 minutes. Unmold onto a kitchen towel.

6~ In a small bowl, combine the cream cheese with 3 tablespoons of the sour cream. Spread over the cake. Starting with a short side, roll the cake up like a jellyroll. *(The recipe can be made to this point up to 3 hours ahead. Set aside, covered, at room temperature.)*

7~ To serve, carefully slice the roll with a serrated knife. Serve each slice with a heaping spoonful of the remaining sour cream and top with a dollop of caviar. Serve warm or at room temperature.

SERVES 8 TO 12
RECIPE BY CRAIG CLAIBORNE

171

172

A Bit about *Foie Gras*

Foie gras, *the fatted liver of either goose* (foie gras d'oie) *or duck* (foie gras de canard), *is a rare and costly ingredient that tastes like nothing else in the world. It may be purchased raw,* mi-cuit *or as a terrine. The raw* foie gras *will require soaking, cleaning and cooking, a job best done by someone with experience.* Mi-cuit foie gras *is cooked and vacuum-packed, ready to eat without further cooking. A terrine of* foie gras *is cooked and ready to serve either slightly chilled or at room temperature. It is best spread on toast and savored, along with sips of a honeyed fine Sauternes. For this extravagant dinner, serve each guest two thin slices of* foie gras, *layered on slices of toasted brioche or other special bread.*

RAGOUT OF SNAILS AND WILD MUSHROOMS WITH TARRAGON

You get your choice with this recipe. Use it in this menu in lieu of *foie gras,* or save it to serve as a rich, appealing first course with any roasted or broiled entrée.

6 TABLESPOONS UNSALTED BUTTER
¼ CUP MINCED ONION
1 LARGE GARLIC CLOVE, MINCED
½ POUND FRESH SHIITAKE OR OTHER FLAVORFUL WILD MUSHROOMS, STEMMED AND QUARTERED
⅓ CUP CANNED CRUSHED ITALIAN PEELED TOMATOES
¾ CUP CHICKEN STOCK OR CANNED BROTH
1 CAN (7 OUNCES) SNAILS, JUICE RESERVED
¼ CUP PLUS 1 TABLESPOON SWEET MARSALA
1½ TABLESPOONS MINCED FRESH TARRAGON
4 LARGE SLICES OF STALE FRENCH OR ITALIAN BREAD
¾ TEASPOON SALT
½ TEASPOON FRESHLY GROUND BLACK PEPPER
2 TEASPOONS FRESH LEMON JUICE

1~ Preheat the oven to 400°.
2~ In a large skillet, melt 2 tablespoons of the butter over moderate heat. Add the onion and garlic. Reduce the heat to low and cook until the onion is soft but not brown, about 5 minutes. Add the mushrooms and cook, stirring occasionally, until wilted, about 10 minutes.

3~ Increase the heat to moderate and stir in the tomatoes, chicken stock, reserved snail juice, ¼ cup of the Marsala and 1 tablespoon of the tarragon. Bring to a boil, reduce the heat to low and simmer until reduced by about one-third, about 15 minutes.
4~ Meanwhile, in a small saucepan, melt 2 tablespoons of the butter. Brush both sides of each bread slice with the melted butter. Place the bread on a baking sheet and bake until golden brown on the bottom, about 8 minutes. Turn the bread slices and cook until browned on the second side, about 5 minutes. Place each slice of bread in a shallow gratin dish.
5~ Add the snails to the ragout. Stir in the remaining ½ tablespoon tarragon, 1 tablespoon Marsala, the salt, pepper and lemon juice. Increase the heat to high and bring the mixture to a boil. Turn off the heat and swirl in the remaining 2 tablespoons butter.
6~ To serve, spoon the ragout over each slice of bread and serve hot.

MAKES 4 FIRST-COURSE SERVINGS
RECIPE BY MARCIA KIESEL

BUTTERFLIED LEG OF LAMB

This entrée is a cinch to prepare since the butcher does all of the hard work for you.

LAMB:

1 TABLESPOON PLUS 1 TEASPOON OLIVE OIL
1 TEASPOON SOY SAUCE
1 TABLESPOON FINELY CHOPPED FRESH
    ROSEMARY OR TARRAGON OR
    1 TEASPOON DRIED, CRUMBLED
1 LEG OF LAMB (ABOUT 7 POUNDS)—
    TRIMMED OF FAT, BONED AND
    BUTTERFLIED
2 LARGE GARLIC CLOVES, EACH CUT INTO
    12 SLIVERS
3 TABLESPOONS FRESH LEMON JUICE

SAUCE:

1 LARGE GARLIC CLOVE, CRUSHED AND
    CHOPPED
1 TABLESPOON FRESH LEMON JUICE
¾ TEASPOON FRESH THYME OR
    ¼ TEASPOON DRIED, CRUMBLED
1 TABLESPOON MINCED FRESH PARSLEY

1~ *Prepare the Lamb:* Preheat the oven to 400°.
2~ In a small bowl, combine 1 tablespoon of the olive oil with the soy sauce and 2 teaspoons of the fresh rosemary or ¾ teaspoon of the dried. Rub the lamb all over with the mixture.
3~ With a small sharp knife, make 24 slits in the boned side of the lamb and insert a garlic sliver in each. Rub the lamb with the remaining olive oil and rosemary and pour the lemon juice over all.

4~ Place the lamb, boned side down, on a broiler rack with a broiler pan underneath to catch the drippings. Roast in the oven for about 20 minutes, or until the internal temperature reaches 120°.
5~ Increase the oven temperature to broil and place the lamb under the broiler about 5 inches from the heat. Broil for 2 to 3 minutes, or until the meat starts to brown. Transfer the lamb to a carving board and let rest for about 10 minutes.
6~ Meanwhile, *prepare the Sauce:* Stir the garlic, lemon juice and thyme into the pan juices, cover and keep warm.
7~ To serve, carve the lamb and transfer the slices to a serving platter. Stir the parsley into the sauce and pour over the lamb or pass separately.

SERVES 8 TO 12
RECIPE BY JANE AND BEN THOMPSON

SCRAMBLED EGGS WITH BLACK TRUFFLES

A pull-out-the-stops dinner has to include truffles in order to be complete. We'd serve just a spoonful of these truffled eggs on or next to the *rösti*. Or you can even save this treat for breakfast the morning after.

8 EGGS
2 OUNCES FRESH BLACK TRUFFLES
1 GARLIC CLOVE, PEELED
8 TABLESPOONS UNSALTED BUTTER
¼ TEASPOON SALT
⅛ TEASPOON FRESHLY GROUND PEPPER

1~ Place the uncracked eggs in a bowl with the whole truffles, cover tightly and refrigerate overnight.
2~ Break the eggs into a medium bowl. Spear the garlic clove on a fork and use it to beat the eggs. Set aside with the garlic in the eggs.
3~ Cut the truffles into very thin slices or shavings. Add them to the beaten eggs and let stand for 15 minutes.
4~ In a small saucepan, melt 5 tablespoons of the butter over low heat; set aside. Thinly slice the remaining 3 tablespoons butter into the eggs.
5~ Pour 3 tablespoons of the melted butter into a heavy nonreactive double boiler or medium saucepan set in a larger pan of hot water. Remove the garlic and pour the beaten eggs into the double boiler. Add the salt and pepper. Cook over steaming water, whisking constantly, until the eggs have a thick, custardlike consistency, 15 to 20 minutes. Do not let the eggs curdle. Whisk in the remaining melted butter and serve at once.

SERVES 3 TO 4 AS AN ENTRÉE
RECIPE BY JUDITH OLNEY

RÖSTI

There's nothing neutral about *rösti*, the sublime Swiss shredded-potato pancakes. They are magnificent. This recipe makes four 8-inch *rösti*—you'll need only one, or at most two, for your dinner, so halve the recipe accordingly.

4 MEDIUM BAKING POTATOES
½ CUP LARD
ABOUT 2 TABLESPOONS UNSALTED BUTTER
SALT AND FRESHLY GROUND PEPPER

1~ In a large saucepan of boiling salted water, cook the whole, unpeeled potatoes over moderate heat for about 15 minutes, until a skewer or knife point easily pierces the outer ½ inch of potato but meets resistance in the center (the potatoes will finish cooking later). Drain the potatoes and rinse under cold running water. Refrigerate uncovered until well chilled, 3 to 4 hours or overnight.

2~ Peel the potatoes. In a food processor fitted with a shredding blade or on the large holes of a hand grater, shred the potatoes lengthwise to make long, even shreds.

3~ In a heavy 8-inch skillet with sloping sides or in an omelet pan, melt 2 tablespoons of the lard over high heat until the lard begins to smoke.

4~ Sprinkle one-quarter (about ¾ cup) of the shredded potato into the skillet. Season lightly with salt and pepper. Quickly push any stray shreds in from the outer rim of the pan to form an even round pancake. Lightly tamp down the top of the *rösti*.

5~ Reduce the heat to moderately high, and cook the *rösti*, shaking and rotating the pan occasionally to loosen the potatoes, until well browned on the bottom, about 3 minutes. (If the potatoes stick, remove the pan from the heat and rap it sharply on a hard surface, such as a cutting board, to loosen them.)

6~ Add ½ tablespoon butter to the edge of the pan. Rotate quickly to melt and distribute the butter. Flip the *rösti* like a flapjack or turn over with a wide spatula.

7~ Season lightly again with salt and pepper. Continue cooking over moderately high heat, adding additional butter if the pan becomes dry, until browned on the second side, about 3 minutes longer. Keep warm in a low oven while you make the other *rösti* with the remaining ingredients.

MAKES 4 PANCAKES
RECIPE BY JOHN ROBERT MASSIE

SALADE BLANCHE

A long meal needs a salad course, if only to add a bit of resting time between richer foods. This simple salad will give you a refreshing interlude between the main course and two very appealing desserts.

1 HEAD OF CURLY ENDIVE, CUT INTO
  A CHIFFONADE
1 HEAD OF BELGIAN ENDIVE, CUT INTO
  A CHIFFONADE
1 SMALL HEAD OF BOSTON LETTUCE,
  CUT INTO A CHIFFONADE
¼ CUP EXTRA-VIRGIN OLIVE OIL
1 TABLESPOON WHITE WINE VINEGAR
½ TEASPOON DIJON-STYLE MUSTARD
½ TEASPOON SALT
½ TEASPOON FRESHLY GROUND PEPPER

1~ Combine the lettuces in a large bowl and toss together. Cover and refrigerate.

2~ In a jar, combine the oil, vinegar, mustard, salt and pepper. Cover and shake well.

3~ To serve, shake the dressing and pour over the lettuces. Toss well to coat. Divide the salad among chilled salad plates and serve.

SERVES 6
RECIPE BY FOOD & WINE

FROZEN CHOCOLATE MASCARPONE CREAM

Ummm—creamy, smooth and rich with chocolate. How can you miss? This dessert adds a glamorous finish to a special meal.

½ CUP HAZELNUTS
3 OUNCES BITTERSWEET CHOCOLATE
2 EGG YOLKS, AT ROOM TEMPERATURE
2 TABLESPOONS SUGAR
6 OUNCES (¾ CUP) MASCARPONE CHEESE, AT ROOM TEMPERATURE
¼ TEASPOON VANILLA EXTRACT
1 TABLESPOON COFFEE LIQUEUR
½ CUP HEAVY CREAM

1~ Preheat the oven to 350°.
2~ Spread the hazelnuts on a small baking sheet and roast until the skins begin to crack and the nuts are browned, about 10 minutes. Transfer to a kitchen towel and rub off as much of the brown outer skin as possible. Let the nuts cool, then coarsely chop.
3~ In a small saucepan over hot water or in a microwave oven, melt the chocolate, stirring until smooth.
4~ In a medium bowl, beat the egg yolks lightly. Add 1 tablespoon of the sugar and beat with an electric hand mixer on medium speed for 1 minute. Add the remaining 1 tablespoon sugar and beat for 3 to 4 minutes, until thick and pale yellow.
5~ Blend in the melted chocolate. Beat in the mascarpone, vanilla and coffee liqueur.
6~ In another bowl, beat the cream until it stands in soft peaks. Stir one-fourth of the whipped cream into the chocolate mixture. Fold in the remaining whipped cream and the nuts.
7~ Scrape into a small (3-cup) loaf pan or bowl. Cover and freeze for 3 hours or until firm.

SERVES 4 TO 6
RECIPE BY FOOD & WINE

PEARS POACHED IN SAUTERNES

If you are serving a second dessert, you'll want to halve this recipe so your guests will be able to sample both sweets.

6 LARGE PEARS, SUCH AS ANJOU— PEELED, CORED AND QUARTERED (ABOUT 3¼ POUNDS)
2 TABLESPOONS FRESH LEMON JUICE
1 BOTTLE SAUTERNES
3 TABLESPOONS SUGAR
4 WHOLE CLOVES
1 TEASPOON PEAR BRANDY (OPTIONAL)
FRESHLY GROUND BLACK PEPPER
FRESHLY GRATED LIME ZEST

1~ In a medium bowl, toss the pears with the lemon juice.
2~ In a large shallow nonreactive pan, combine the Sauternes, sugar and cloves. Bring to a boil over moderately high heat. Add the pears. When the liquid returns to a simmer, reduce the heat to moderately low and cook until the pears are tender when pierced, 8 to 10 minutes. Remove the pears and set aside. Discard the cloves.
3~ Boil the poaching liquid over moderate heat until reduced to ½ cup, 8 to 10 minutes. Remove from the heat and let cool. Stir in the pear brandy, if using. *(The recipe can be prepared ahead to this point. Combine the pears and the syrup, cover and refrigerate.)*
4~ To serve, divide the pear quarters among the dessert plates. Sprinkle each serving with 1 tablespoon of the syrup and garnish with a light dusting of pepper and lime zest.

SERVES 8
RECIPE BY W. PETER PRESTCOTT

■ ■ ■

A
MIDDAY MEAL ON
THE COLDEST
DAY OF THE YEAR

The mercury is shivering at the zero mark, the
windchill factor is sending the temperature deep
into the negative numbers, and there is no way
you're going to budge from your warm and cozy lair.
Instead, you'll cook. You'll cook for anyone who'll
brave the cold to get to your kitchen. ～ To warm
you thoroughly, we start with a bowl of potato soup
strewn with potato skin croutons and accompanied
by chunks of crusty peasant bread. Next comes
France's ultimate homey, wintertime dish – Cassoulet de Castelnaudary. If you don't make your own
confit, buy it already made. If you forget to get it at
the store, go on without it; this cassoulet still will be
delicious. Serve it with a mustardy celery root salad
and savor the combination of flavors. ～ After dinner, sit back with some coffee or hot chocolate to
decide which dessert you'll have first – the gingerbread or the allspice bread pudding. Don't ponder
the question too long, though. Over the course of the
afternoon you're bound to have some of each.

■ ■ ■

Celery Root
with
Celery Dressing

Cassoulet de
Castelnaudary

POTATO SOUP WITH GREENS AND CRISP POTATO SKIN CROUTONS

A MIDDAY MEAL ON THE COLDEST DAY OF THE YEAR

Serves 6 to 8

HEARTY RED WINE
Potato Soup with Greens and Crisp Potato Skin Croutons
crusty peasant bread

Cassoulet de Castelnaudary
Celery Root with Celery Dressing

COFFEE OR HOT CHOCOLATE
Gingerbread Cake
Allspice Bread Pudding

This hearty soup really hits the spot on cold nasty days. The potato skin croutons not only make a fine garnish for the soup but are a treat (cut into strips instead of small pieces) to nibble on with drinks.

3 RUSSET OR OTHER BAKING POTATOES
¼ POUND SMOKED SLAB BACON
   WITH RIND
1 MEDIUM ONION, COARSELY CHOPPED
2 GARLIC CLOVES, COARSELY CHOPPED
½ POUND KALE, LARGE STEMS REMOVED,
   COARSELY CHOPPED (ABOUT 8 CUPS)
2 CUPS CHICKEN STOCK OR CANNED BROTH
3 TABLESPOONS OLIVE OIL
1 TEASPOON SALT
¼ TEASPOON FRESHLY GROUND PEPPER
1 BUNCH OF WATERCRESS, COARSELY
   CHOPPED
2 TABLESPOONS UNSALTED BUTTER
   (OPTIONAL)

1~ Preheat the oven to 400°.
2~ Pierce the potatoes several times with a fork. Bake for about 50 minutes, or until tender when pierced with a fork.
3~ Meanwhile, remove the rind from the bacon in one piece and reserve. Slice the bacon into ¼-inch-thick slices and then slice crosswise into ¼-inch-wide julienne. In a stockpot, fry the bacon over moderate heat until browned. Remove with a slotted spoon and drain on paper towels; reserve the bacon for soup garnish.
4~ Pour off all but 2 tablespoons of the bacon fat. Add the onion and garlic to the pan. Cover and cook over low heat until softened but not browned, about 5 minutes.
5~ Add the kale, chicken stock, reserved bacon rind and 4 cups of water. Bring to a simmer and cook, partially covered, for 1 hour. Remove and discard the bacon rind.
6~ When the potatoes are done, leave the oven on at 400°. Cut the potatoes in half and scoop out the insides; set aside. Halve each potato skin lengthwise. Brush liberally on both sides with the oil. Place on a baking sheet and bake, turning once, for 15 minutes, until browned and crisp. Remove from the oven and sprinkle with ½ teaspoon of the salt. Chop into bite-size croutons.
7~ Mash half of the reserved potato pulp and stir into the soup. Break the remainder into small pieces and drop into the soup. Simmer until warmed through, about 10 minutes. Season with the remaining ½ teaspoon salt and the pepper.
8~ Stir the watercress into the soup. Swirl in the butter. Ladle the soup into individual soup bowls and sprinkle the potato skin croutons and bacon on top.

SERVES 8 TO 10
RECIPE BY ANNE DISRUDE

CASSOULET DE CASTELNAUDARY

There are many versions of cassoulet; three are widely recognized. The most famous, cassoulet of Toulouse, was nicknamed "God the Father" by Anatole France. It contains pork, sausages, confit, mutton and white kidney beans. The cassoulet of Carcassonne, "God the Son," adds chicken livers and red partridge; while the cassoulet of Castelnaudary, "God the Holy Spirit," is said to be the essence of them all.

1½ POUNDS DRIED WHITE KIDNEY BEANS, SOAKED OVERNIGHT AND DRAINED

1½ TEASPOONS SALT

½ POUND GARLIC SAUSAGE

1 POUND SLAB BACON, CUT INTO ½-INCH DICE

3 PIECES OF DUCK CONFIT

1½-POUND BONELESS PORK LOIN, CUT INTO 2-INCH CUBES

½ POUND FRESH PORK SAUSAGES, SUCH AS SWEET ITALIAN

2 MEDIUM ONIONS, CHOPPED

2 POUNDS TOMATOES—PEELED, SEEDED AND COARSELY CHOPPED

¾ CUP DRY WHITE WINE

3 OR 4 GARLIC CLOVES

1 TABLESPOON TOMATO PASTE

BOUQUET GARNI: 8 PARSLEY STEMS, ½ TEASPOON THYME AND 1 BAY LEAF TIED IN A DOUBLE THICKNESS OF CHEESECLOTH

¼ TEASPOON FRESHLY GROUND PEPPER

⅔ CUP DRY BREAD CRUMBS

1~ Place the beans in a large saucepan or stovetop casserole and add enough cold water to cover generously, about 8 cups. Bring to a boil over high heat, reduce the heat to low, cover and simmer for 30 minutes. Add ½ teaspoon of the salt and continue to cook for 30 minutes longer. Drain the beans, reserving the cooking liquid.

2~ Preheat the oven to 350°.

3~ Prick the garlic sausage all over with a fork and place in a medium saucepan; add water to cover. Bring to a boil, reduce the heat to moderately low and poach just below the boil for 30 minutes. Drain and let rest until cool enough to handle. Cut the sausage into 1½-inch lengths.

4~ Meanwhile, in a medium saucepan of boiling water, blanch the bacon for 2 minutes. Drain and rinse under cold running water to refresh; pat dry.

5~ Place the pieces of confit, skin-side down, in a large flameproof casserole and cook over moderately high heat until browned, about 5 minutes. Remove with a slotted spoon.

6~ Add the pork loin pieces to the hot fat in the casserole and cook, turning, until browned on all sides, about 5 minutes. Remove the pork with a slotted spoon.

7~ Prick the fresh sausages all over with a fork. Add them to the pan and cook, turning, until browned, about 5 minutes. Remove with a slotted spoon.

8~ Add the blanched bacon to the pan and cook without browning, stirring once or twice, for 2 minutes. Add the onions and cook with the bacon, stirring occasionally, until both are browned, about 8 minutes.

9~ Stir in the tomatoes, wine, garlic, tomato paste, bouquet garni, 3 cups of the reserved bean liquid, the remaining 1 teaspoon salt and the pepper. Add the cubes of pork and bring to a boil. Cover and cook in the oven until the pork is almost tender, 50 to 60 minutes.

10~ Cut each piece of duck confit in half. Cut the fresh sausages into 1½-inch lengths. Add the garlic sausages, confit, fresh sausages and the beans to the casserole, stirring to mix them together with the meats. Add 2 more cups of the reserved bean liquid, cover and return to the oven. Cook for 1 to 1½ hours, until moist but not soupy.

11~ Remove and discard the bouquet garni. Season with additional salt and pepper to taste. Sprinkle the bread crumbs over the cassoulet. *(The recipe can be prepared to this point up to 3 days ahead. Cover and refrigerate; let return to room temperature before proceeding.)*

12~ Preheat the oven to 400°.

13~ Bake the cassoulet, uncovered, until a golden brown crust forms on top, 30 to 45 minutes. Serve from the pot.

SERVES 6
RECIPE BY ANNE WILLAN

CELERY ROOT WITH CELERY DRESSING

180 Celery root, a.k.a. celeriac, is a crunchy and flavorful ingredient that deserves more frequent use in our kitchens.

2 CUPS CHOPPED CELERY (4 TO 6 RIBS), INCLUDING SOME OF THE LEAVES
1 LARGE GARLIC CLOVE, SLICED
1 SMALL ONION, CHOPPED
1 TEASPOON SALT
½ CUP PLUS 1 TABLESPOON OLIVE OIL
2 EGG YOLKS, AT ROOM TEMPERATURE
3 TABLESPOONS FRESH LEMON JUICE
⅓ CUP SOUR CREAM
1½ TABLESPOONS DIJON-STYLE MUSTARD
1 TEASPOON SUGAR
½ TEASPOON GROUND CUMIN
¼ TEASPOON CELERY SEEDS
¼ TEASPOON FRESHLY GROUND PEPPER
2 POUNDS CELERY ROOT, PEELED AND CUT INTO ¼-INCH THICK JULIENNE

1~ In a medium saucepan, combine the celery, garlic, onion, ½ teaspoon of the salt, 1 tablespoon of the oil and 2 cups of water. Bring to a boil over moderately high heat. Boil, uncovered, until the water has evaporated and the vegetables begin to sauté in the oil, 15 to 20 minutes. Continue to cook, stirring constantly, until the celery is dry, about 2 minutes.

2~ Puree the celery mixture in a food processor or through the medium disk of a food mill. Transfer the puree to a fine sieve set over a bowl and let any excess moisture drain off.

3~ In a food processor, mix the egg yolks and 1 tablespoon of the lemon juice until blended. With the motor running, gradually add the remaining ½ cup oil in a thin stream to make a smooth, thick mayonnaise. Scrape into a bowl and stir in the celery puree, sour cream, mustard, sugar, cumin, celery seeds, the remaining ½ teaspoon salt, the pepper and the remaining 2 tablespoons lemon juice. Cover and refrigerate.

4~ Bring a large pot of lightly salted water to a boil. Add the celery root, return to a boil and cook for 1 minute. Drain and rinse under cold running water; drain well. Dry with paper towels.

5~ Toss the celery root with the celery dressing. If desired, stir in additional lemon juice or mustard to taste. Cover and refrigerate until chilled before serving.

SERVES 8
RECIPE BY FOOD & WINE

GINGERBREAD CAKE

This is how most of us remember the gingerbread cakes of our childhood: simple and even-textured, with a pleasantly spicy taste. Serve it with whipped cream, ice cream or toast a slice and spread it with butter for breakfast.

1½ TEASPOONS GROUND GINGER
1½ TEASPOONS GROUND CINNAMON
¼ TEASPOON GROUND NUTMEG
¼ TEASPOON GROUND CLOVES
1 TEASPOON BAKING SODA
½ TEASPOON SALT
½ CUP DARK UNSULPHURED MOLASSES
¼ POUND (1 STICK) UNSALTED BUTTER, AT ROOM TEMPERATURE
½ CUP PACKED DARK BROWN SUGAR
3 EGGS
2 CUPS ALL-PURPOSE FLOUR

1~ Preheat the oven to 350°. Butter an 8-inch square baking pan.

2~ In a small bowl, combine the ginger, cinnamon, nutmeg, cloves, baking soda and salt.

3~ In a small saucepan, preferably nonstick, heat the molasses over low heat until bubbles begin to form around the sides. Remove from the heat and stir in the butter, 1 tablespoon at a time, until melted and blended.

ALLSPICE BREAD PUDDING

4~ Scrape the molasses into a large mixer bowl. Gradually beat in the spice mixture, brown sugar and ¼ cup of water. Add the eggs, 1 at a time, beating until well blended, 3 to 5 minutes. Add the flour and beat on low speed for 1 minute, then increase the speed to moderate and beat until well combined.

5~ Pour the batter into the prepared pan. Bake for 45 to 50 minutes, or until a skewer inserted into the center of the cake comes out clean. Let cool in the pan on a rack. Cut into squares to serve.

SERVES 9
RECIPE BY LINDA MERINOFF

On winter's coldest day, two desserts are not too much. After all, sugar produces heat, or so we like to think.

1½ CUPS MILK
1 CUP HEAVY CREAM
¾ CUP PACKED LIGHT BROWN SUGAR
1½ TABLESPOONS WHOLE ALLSPICE BERRIES, BRUISED
8 THIN SLICES OF FIRM-TEXTURED WHITE BREAD, CRUSTS REMOVED
¾ CUP (4 OUNCES) PITTED PRUNES, CUT INTO ⅜-INCH DICE
3 WHOLE EGGS
2 EGG YOLKS
¾ TEASPOON VANILLA EXTRACT
2 TABLESPOONS GRANULATED SUGAR

1~ In a heavy medium nonreactive saucepan, combine the milk, cream, brown sugar and allspice berries. Bring to a boil. Remove from the heat, cover and let steep for 10 minutes; the mixture will look curdled.

2~ Preheat the oven to 375°. Butter eight 6-ounce ramekins or custard cups.

3~ Cut the bread into ½-inch dice. Place the bread in a bowl and toss with the prunes; distribute the mixture among the ramekins.

4~ In a large bowl, whisk together the whole eggs, egg yolks and vanilla. Strain the allspice milk mixture, discarding the berries. Whisk the liquid into the eggs.

5~ Place the ramekins in a large roasting pan. Ladle about ⅓ cup of the custard into each ramekin. Push the bread down into the custard. Add additional custard to fill the cups. Let stand for 10 minutes.

6~ Sprinkle the granulated sugar on top of the puddings. Fill the roasting pan with enough cold water to reach almost halfway up the sides of the ramekins. Bake in the center of the oven for 20 to 25 minutes, or until a knife inserted near the center of a pudding comes out clean and the tops are puffed and golden. Remove the ramekins to a rack and let cool.

7~ Serve warm, at room temperature or chilled.

SERVES 8
RECIPE BY DORIE GREENSPAN

181

■ ■ ■

A MENU
FOR ALL SEASONS

Most of us find a great deal of comfort in the familiar. We grow accustomed to things and places, and we look forward to them; they become our friends. The same can be said of certain foods. It's so enjoyable to sit down to a favorite meal, not a detail of which is different from the last time it was served. ∽ Here, then, is a menu for all seasons. Serve it as frequently or as rarely as you please. It is never inappropriate, since its recipes include a pleasing combination of ingredients that always are available. You can make this dinner during any month of the year, at midday, afternoon or evening on any day of the week. The roasted pepper soup and double-corn and Cheddar muffins can be served as a duet to make a filling and tasty lunch, or as preface to the dinner's main course, as they are here. You'll be having an all-in-one chicken dish for your entrée, accompanied, if you like, by an excellent green salad scattered with Roquefort and roasted walnuts. For dessert, the lavender-pepper pears and a wedge of your favorite cheese add a civilized note to the end of the meal.

■ ■ ■

Mixed Salad
with
Roasted Walnuts and
Roquefort

Roasted Pepper
Soup with
Zucchini

ROASTED PEPPER SOUP WITH ZUCCHINI

184

This soup is adapted from a recipe that appeared in *Cucina Fresca* by Viana La Place and Evan Kleiman. Extra-virgin olive oil not only emulsifies and smooths out this soup but adds, along with the balsamic vinegar, a distinct fruity flavor. Note that the soup is served at room temperature.

4 LARGE RED BELL PEPPERS
2 CUPS PEELED, CHOPPED AND SEEDED
   FRESH TOMATOES, OR 1 CAN
   (35 OUNCES) ITALIAN PEELED TOMA-
   TOES, DRAINED
¼ CUP EXTRA-VIRGIN OLIVE OIL
2 GARLIC CLOVES, MINCED
3 CUPS CHICKEN STOCK OR CANNED BROTH
½ TEASPOON SALT
¼ TEASPOON FRESHLY GROUND BLACK
   PEPPER
1 MEDIUM ZUCCHINI, CUT INTO 2-BY-
   ¼-INCH JULIENNE
1½ TABLESPOONS CHOPPED FRESH BASIL
2 TABLESPOONS BALSAMIC VINEGAR

1~ Roast the peppers under a broiler or directly over a gas flame, turning, until the skin is charred all over, about 10 minutes. Enclose in a plastic bag and let stand for 10 to 15 minutes. Peel off the skin; remove the stems and seeds.
2~ In a food processor, combine the roasted peppers and tomatoes. Process to a smooth puree. Set aside.

3~ In a medium nonreactive saucepan, heat 3 tablespoons of the olive oil. Add the garlic and sauté over moderately high heat until fragrant but not browned, about 30 seconds. Add the pepper-tomato puree and the stock. Simmer over low heat, stirring occasionally, until slightly thickened, 10 to 12 minutes.
4~ Pour the soup into a serving bowl, season with the salt and black pepper and let cool to room temperature.
5~ Just before serving, warm the remaining 1 tablespoon olive oil in a medium skillet over high heat. Add the zucchini and sauté, stirring occasionally, until barely softened, about 2 minutes. Stir the zucchini into the soup and add the basil and balsamic vinegar. Season with additional salt, black pepper and vinegar to taste.

SERVES 4 TO 6
RECIPE BY MARCIA KIESEL

DOUBLE-CORN AND CHEDDAR MUFFINS

Serve these muffins hot from the oven along with the soup course.

1½ CUPS UNBLEACHED ALL-PURPOSE FLOUR
⅔ CUP YELLOW CORNMEAL, PREFERABLY
    STONE-GROUND
2 TABLESPOONS SUGAR
1 TABLESPOON BAKING POWDER
1 TEASPOON SALT
2 EGGS
1 CUP MILK
5 TABLESPOONS UNSALTED BUTTER,
    MELTED
1 CUP CORN KERNELS, THAWED AND
    PATTED DRY, IF FROZEN
1 CUP GRATED CHEDDAR CHEESE
    (4 OUNCES)

1~ Preheat the oven to 400°. Butter twelve
   2½-inch muffin cups.
2~ In a large mixing bowl, combine the flour,
   cornmeal, sugar, baking powder and salt.
3~ In a separate bowl, beat the eggs lightly. Then
   whisk in the milk and melted butter. Make a
   well in the dry ingredients, pour in the liquids
   and stir gently, just until combined. Fold in the
   corn and cheese. Divide the batter among the
   12 cups, filling each about three-quarters full.
4~ Bake the muffins in the middle of the oven for
   about 25 minutes, until lightly browned.
   Transfer the muffin pan to a rack and let cool
   for several minutes before removing the
   muffins.

MAKES 12 MUFFINS
RECIPE BY KEN HAEDRICH

MIXED SALAD WITH ROASTED WALNUTS AND ROQUEFORT

Slow roasting is the key to bringing out the true character of the walnuts in this salad. Any mix of greens can be used as the base, so don't feel confined by those listed below.

½ CUP COARSELY CHOPPED WALNUTS
1 TABLESPOON RED WINE VINEGAR
1 TABLESPOON DIJON-STYLE MUSTARD
⅛ TEASPOON SALT
3 TABLESPOONS EXTRA-VIRGIN OLIVE OIL
2 TEASPOONS MINCED FRESH PARSLEY
FRESHLY GROUND PEPPER
4 CUPS MIXED SALAD GREENS, SUCH AS
    ARUGULA, RADICCHIO, CHICORY AND
    RED LEAF LETTUCE
⅓ CUP CRUMBLED ROQUEFORT CHEESE

1~ Preheat the oven to 275°.
2~ Spread the walnuts on a baking sheet and roast
   in the oven for 45 minutes, until fragrant and
   golden. Let cool.
3~ In a small bowl, combine the vinegar, mustard
   and salt. Gradually whisk in the olive oil. Stir
   in the parsley and season with pepper to taste.
4~ In a large bowl, toss the salad greens with the
   roasted walnuts, Roquefort and the vinaigrette. Divide the salad between 2 plates and
   serve immediately.

SERVES 2
RECIPE BY BOB CHAMBERS

■ ▬▬▬▬▬▬ ■■ ▬▬▬▬▬▬ ■   185

Ripening Time: on or off the Vine?

Some fruits need to ripen fully on the vine or tree, while other mature fruit can continue the ripening process after being picked. It pays to know which are which.

FRUIT RIPENS ONLY BEFORE PICKING:

blackberries	grapes	pineapples
blueberries	lemons	plums
cherries	limes	raspberries
cranberries	melons	strawberries
figs	nectarines	tangerines
gooseberries	oranges	
grapefruits	peaches	

MATURE FRUIT RIPENS AFTER PICKING:

apples	cactus pears	mangos
apricots	carambolas	papayas
atemoyas	cherimoyas	passion fruits
avocados	feijoas	pears
bananas	guavas	persimmons
breadfruits	kiwifruits	tamarillos

■ ▬▬▬▬▬▬ ■■ ▬▬▬▬▬▬ ■

MUSTARD CHICKEN WITH CABBAGE AND APPLES

Since the chicken in this recipe is cooked with onions, cabbage and apples, it makes a good, one-dish meal. There's really no need for accompaniments other than, perhaps, a salad.

1 TABLESPOON DIJON-STYLE MUSTARD
½ TEASPOON CRUMBLED DRIED SAGE
½ TEASPOON DRIED THYME
½ TEASPOON SALT
½ TEASPOON FRESHLY GROUND PEPPER
2 SKINLESS, BONELESS CHICKEN BREAST
    HALVES (4½ OUNCES EACH)
1 TABLESPOON UNSALTED BUTTER
½ CUP THINLY SLICED ONION
1 TABLESPOON PLUS 1 TEASPOON CIDER
    VINEGAR
2 TEASPOONS CHOPPED FRESH PARSLEY
1 CUP THINLY SLICED RED CABBAGE
1 CUP THINLY SLICED GREEN CABBAGE
1 GRANNY SMITH APPLE—PEELED, CORED
    AND CUT INTO EIGHTHS
1 TEASPOON SUGAR

1~ In a small bowl, combine the mustard, sage, thyme and ¼ teaspoon each of the salt and pepper. Rub all over the chicken. Cover and refrigerate for at least 2 hours.

2~ In a heavy medium saucepan, melt ½ teaspoon of the butter over high heat. When the butter starts to brown, add ¼ cup of the onion. Reduce the heat to moderate and stir well. Cover and cook, stirring occasionally, until the onion is translucent, 5 to 7 minutes. Add ½ tablespoon of the vinegar, 1 teaspoon of the parsley and ⅛ teaspoon each of the salt and pepper. Stir in the red cabbage. Cover and cook, stirring occasionally, for 5 minutes. Uncover and cook over high heat, stirring constantly, until the cabbage browns lightly, 3 to 4 minutes. Set aside and keep warm.

3~ Repeat with ½ teaspoon of the butter, the remaining onion, ½ tablespoon of the vinegar, the remaining parsley, salt and pepper and the green cabbage.

4~ Melt 1 teaspoon of the butter in a medium nonstick skillet. Add the apple slices and cook over moderate heat, tossing, until evenly browned, 5 to 7 minutes. Sprinkle with the sugar and cook for 2 minutes. Stir in the remaining 1 teaspoon vinegar, toss well and remove from the skillet; keep warm.

5~ Wipe the skillet clean. Add the remaining 1 teaspoon butter and melt over high heat. Add the chicken breasts and sauté until nicely browned, about 2 minutes per side. Reduce the heat to moderately low and cook, turning once, until the chicken is just white throughout but still moist, about 4 minutes.

6~ On each plate, mound the two colors of cabbage, side by side. Top with the chicken breasts and garnish with apple slices.

SERVES 2
RECIPE BY MARCIA KIESEL AND BOB CHAMBERS

LAVENDER-PEPPER PEARS

Pears are delectable in any form, but here they are especially pleasing to both the eye and palate. Choose your favorite mild cheese to serve alongside.

1 TABLESPOON FRESH LEMON JUICE
2 LARGE RIPE BARTLETT PEARS, PEELED
⅛ TEASPOON LAVENDER,* CRUMBLED
½ TEASPOON COARSELY CRACKED BLACK
    PEPPER
*AVAILABLE AT SPICE MARKETS AND
    SPECIALTY FOOD SHOPS

1~ Sprinkle the lemon juice over the pears. Combine the lavender and pepper and sprinkle over the pears.

2~ Serve on a plate with a knife and fork, accompanied with cheese.

SERVES 2
RECIPE BY FOOD & WINE

INDEX

190

Recipes by Diana Sturgis, Marcia Kiesel, John Robert Massie, Anne Disrude and Mimi Ruth Brodeur were developed in the course of their work in Food & Wine's *test kitchen. Other former or current* Food & Wine *staff members who contributed recipes include: W. Peter Prestcott, Jim Brown, Susan Wyler and Anne Montgomery.*

Food professionals who have contributed to this book include the following:

Jean Anderson is a food writer, cookbook author, syndicated newspaper columnist and accomplished photographer. She has written 14 cookbooks, including a microwave cookbook (with Elaine Hanna) for Doubleday. She is currently working on two new books, the subjects of which are a secret at this time.

Lee Bailey is a designer, cookbook author and writer of the "Entertaining with Lee Bailey" column in Food & Wine. *His most recent book is* Soup Meals, *and he is currently working on* Southern Food and Plantation Houses *due in March 1990 and* Wine Country Cooking *due in 1991, all to be published by Clarkson Potter.*

Nancy Verde Barr is a food writer and cooking teacher who is currently writing a book on southern Italian cooking for Knopf.

Rose Levy Beranbaum's most recent books are The Cake Bible *and* Passion for Chocolate *(both from William Morrow).*

Ella and Dick Brennan are owners of Commander's Palace restaurant in New Orleans. They are collecting recipes for a new but as yet untitled cookbook.

Bob Chambers is an executive chef and New York-based food stylist.

Christian Chavanne is working in research and development for the Galaxy Cheese Company in New Castle, Pennsylvania. He is also an adviser for the Kaiser Foundation, in Menlo Park, California.

Craig Claiborne, former food editor of The New York Times, *is the author or co-author of over 20 cookbooks, most recently,* Craig Claiborne's Southern Cooking *(Times Books).*

Peggy Cullen is a pastry chef, bakery production manager and freelance writer who lives in New York City.

Robert Del Grande is chef/owner of Cafe Express, which has two locations in Houston.

Jim Dodge, formerly the pastry chef at the Stanford Court Hotel, is preparing to open his own pastry shop in San Francisco.

Jim Fobel, former test kitchen director of Food & Wine, *is a freelance food writer and cookbook author. His most recent book,* Jim Fobel's Old-Fashioned Baking Book *(Ballantine), will be followed by* Jim Fobel's Diet Feasts *(Doubleday) in 1990.*

Margaret Fox is chef/owner of Cafe Beaujolais in Mendocino, California. Her most recent book is Morning Food from Cafe Beaujolais, *co-authored with John Bear (10 Speed Press).*

Arthur Gold and Robert Fizdale are freelance writers whose highly acclaimed book, The Gold and Fizdale Cookbook *(Random House), won an R.T. French award when it was published in 1984.*

Dorie Greenspan is a New York-based food writer who is at work on a dessert cookbook to be published by William Morrow in 1990.

Ken Haedrich is a freelance writer and bi-monthly columnist for Country Journal *magazine. He is at work on a baking book for Bantam, due out in the fall of 1990.*

Mary Marshall Hynson is a writer and food consultant.

Michael James is a chef, food writer and cookbook author currently working on a book entitled American Pie.

Nancy Harmon Jenkins is the editorial director of the American Institute of Wine & Food. She is a regular contributor to The New York Times *and is working on a book about the history of American ethnic and immigrant foods, to be published in 1992 by Bantam Books.*

Barbara Kafka is a cookbook author, newspaper and magazine columnist and restaurant consultant. Her newest book is Microslim Gourmet, published by William Morrow.

Edna Lewis is executive chef at Gage & Tollner in Brooklyn, New York. Her most recent books are In Pursuit of Flavor and The Taste of Country Cooking, both published by Knopf.

Eileen Yin-Fei Lo is a chef, cookbook author and cooking teacher who teaches at The China Institute of America in New York City. Her most recent book, Eileen Yin-Fei Lo's New Cantonese Cooking, was published in 1988 by Viking.

Nicholas Malgieri, pastry chef and teacher at Peter Kump's New York Cooking School, is the author of the new Nicholas Malgieri's Perfect Pastry (Macmillan) and has a book of Italian desserts due in 1990 from Little, Brown.

Lydie Marshall is a cooking teacher (A La Bonne Cocotte) in New York City. Her book Cooking with Lydie Marshall was published by Knopf in 1982.

Robert McGrath is executive chef at the Four Seasons Hotel in Houston.

Michael McLaughlin is a Brooklyn-based freelance food writer whose next book, The New American Kitchen, is due in 1990 from Simon & Schuster.

Linda Merinoff is a cookbook author and food writer who has two new books: Gingerbread from Fireside Press and Pig-Out with Peg: Secrets from the Bundy Kitchen (co-authored with Peg Bundy) from Columbia Pictures Television.

Perla Meyers is a cookbook author and restaurant consultant. Her two new books are Peasant Kitchen and New Seasonal Kitchen (fall 1990), both with Simon & Schuster.

Leslie Newman is "a writer by profession, a cook by obsession" who is writing a cookbook entitled Feasts, to be published in the fall of 1990 by Harper & Row.

Jo Northrup is a freelance writer for such publications as The Washington Post and Good Housekeeping. She has been a contributing editor of Country Living for the past ten years.

Judith Olney, founder of the Judith Olney Cookery School in Durham, North Carolina, has written four cookbooks and currently is working on a fifth about American farm markets.

Molly O'Neill is a former chef who is the restaurant critic for New York Newsday. She co-authored, with Stanley Dry, the upcoming New York Cooking, to be published by Workman.

Seppi Renggli is executive chef at New York's The Four Seasons restaurant. He is the author of The Four Seasons Spa Cuisine, published by Simon & Schuster.

Julie Sahni is a chef, cookbook author, food writer, cooking school teacher and consultant whose newest title, Moghul Microwave, will be published by William Morrow in the spring of 1990.

Shirley Sarvis is a food and wine writer and consultant who conducts Wine-With-Food tastings.

Jean-Michel Savoca and Boyce Brawley are co-owners of the New York catering firm, New York Parties. They are publishing a cookbook by that name with Rizzoli.

Richard Sax is a cookbook author and food consultant currently at work on a dessert cookbook to be published in 1991 or 1992 by Simon & Schuster.

Jimmy Schmidt is executive chef/owner of The Rattlesnake Club in Detroit. He is writing A Cook for All Seasons for publication by Macmillan in 1990.

Elizabeth Schneider is a food journalist, cookbook author and specialty produce consultant. Her two most recent cookbooks are Dining in Grand Style (with Dieter Hannig and the chefs of Hilton International; Thorsons Publishers) and the encyclopedic Uncommon Fruits and Vegetables: A Commonsense Guide (Harper & Row).

Phillip Stephen Schulz is a cookbook author and freelance writer who is promoting top-quality American food products in Japan and working on two cookbooks: Better by the Dozen (Simon & Schuster) and the America the Beautiful Cookbook, due in 1990.

Annie Somerville is executive chef of Greens restaurant in San Francisco.

Jerrie Strom is a cooking teacher who conducts classes at her home, Rancho Santa Fe, north of San Diego.

Jane Thompson, owner of Harvest Restaurant in Cambridge, Massachusetts, and her husband, Ben Thompson, have founded and owned four banquet/restaurant operations in the Boston area. She is writing a book of culinary memoirs.

Michèle Urvater is a cookbook author and executive chef currently at work on a book for Harper & Row to be published in 1991.

Brendan Walsh, formerly executive chef at Arizona 206 restaurant in New York City, is preparing to open a new restaurant also in New York. He is writing a book about New York cooking.

Patricia Wells lives in Paris, where she is restaurant critic for The International Herald Tribune and L'Express. Her existing books, A Food Lover's Guide to Paris and A Food Lover's Guide to France will be joined by The French Bistro Cookbook (all published by Workman) later this year.

Anne Willan, president of the esteemed La Varenne cooking school in Paris, has written four cookbooks, is working on two more and is president-elect of The International Association of Cooking Professionals.

2 0 0   If you are not already a subscriber to
Food & Wine magazine and would be
interested in subscribing, please call
Food & Wine's toll-free number:
800-333-6569.